6 Endorsements for *Homeschool Heroes* by Chris Klicka

"*Homeschool Heroes* is a book that is long overdue. This is a must read for every homeschooler as it details the struggles faced to gain the freedom to homeschool. No one is more qualified to bring this story than Chris Klicka. More than any other person, he has been on the front lines of this battle for twenty-four years. His summary of the homeschool law for the fifty states is the single most important resource that has been developed to advance homeschool freedom."

—Michael Smith, president
Home School Legal Defense Association

"Chris Klicka chronicles the history of the modern-day homeschooling movement with the detail and impact that only an eyewitness can deliver. From the battles on the snowy plains of North Dakota to the long road to the Michigan Supreme Court, Chris was there. Chris reminds us with the many examples from his own life and others that trusting in the mighty hand of God will bring deliverance for those who follow his ways and that perseverance brings victory. This book shows all of us how one man, sold out to God for a noble, ambitious purpose, can accomplish great things by God's wisdom and power. May this book spur the next generation to even greater feats of glory."

—Jordan Lorence, vice president and senior counsel
Alliance Defense Fund

"In the early 1980s thousands of courageous parents quietly decided to keep their children out of conventional schools in order to teach them at home. Though it was very painful at the time, many such parents were discovered by state authorities, hauled into court (some were even jailed), and in those legal conflicts state laws were changed. Freedom for the many was won by the few. In many of those cases, Chris Klicka was there. In his new book *Homeschool Heroes*, Chris tells their stories. In doing so, he captures a precious piece of history for all who love freedom and long to preserve it."

—Gregg Harris, homeschool pioneer, speaker, and author of
The Christian Home School

"*Homeschool Heroes* is an informative and inspiring account of the history and social impact of the homeschool movement in the United States. It is an important book because it remembers and honors the pioneers whose sacrificial work made possible the freedom homeschool parents enjoy today. I highly recommend it to all who love home education and seek to make it even stronger for future generations."

—Justice Tom Parker, Alabama Supreme Court

"This book proves that individuals can make a difference and, in the process, change the course of history."

—John W. Whitehead, president, The Rutherford Institute

"Chris Klicka has written an important book on one of the most encouraging movements of our time—homeschooling— and gives God all the glory. He shatters the myth that there is anything illegal about it. I am impressed that Chris, though suffering with MS, still engages in evangelism on a regular basis."

—D. James Kennedy, president of Evangelism Explosion; president of Coral Ridge Ministries

Home School Heroes

Home School

Heroes

the Struggle & Triumph
of Home Schooling in America

Christopher
KLICKA

B&H
EDUCATIONAL
Nashville, Tennessee

Ten-digit ISBN: 0-8054-2600-0
Thirteen-digit ISBN: 978-0-8054-2600-7

Published by B&H Publishing Group,
Nashville, Tennessee

Dewey Decimal Classification: 371.042
Subject Heading: HOME SCHOOLING \ TEACHING

1 2 3 4 5 6 7 8 9 10   10 09 08 07 06

I dedicate this book to the countless homeschooling families who have sacrificed so much—and leaned on Jesus—in those early years to win our rights to homeschool in America.

I also dedicate this book to my greatest supporters and prayer warriors, who made it possible for me to minister to homeschoolers for the last twenty years: my wife, Tracy; daughters, Bethany, Megan, Susanna, Charity, and Amy; my sons, Jesse and John; and my parents, George and Ardath Klicka, who had the wisdom to put me in Christian school, where I was saved, by the grace of God.

Table of Contents

Acknowledgments

First and foremost, I thank the Lord Jesus for His great mercy in saving my soul for all eternity and blessing me so abundantly. God has given me a job that is better than any in the whole world: protecting the rights of moms and dads to faithfully teach their children at home. No other work could bring me such great joy and satisfaction. I am blessed.

I give special thanks to Tracy, my wife of twenty-two years, who has faithfully loved me and supported me through many years of extremely pressing and time-consuming work with HSLDA. I admire her greatly for her perseverance and diligence in training our seven children up the way they should go. She is a true helpmeet. Her unconditional love has been a gift of God, even as my body deteriorates from multiple sclerosis. I am blessed.

I thank all of my children for their constant love, compassion, and service to me. They have to help me in ways most children don't have to help their dads. I always wondered why God gave me seven children—it seemed so many. But now, as MS gradually takes away the use of my legs, arm, hand, and bodily functions, my children are there, always giving and enabling me to continue serving the body of Christ and working full-time at HSLDA. I am blessed.

I thank Michael Farris and Michael Smith for giving me this job way back in June 1985. Without their believing in me and giving me a chance, I would never have had the privilege to serve the homeschool community, whom I have come to love so dearly. Their vision, foresight, and legal expertise have always been an example to me. I especially thank Michael Smith for his faithful friendship and patience through the good times and the hard times. He is the best boss I could ever have. I am blessed.

I thank the members of Gainesville Presbyterian Church, who have faithfully prayed for me and our family and have showered us with God's love. In so many practical ways, they have always been there for us. I am blessed.

And I give especially warm thanks for the homeschool leaders across the fifty states—men and women whom I have come to know as my good friends and fellow warriors. Most of these individuals have sacrificed for years without pay or reward to serve the homeschool community in the name of Jesus Christ. I can do nothing worthy of truly expressing the depth of my gratitude and love for them. I am blessed.

Finally, I thank all the homeschool families who have made this book possible. Without their stories to tell, there would be no book. Their faithfulness against great odds and their perseverance in the midst of trials and difficulty have been an inspiration to me and helped me persevere in the face of the disease that is racking my body.

I am blessed among men.

—Christopher J. Klicka

Foreword

In 1980, at the age of five, I became a homeschool student. My parents, Gregg and Sono Harris, were among the pioneer generation of Christian families captured by the biblical vision of making the home a center for training and discipleship. They refused to delegate the responsibility for my education and spiritual formation to someone else. So they chose to keep me at home, even when it flew in the face of society's norms. And even a few of society's laws.

Because of the legal restrictions of the time, homeschooling at that time required a bit of stealth. I wasn't allowed to go outside and play while the other kids were at school so the neighbors wouldn't become suspicious. And whenever strangers saw me with my mom in public during school hours, I would just nod and smile politely when they frowned and asked, "Is school out today?"

I owe so much of who I am today to the influence and teaching of my dad and mom. I'm grateful that they took the risks and braved the questions and the criticism that came with homeschooling back then.

Today I'm a father with my own five-year-old. My wife and I are just beginning to homeschool our child, but we do so without fear. We can do so because others, like my dad and mom, have gone before us and fought the battles. Because of their faithfulness, we enjoy the freedom to teach our child at home, and I never want to forget that this freedom was hard won.

Chris Klicka is a dear old friend of our family. And even if you've never met him, if you homeschool or simply cherish your freedom to do so, Chris has been a good friend of yours too. He has dedicated his life to preserving parents' rights to teach their children at home.

I'm grateful to Chris for writing this book so that young parents like me who are choosing to homeschool can learn about our unique heritage. It's so easy to take for granted the rights we enjoy today. Chris's work as a historian and eyewitness to so many key legal struggles helps us to remember where we've come from—and where we could return if we're not watchful.

What I respect most about Chris is his heart for God. For him, the history of homeschooling isn't ultimately about skilled attorneys or even courageous parents. It's the story of a faithful, sovereign God who gave a generation of parents a vision to train and disciple their kids—and then fought on their behalf so that they would be free to fulfill their God-given mandate.

May God be glorified as this story is retold. May He be glorified as my parents' generation is appropriately honored in these pages.

Thanks, Dad and Mom. Thank you for homeschooling me and for teaching me God's ways.

And thank you, Chris, for being a defender of parents like mine—and parents like me.

—Joshua Harris

Introduction

The history of the modern homeschool movement is an incredible and inspirational story. It is a story of God's faithfulness, demonstrating God's promise that "He will honor those who honor Him."

The great odds faced by a tiny band of faithful families following God's call reminds us of the advantage in size and strength Goliath had over young David. The teachers' unions with their millions of dollars, the national organizations of educational elite, and the monolithic public school system were all lined up in great array against this small cadre of parents, many of whom had no finances to fight back. It appeared to the world that they were simply lambs proceeding to the slaughter.

But there was a secret weapon in the arsenal of these homeschoolers: God was on their side.

As a result, the "iron curtain" of state education laws prohibiting homeschooling in the early 1980s crumbled in little more than a decade. The powerful educational elite said all along it could not be done. They were wrong. Nothing is impossible with God, and the unprecedented advancement of the freedom to homeschool proves this truth.

As an active participant in this struggle, God has given me a bird's-eye view of the battle. I have seen His hand move on behalf of His people in a visible way. As an attorney working full-time in the defense of this small minority, I saw the hearts of judges turned, miraculous victories in state legislatures won, and the public schools' virtual monopoly dissolved.

When I started working for the Home School Legal Defense Association (HSLDA) in 1985, only in a handful of states was it clearly legal to homeschool. After many sacrifices and risks taken by committed parents, tireless work by home-school state leaders, and thousands of hours of legal work by HSLDA, homeschooling is now legal in all fifty states.

Having solidarity with homeschoolers in all fifty states through HSLDA gave homeschoolers the financial backing to fight back in the courts and legislatures. As HSLDA linked up with the fledgling state homeschool organizations, the tide began to turn.

Many unheralded but significant miracles happened all along the way as faithful parents committed their families to God's hands. I have witnessed thousands of examples of God protecting His families against social workers, truant officers, prosecutors, legislatures, school boards, state departments of education, and judges.

I hope to capture some of these amazing stories in this book so that generations to come will remember God's faithfulness and deliverance. My prayer is that this book will help home-schoolers be vigilant and never let their guard down. The same forces today that tried to regulate homeschooling to death still remain, waiting for their chance to take away parents' rights and "turn back the clock."

I believe, as you read these accounts, you will know of God's faithfulness on behalf of His people; and your trust in Him will increase. You will be motivated to do your part to keep our families free, inspired by the courage of these homeschool heroes.

This book is their story.

❈ 1

Fear for the Children and Fear of the Authorities

"With people this is impossible, but with God all things are possible."

MATTHEW 19:26

In the late 1970s, American families began to become disgruntled with the public school system. The statistics and information concerning the downward trend of public education was trickling out to the people. Christian parents, in particular, were becoming disenchanted with this system of education that was actively working against their interests and convictions. As a result, people began looking for alternatives—and still are.

Interestingly enough, as I travel in foreign countries, I find similar concerns among the people. Government-run schools everywhere are plagued with the same gradual secularization, growing immorality, and the shortcomings of factory-made, one-size-fits-all education. Homeschool movements in other countries are twenty years behind America and are only beginning to experience the same legal conflicts and difficulties as their American forerunners. Therefore, we have much to share with these parents in foreign countries to help them employ successful legal strategies and avoid some of the mistakes that were made here in America.

A Nation at Risk

The Reagan administration, in 1982, had come into power with a mandate to "fix" our nation's public school system. Reagan appointed a panel to examine the modern school system and found that our public schools were in desperate shape. The panel issued a report titled "A Nation at Risk," which said that if a foreign government had perpetrated what was taking place academically and morally in our public schools, we would consider it an act of war! This was a severe indictment handed down by the highest levels of our own government.

The message was trumpeted loud and clear to parents everywhere in our country: The public schools are in trouble. You need to think twice about where your children are being educated.

Needless to say, many Christian parents began to seek God for the answer. And God made the path clear to them from the Scriptures, where He said, "Learn not the way of the heathen" (Jer. 10:2 KJV). As parents began to scrutinize the public school curriculum and heard reports from their children, they realized this is exactly what their children were learning: the ways of the heathen. In the 1960s, a number of U.S. Supreme Court cases were handed down barring any teaching of the Bible and Christianity in public schools as it supposedly violated the constitutional amendment prohibiting the government from establishing a religion. Further decisions came down prohibiting the display of the Ten Commandments in schools. Other rulings would eventually prohibit school prayer, Bible reading, and even a "minute of silence."

Textbook publishers responded by removing every reference to Christianity and vestige of Christian moral truth from their texts. By the end of the 1970s, there was no longer a rudder steering this huge ship of public education.

A new philosophy prevailed. Children were taught, "If it feels good, do it." The nation's moral foundations were all but destroyed. As we "sow[ed] the wind," we began to "reap the whirlwind" (Hosea 8:7).

This danger was exposed in the "Nation at Risk" report. And so, as it says in Malachi 4:6, the hearts of fathers began to be turned back to their children, and their children to their fathers.

The Hearts of the Fathers Are Turned

The Holy Spirit was working, one by one, in the hearts of families and parents all across America. Parents were being convicted by passages like Deuteronomy 6:7, which states that parents need to teach their children God's principles all the time: "You shall teach them diligently to your sons and shall talk of them when you sit in your house and when you walk by the way and when you lie down and when you rise up." In other words, a comprehensive view of Christian education is required.

Parents began to look closely at Ephesians 6:4, where fathers are given a heavy responsibility: "Fathers, do not provoke your children to anger; but bring them up in the discipline and instruction of the Lord."

These Scriptures and many others were speaking to God's people and waking them from a prolonged slumber. No longer would their consciences allow their children to be taught a completely opposing worldview than that which God required of them. Parents realized they needed to make a choice.

Christian School Battles

Meanwhile, Christian schools were battling for their very existence in the 1970s. Many states required all educators to be certified, licensed teachers, all curriculum to be approved by the department of education, and all schools to be accredited. Small Christian schools with low tuitions were already at a disadvantage, and their teachers were sacrificing everything in order to teach Christian truths to their students. (I attended one of these schools in Brookfield, Wisconsin. It was called Christian Liberty Academy—affiliated with Christian Liberty Academy Satellite Schools [CLASS]. I thank God for the headmaster, John Vouga, and the school's teaching, because that's how I was saved and became a born-again Christian. It was there I saw firsthand the huge personal sacrifice of those teachers.)

The Christian schools fought back. But in a long line of cases, the schools lost in state court after state court. The courts almost universally held that the Christian schools were to bow to the whims of the state, including complicated accreditation processes and approval of requirements. By God's grace, most state legislatures came to their rescue and passed laws exempting Christian schools from many of the worst compulsory attendance law restrictions.

Homeschooling—Is It Legal?

Meanwhile many parents began to turn to homeschooling. Little by little the word was spreading. Parents began to talk about how wonderful it would be if they could just keep their children at home. Many Christian school textbook companies like A Beka and Bob Jones University provided texts to these early homeschool pioneers.

There was just one problem: Homeschooling was not legal in most states.

In 1983, unbeknownst to me, God was preparing me to join the fight by allowing me to witness the attacks on Christian education at every level. I was then a young law student attending O. W. Coburn School of Law in Tulsa, Oklahoma, a Christian law school battling the monolithic American Bar Association for accreditation so its graduates could become lawyers—a battle they finally won.

I had just graduated from a Christian university, Grove City College (GCC), which itself was taken to court by the Department of Education and Welfare. The government claimed that Grove City was in violation of myriad federal regulations. Grove City said, "We don't have to comply because we don't receive any federal aid. Therefore, we're free from government strings and can operate our college the way we see fit."

The government rejected this argument, noting that some of GCC's students received federal guaranteed student loans and grants. Therefore, they said, GCC was receiving government money and must submit to government authority.

The case made it all the way to the Supreme Court, who finally ruled in the college's favor. The high court ruled that Grove City College was not required to submit to government regulations—except in one area. Their financial aid department, the Court reasoned, indirectly received federal funds via government-guaranteed student loans and various federal student scholarship grants.

Grove City College's response was to ban any student who receives government money from attending GCC. They did not want *any* federal regulation. They quickly set up private scholarships and grants and loans through local banks and investors, thus allowing students to receive *more* financial aid than if they had worked through the federal government.

This is the kind of background God was using to prepare me to fight for Christian education to make it free from state controls. I was being called into a specialized area of constitutional law.

One of my professors in law school was John Whitehead, who had recently started the Rutherford Institute in 1983. He had urged me that summer to join him as an intern at the institute in Woodbridge, Virginia. This I excitedly did. However, I was in for a big surprise. There were only two offices, a secretary, and three interns, and John Whitehead worked from home. The project I was given for the next four months was to analyze all the compulsory education laws and attendance laws in all fifty states. I found that in only five states was it clearly legal to homeschool. In the rest of the states, it was "open season" on anyone who dared to teach their children at home.

I buried myself in the law library at Georgetown University in Washington, DC, where I dug up nearly every attorney general opinion, case, and statute that remotely related to the possibility of a person's legally homeschooling. I learned to be creative in my legal analysis. For instance, I began thinking of ways homeschools could be classified as private schools because in many states private schools were not heavily regulated. In fact, there were actually some reported cases where homeschoolers were recognized as private schools. So I applied this reasoning to other states.

The argument was that the "private school" was located at home with the father as principal, the mother as teacher, and a student body comprising the children of the one family!

During my third year of law school, I sent my résumé to Concerned Women for America, among other places, because I had heard that a man named Mike Farris was heading up the legal department there. He was engaged in a lot of First Amendment law concerning Christians' rights in the public sector. This was exciting to me. I felt strongly called by God to go and work the rest of my life in this area. When Mike got my résumé, he called within a few days and exclaimed, "You know more about homeschooling laws than I do!" He wanted to interview me for the job of the executive director of the Home School Legal Defense Association. I had never heard of such an organization. Mike said it was founded in 1983 but was small and needed some full-time attention. I got the job, the first in my new law career; and twenty years later I am still here.

In 1985 my new bride, Tracy, and I moved to Virginia to work in Washington, DC, for HSLDA. Before we had children, we had already committed to homeschooling them.

Legal Atmosphere: Fear and Intimidation

It was difficult to go to work each day because the legal atmosphere was so bleak. It was only legal in a few states to homeschool, and in the rest of the states I just had to be creative. I was hearing more and more stories from people trying to fight the government in order to keep the call of God.

To give you an idea of what the legal atmosphere was back then, allow me to describe a few real-life situations.

In North Dakota, where nearly every home educator who was discovered by state officials was taken to criminal court, local TV stations would interview homeschoolers about the joys and successes of homeschooling—with "squiggles" in front of their faces to protect their identity. Or the individuals would be shown in a darkened silhouette so they could not be recognized.

Many families set up escape routes so that their children could run out the back door and hop over a fence if a truant officer came to the door. Dennis Smith, who is now a homeschool leader in Michigan, had such a plan laid out for their children.

One story from Michigan was particularly amazing. A family told me that every Monday they would get up early, take their empty suitcases outside, load everyone into the car, and drive off. They pulled all their shades down before they left—shades that were black on the inside so no one could tell the lights were on! Shortly thereafter they would park away from the house and sneak back into their house through the backyard. There they would stay and do their home-schooling and not leave all week long. Only the father would come and go to work. To the casual observer, it looked like the family was only home on weekends. This is how they avoided investigation by the school authorities.

Fear and intimidation was the order of the day. Home-schooling families everywhere were trembling, not knowing when the officers or social workers would be knocking at their door.

The Resolve of Homeschool Families

Nonetheless, the intense pressure of the state did not affect the resolve of these brave few. These people were following the call of God; no risk was too great, and they trusted God would see them through.

At the same time more and more families were learning about the Home School Legal Defense Association.

As I traveled around the country explaining the value of families pooling their resources together by joining HSLDA, I saw our membership numbers grow rapidly from the twelve hundred we had in 1985. Families became emboldened as they became part of HSLDA; they now enjoyed "solidarity" with homeschoolers everywhere. We began to develop a voice and a reputation.

Homeschooling was hard in those early days. It took a person under great conviction from the Lord to take this big step to challenge the authorities and teach their children at home. The rest of this book will recount many stories of individual families who, hearing the call of God, stood firm.

When all else failed, they still stood firm.

Their God was bigger than the government. God would protect them. God would see them through.

And as you'll see in the next chapters, He did.

2

The Christian Foundations of the Homeschool Movement

For whatever is born of God overcomes the world; and this
is the victory that has overcome the world—our faith.
Who is the one who overcomes the world, but he who
believes that Jesus is the Son of God?

1 JOHN 5:4–5

The modern homeschool movement was started through a miraculous moving of the Holy Spirit. A number of key instruments were used by God to bring about and spread awareness of the concept of homeschooling, but the most important factor was no doubt the Holy Spirit's pricking the hearts of parents to train their children according to God's laws.

The modern homeschool movement is by no means a new phenomenon in America. It is a time-tested and highly successful form of education that first appeared in America in the seventeenth century. Unfortunately, when the public schools were formed and compulsory attendance laws were passed throughout the country in the early 1900s, homeschooling almost died out. It wasn't until the 1970s that the homeschool movement was reborn.

Homeschooling in Colonial America

Until the 1990s, however, homeschooling was the primary method by which most were educated. Education was mainly a family responsibility in colonial America. Children were taught at home to read, write, do math, and perform the skills they would need to earn a living as adults. The role of the Bible was paramount in their education. Every subject was taught as it related to Scripture. Why? Because the Bible had so much to say about every area of life.

Therefore, in early America, a biblical mind-set prevailed. Whether people believed in Christianity or not, they taught the Bible, because in it they saw the answers to many of life's problems—it would help their children to become better parents, better spouses, better citizens.

By the latter half of the twentieth century, this biblical mind-set had been gradually replaced by a humanistic mind-set. The public schools and the growing mass media were (and are) teaching our children to think like non-Christians. Even Christians were starting to think like non-Christians and develop humanistic views due to these influences.

The modern homeschool movement is, in a sense, bringing about a spontaneous restoration of a biblical mind-set. Our children are once again being taught a biblical worldview so that they can apply God's Word to every area of life. Therein lies the hope for this nation. Homeschoolers are becoming the leaders of tomorrow.

Famous Homeschooled Americans

Many presidents of the United States, including George Washington, Thomas Jefferson, James Madison, John Quincy Adams, Abraham Lincoln, John Tyler, and Teddy Roosevelt, were taught at home.

Other people who were home educated include Benjamin Franklin, Patrick Henry, John Jay, John Marshall, and Timothy Dwight, grandson of Jonathan Edwards and later president of Yale University. Jonathan Edwards, William Carey, and Dwight L. Moody were homeschooled, as were renowned military leaders Stonewall Jackson, Robert E. Lee, Douglas MacArthur, and George Patton.

At least seventeen of the delegates to the constitutional convention were home educated. One of these delegates, Rev. John Witherspoon, was a member of the New Jersey senate and the president of Princeton University. His mother had no idea the impact that he would have on this nation. Witherspoon was president of Princeton from 1768 to 1794. In those twenty-six years, 478 young men graduated from the school. Of those 478 graduates, 114 became ministers of the gospel, thirteen became state governors, three would be appointed to the United States Supreme Court, twenty would be elected to the U.S. senate, and thirty-three would serve as U.S. congressmen. In addition, Princeton graduates James Madison and Aaron Burr served as president and vice president of the United States.

I am sure Mrs. Witherspoon never dreamed that the young son she was training at home would someday train the leaders of our country!

I could go on and on recounting examples of famous men and women successfully taught at home, but I have saved that for another book. The early days of homeschooling in America are chronicled in my book *Home Schooling: The Right Choice*, published by Broadman & Holman.

Homeschoolers Must Make Every Day Count

Mike Farris wrote a column back in 1991 in which he stated, "We have precious children whom the Lord has entrusted us, we have been given a high calling, let's use the days and hours to make a difference in their lives. Anything less constitutes a waste of the time the Lord has given us. You never know when your time is going to run out."

As I have struggled with multiple sclerosis since 1994, God has impressed upon me to make every day count for my family, for my children, and for my God. This means that I no longer want to "waste" time on frivolous activities, personal hobbies, and selfish pursuits. I need to do what the Bible tells us to do over and over again: die to self. The Scriptures tell us that to live is Christ, to die is gain. I am to be "crucified" with Christ, for it is not I who lives anymore but Christ. I must put aside the old man and put on the new. I need to carry my brother's burdens. I need to love others and not keep a record of wrongs and give people the benefit of the doubt. God calls me to holiness, not to the pursuit of health and personal satisfaction.

Homeschooling is hard work and the homeschoolers throughout this country are, by and large, families that are called by God. These are families whose eyes have been opened to the decay of the culture around us—the same culture that is seeking to mold and shape our children into its image.

These parents are making a difference by taking their children out of the system, and as they do so, God is pouring out His blessings on them—not only academically and socially but also spiritually. A mighty army has been raised up through the homeschool movement that began primarily in the early 1980s.

Delegated by God to Raise Our Children

Time and time again in my work, I've spoken with superintendents and school officials who really believe that the students are "their children." In other words they believe that our children belong to society, not to their parents. It is Hillary Clinton's "it takes a village" mentality.

But that's not what God tells us. He has a different perspective on child rearing. This is the biblical perspective that has pervaded the homeschool community since the beginning of the modern homeschool movement. This understanding and the inward call of the Holy Spirit have kept families fearless in the midst of a fearful time, enabling them to remain strong and courageous in spite of the pressures that the state would bring to bear on them.

According to the Bible, our children belong to God, but the responsibility and authority to raise and educate them is delegated to their parents:

> Behold, children are a gift of the Lord, the fruit of the womb is a reward. Like arrows in the hand of a warrior, so are the children of one's youth. How blessed is the man whose quiver is full of them; they will not be ashamed when they speak with their enemies in the gate. (Ps. 127:3–5)

We can see in this passage that children are a gift of the Lord. But nowhere in Scripture can a verse be found where God delegates the authority to raise and educate children to the state. God has clearly delegated the responsibility and the authority to teach and raise the children to the parents first. Parents can delegate the *authority* to raise and teach their children to someone else (i.e., a tutor, a church, or a private or public school), but they can never delegate the *responsibility* to teach their children to anyone else. God will always hold parents responsible for whatever education their children receive. We cannot duck this responsibility by sending our children out of the home.

For this reason, parents of children in public or private schools need to be aware of what is being taught verbally in class by both their teachers and peers, and what is being taught in the textbooks and supplemental books and projects. This is an immense responsibility. In this day and age, with children required to be in school so much of each and every day, there is little opportunity for parents to supervise or limit their children's exposure to the things of this world. Keeping them at home is the best way to fulfill our God-given responsibility.

God-Mandated Conditions for Raising Children

Although God has "given" children to parents, God gives the parents certain "conditions" that must be met because He still considers the children His. For instance, God refers to Jacob's children as "the work of My hands" in Isaiah 29:23.

In Ezekiel 16:20–21, the Lord said to Israel, "You took your sons and daughters whom you had borne to Me, and you have sacrificed them to idols to be devoured." God judged these parents severely because they did not meet God's conditions for raising His children. They gave their children up to an idolatrous system, which is opposed to God. Today we are confronted with a public school system that is also opposed to God.

Jeremiah 10:12 (KJV) says, "Learn not the way of the heathen." What way *are* our children learning in the public schools? Such principles and commands of Scripture have weighed heavily on the minds of homeschoolers in recent decades. They also have weighed the public schools on the scales of God's requirements and justice, *and the public schools have been found wanting.*

In Ephesians 6:4, fathers are commanded to "bring [their children] up in the nurture and discipline of the Lord" (KJV). This responsibility is given to fathers first. They will stand before God one day and answer to Him as to how their children were instructed.

Furthermore, the Lord declares, "These words, which I am commanding you today, shall be on your heart; and you shall teach them diligently to your sons and shall talk of them when you sit in your house and when you walk by the way and when you lie down and when you rise up" (Deut. 6:6–9).

Are we teaching God's commands and truths to our children *all the time?*

Rethinking a Christian's Education

Christian parents in the early years of the modern homeschool movement began to ask themselves such questions:

- How can I satisfy God's requirements of me as a parent if my child spends six to seven hours a day receiving an education empty of all references to God's truths?
- How can we fulfill the Scriptures and train our children in God's ways if our children are being taught that we've evolved from an ape and man has no soul?
- How can we fulfill these commands in the Word of God and teach our children to love them with all their heart, soul, and mind when we allow their mind to be taught to accept homosexuality and alternative lifestyles?
- How can sending my children to a school that teaches my children "the way of the heathen" be considered as obeying God's command to diligently teach my children about the Lord and His principles?

Many more questions like these were causing parents to make the important decision to teach their children at home, even in many states where it was still illegal. Parents knew that as they took this step of faith, they would likely be slammed with truancy charges, social worker investigations, and other forms of harassment.

Yet they believed that the call of God is greater than the state's laws.

It is clear from Scripture that a parent's primary responsibility is to teach his or her children "so that your days and the days of your sons may be multiplied" (Deut. 11:21). Biblical commands to educate our children cannot be accomplished in a single Sunday school lesson each week, but instead require a comprehensive approach to education on a daily basis. The commands of God should be taught to our children when we sit in our home, when we rise up, when we lie down, and when we travel. In other words, *all* the time. And this kind of comprehensive educational program must be based on His Word.

Two of the goals of godly education, therefore, are that children will put their confidence in the Lord and that they will keep His commandments:

> For He established a testimony in Jacob, and appointed
> a law in Israel, which He commanded our fathers,
> that they should teach them to their children, that the
> generation to come might know, even the children yet
> to be born, that they may arise and tell them to their
> children, that they should put their confidence in God,
> and not forget the works of God, but keep His com-
> mandments. (Ps. 78:5–7)

The children, likewise, are told to obey these commands that are given to them from God through their parents:

> My son, observe the commandment of your father, and
> do not forsake the teaching of your mother. . . . When
> you walk about, they will guide you; when you sleep,
> they will watch over you; when you awake, they will
> talk to you. For the commandment is a lamp, and the
> teaching is light; and reproofs for discipline are the
> way of life. (Prov. 6:20–23)

David explains that we need to meditate on God's law day and night (see Ps. 1:1–2). Paul writes that we are to take "every thought captive to the obedience of Christ" (2 Cor. 10:5).

This is an immense responsibility for the parent. We need to train our children to think God's thoughts after Him. Jesus, Himself, said, quoting the Old Testament, "'Love the LORD your God with all your heart, and with all your soul, and with all your mind.' This is the great and foremost commandment" (Matt. 22:37–38). "There is no other commandment greater" (Mark 12:31). Our children not only need to know Jesus in their heart and soul but also in their mind. If they are taught to think like a non-Christian, what does that make of our children? Proverbs says, "For as [a man] thinks within himself, so he is" (23:7).

For many years Christian parents had neglected their duty to educate their children and were reaping the whirlwind. Today many adults believe as Christians but think like non-Christians. I have seen many congressmen or senators who faithfully attend prayer breakfast yet turn around the same day and vote in favor of abortion and other alternative lifestyle issues.

The Content of a True Education

Third John 1:4 says "I have no greater joy than this, to hear of my children walking in the truth." But it is also clear that God will hold us responsible for how we direct the education of our children. We must be careful not to cause "one of these little ones . . . to stumble" by subjecting them to an ungodly education (Matt. 18:6). Paul further reminds us that if we do wrong, we "will receive the consequences of the wrong, . . . and that without partiality" (Col. 3:25).

We have to make certain, of course, that our homeschool education isn't a secular education in disguise, where we simply pray over humanistic textbooks. We must provide a godly education based on His Word. Paul promises, "All Scripture is inspired by God and profitable for teaching, for reproof, for correction, for training in righteousness so that the man of God may be adequate, equipped for every good work" (2 Tim. 3:16–17).

Scripture speaks to every area of life. Every subject, as a result, needs to be studied through the lens of God's Word. If we do this, our children will be equipped for every good work and able to apply God's principles to every part of life. Their beliefs will not be separated from their thoughts and their actions, and they will not become spiritual schizophrenics like so many Christian youth today.

The Homeschool Movement Grows Up

I have been blessed to see the fulfillment of many of these passages that the early homeschoolers hung onto so dearly as their families were being threatened by the might of the state. Homeschool graduates that I have met, some of whom work for us at HSLDA, are living proof that God's blessings have been poured out in abundance on the homeschool movement.

Patrick Henry College in Purcellville, Virginia, which HSLDA helped start, is graduating students who were home-schooled through high school. These students are now entering the halls of government and other places of influence, making a difference for God and His kingdom. As parents apply God's Word faithfully and certainly, God is raising the leaders of tomorrow from within the homeschool movement. Our children are arrows in the hands of the homeschooling warrior and now, as they are launched into the culture, these arrows are flying straight and true. They have a purpose and an aim, and they are hitting their targets. God will continue to bless the homeschool movement—*but only as long as we keep Christ first and foremost.*

A Solid Foundation

In 1980 Gregg Harris and his wife, Sono, elected to take a giant step and homeschool their son, Joshua, in a hostile climate. Gregg signed up Josh as an "extension student" with Bud Schindler's Christian school in Dayton, Ohio, even though the Harris family lived in Oregon. (Homeschoolers had to be creative in those days!)

Gregg was called by God to homeschool, but God also put in his heart a greater vision. Gregg wanted to start a ministry to encourage other families to homeschool. He saw homeschooling as a means of restoring the model of the Bible-centered family, a place to train future leaders for the local church.

His ministry, Christian Life Workshops (CLW), offered these two-day homeschool workshops, which were seminars organized to give parents the "big picture" of homeschooling. Gregg, a master storyteller and eloquent speaker, would weave all the aspects of a Christian family into homeschooling. His first workshop drew sixty-one people and was held in Dayton.

On Friday night he would introduce the benefits of homeschooling. All day Saturday he would teach parents how to teach and to live what really matters. Using overheads, illustrations, humor, and a thorough saturation in the Bible, Gregg would challenge families to live more holy lives. He stressed the need for families to build closer bonds together and encouraged fathers to lead their families spiritually. The importance of making family devotion a priority was emphasized. Gregg covered many practical tips on biblical child training, including the necessity of consistently exercising discipline. He urged parents to have their children apprentice in a skill or trade and even start a home business as a family. He urged all to be faithful witnesses for Christ and to join a solid church. He inspired families to engage in family storytelling and family hospitality to show the children firsthand what it means to apply God's principles in our world.

Gregg offered numerous resources for parents, including "How to Home School" books, homeschool curriculum, "21 Rules of the House," chore charts, devotion books, and anything else a family needed to train their children in God's ways.

The workshops were used by God to give a solid biblical foundation to the homeschool movement—exactly the start it needed. Gregg Harris taught families that they should not homeschool for just the academic benefits but also as the crucial piece to completing the child-training puzzle. He urged families to homeschool in order to fulfill God's commands to train our children.

His homeschool workshops at first drew a few hundred. But since there were so few homeschoolers, Gregg needed to attract *new* people to keep the workshops viable. He published flyers in local churches, grocery stores, and through the early homeschool support groups. He developed a kit to help his local hosts in each city to promote the homeschool seminars on the radio, in newspapers, and throughout their community. Pretty soon the workshops grew in attendance to nearly fifteen hundred. Over 180,000 families were trained by Gregg Harris from 1984 to 1995. At least thirty-five of the now large statewide homeschool associations got their start as Gregg shared his attendee and mailing lists. Many had their founding organizing meetings at Gregg's workshops.

Without Gregg Harris's early *influence*, I am convinced that the homeschool movement would not be the thriving Christian *influence* on our society that it is becoming today.

Sacrificing All for the Kingdom

The work to defend the rights of homeschoolers is hard work. Everyone at our office at the Home School Legal Defense Association can testify to that.

Every leader of every statewide homeschool organization can also testify to that fact. Many of these leaders are volunteers who have sacrificed much time and effort to help protect, promote, and support the homeschool movement.

I personally have been blessed by the many leaders across the country who have been there since the beginning of the movement and have not flinched in the face of adversity. I cannot give them all credit in this book because there are too many, but I so admire and thank these faithful witnesses.

We all need to express our thanks and gratitude to these tireless and often reluctant leaders. I know their rewards in heaven will be great. Some of the faithful homeschool leaders who have gone before us or are still active in leadership include Dennis and Roxanne Smith of INCH of Michigan; Phil and Evella Trout, Mary Scofield, Roy Hanson, and Susan Beatey of CHEA in California. Other valiant leaders: Zan and Joe Tyler of South Carolina; Kevin and Sandy Lundberg, Kevin Swanson and Treon Goossen in Colorado; and Jack Phelps in Alaska. Clinton Birst in North Dakota and Roy Lind of FPEA of Florida also led homeschoolers by their example and passion until the Lord took them home.

More tireless leaders during the toughest times were Barry and Res Peters of Idaho; Sharon Grimes, Rich and Pam Stauter of LEAH of New York; Tom Lewis of Arizona; Ken and JoAnn Patterson of CHEA of Georgia; Don and Debbie Woolet and Joe and Saundra Adams of CHEK of Kentucky; Raymond and Holly Sheen of Connecticut; Ken and Joyce Johnson of Indiana; Ken and Jerri Sisson of Illinois; Bruce Eagleson of CHAP of Pennsylvania; and Anne Miller and Yvonne Bunn of HEAV of Virginia. Also, we give thanks for the constant and diligent leadership of Ed and Kathy Green of HOME of Maine, Jan and Allen Gnaczinski of CHEA of Wisconsin, Roger Shurkee of Minnesota, and Dick and Dorothy Karmen of OCEAN of Oregon. Also, Steve and Kathy Lunsford, Kirk and Bev McCord, Gavino and Ruth Perez, Donna Harp, Jonathan and

Debra Weidner, all of Texas. Also, Joe Esposito of CHEF and Jonathan Smoll of OCHEC of Oklahoma, Claiborne and Lana Thornton of Tennessee, and Steve White of Montana, just to name a few.

God has been good to the homeschool movement to bless us with these leaders.

Establishment of Statewide Christian Homeschool Organizations

The Christian foundations of the homeschool movement are evidenced in the establishment of Christian homeschool organizations in every state. For instance, the Home Education Association of Virginia was established in the 1980s, and their mission statement includes that they will "operate within the context of a biblical worldview" and "help and encourage parents to fulfill their God-given rights and responsibilities to educate their own children."

Another such organization is CHECK, Christian Home Educators Confederation of Kansas, founded in the 1980s. Article II of the CHECK constitution states, "CHECK-sponsored activities and publications will be consistently Christian and dedicated to the honor and glory of God in keeping with the biblical commands of Deuteronomy 6:4–10, Proverbs 22:6, and Ephesians 6:4." Furthermore, the CHECK constitution includes a statement of faith that "the Bible is the inspired, infallible, divinely preserved Word of God; the supreme and final authority for all faith and life." It goes on to explain that "salvation is the free gift of God brought to the sinner by grace and received by personal faith in the Lord Jesus Christ whose substitution death on the cross paid the penalty for man's sin."

CHEA of California, founded in 1982, says in their mission statement, "The mission of the Christian Home Educators Association of California is to advance the kingdom of Jesus

Christ by promoting private Christian home education as an outstanding educational opportunity . . . and protecting the God-given right of parents to direct the education and training of their children to the glory of God."

The Alaska Private and Home Educators Association cites in their constitution a statement of faith that recognizes the Bible to be "the inspired and infallible Word of God constituting God's completed and final revelation." It goes on to say that they "believe in salvation by grace and faith alone. The atonement of Christ has provided all that is necessary for the salvation of men, and his faith and his completed work is the only means of salvation. All who reject the Savior will suffer eternal punishment of a righteous God."

In New York, the Loving Education at Home organization was established as "a Christian organization, the members of which are like-minded Christian home education support groups." They "promote home education as the Scriptural design for education, whereas institutional education is alternative to the home." To this day the organization continues to help homeschoolers throughout the state of New York.

There are similar examples, throughout each of the fifty states, of the statewide homeschool organizations that embrace these Christian foundations. This is testimony that the Lord was at work in the foundations of the homeschool movement.

All of these Christian statewide homeschool organizations still exist today and have grown substantially in size and influence. They continue to serve all homeschoolers by providing information on how to start homeschooling, organizing conventions, and providing a lobbying presence at each state capitol to protect homeschool freedoms.

These state organizations host large conferences—from fifteen hundred to fifteen thousand people!—where invited speakers challenge and energize veteran homeschoolers and encourage new parents to begin the blessing of homeschooling. They speak from a biblical worldview and point parents to the

Scriptures. The gospel is presented freely, and the Holy Spirit is at work at these conventions. I have experienced this personally as I have spoken at nearly three hundred fifty of these conventions since 1985.

These same state organizations encourage secular homeschoolers to use Christian curricula. I have heard many testimonies of parents who began homeschooling by using Christian curricula and ended up getting saved in the process.

God is blessing the homeschool movement. This is not because people are homeschooling for the sake of homeschooling; rather, they are homeschooling for the glory and honor of God. If parents and homeschool leaders ever relegate Jesus Christ to second place, the movement will begin to falter. However, if they keep Christ first, I believe that they will continue to be protected from the annual attempts by public schools to turn back the clock and reintroduce old rules restricting home education.

3

The Home School Legal Defense Association Is Born

I can do all things through Him who strengthens me.

PHILIPPIANS 4:13

In the midst of the hostile legal atmosphere for homeschoolers in the 1980s, God was putting on the hearts and minds of a chosen few the beginnings of the solution to provide legal protection for homeschooling families facing intimidation and persecution from the state.

One such man was Michael Farris. An attorney in the state of Washington, Michael founded a public advocacy legal organization called the Bill of Rights Legal Foundation. God had put a fire in his heart to fight legal battles on behalf of God's people, particularly in the area of religious freedom.

Michael and his wife, Vickie, decided in 1982 to homeschool their second-grader, Christy, after hearing a radio interview with James Dobson and Raymond Moore that helped them solidify their conviction in this area. Moore had said that kids learn from their peers and Mike Farris thought, *My wife and I are smarter than second graders. We're going to do the teaching of our children.*

It wasn't long before Mike Farris and Vickie appeared on the front page of *The Seattle Times* with a picture of them homeschooling their children. Calls began increasing as desperate parents saw that there was an attorney who was boldly homeschooling in a negative legal environment. It wasn't long before Mike realized that he couldn't sustain the legal load because many of these homeschool families simply didn't have the money to afford an attorney.

Legal Defense Association Conceived

God put on his heart the concept of the Home School Legal Defense Association, where families could pool their resources for a minimal fee and thereby have the financial wherewithal to fight the cases and provide legal representation as needed.

At a conference hosted by Dr. Moore in Dallas, Mike met Kirk and Beverly McCord, early pioneering homeschoolers in Texas, and Jim Carden, a businessman who was also homeschooling his children. Mike was greatly encouraged to move forward with the founding of HSLDA. At another homeschool conference in Sacramento, California, in late 1982, Mike met Michael Smith.

As Mike Farris had been considering establishing HSLDA, he had contacted Michael Smith by phone and asked him to be a board member of this new organization. Michael Smith was open to the idea; he had been working with the Christian Home Education Association (CHEA) of California to help defend homeschool families in 1982. He and his wife, Elizabeth, had also been moved by the Holy Spirit to teach their three children at home, in spite of the negative legal atmosphere in California.

He too had heard Ray Moore on the radio. In Mike Smith's own words:

> As I was driving to court, I was listening to
> Dr. James Dobson's *Focus on the Family* radio program.
> He had as his guest that day Dr. and Mrs. Raymond
> Moore. Dr. Moore and his wife Dorothy had writ-
> ten two books that addressed early education. Among
> their conclusions was that little boys are typically two
> to three years behind their counterparts in maturity.
> They stated on that program that many times little
> boys from three years up to eight or nine years old are
> considered slow learners, when the problem is not the
> ability but the lack of maturity to handle what is being
> asked of them, such as reading.
>
> When I heard this, it immediately made sense.
> I knew from reading to Andrew, and many other types
> of interaction, that he was not stupid. He had tremen-
> dous memory and a real quick mind, but it had to be
> something he was interested in. He loved sports, he
> picked up information quickly, and he could under-
> stand complicated concepts. Well, I went to court and
> concluded the hearing I had that day. On my way back
> to the office, I continued to think about what I had
> heard. I thought this is just what Andrew needs,
> homeschooling.
>
> When I came home, I asked my wife, Elizabeth,
> to sit down and told her I had something important
> to talk to her about. I repeated what I heard on the
> radio show. After I finished the presentation, I asked
> Elizabeth what she thought. She surprised me with her
> response: "And what would your role in homeschooling
> be?" I must admit I had not considered what *my* role
> would be, but I sure had hers figured out: hours and
> hours of one-on-one tutoring of Andrew at the kitchen

table. If it was good enough for Thomas Jefferson and James Madison, it was good enough for Andrew. After just a few seconds she said that it made sense to her and she was game to find out more.

Mike and Elizabeth Smith continued to homeschool all their children all the way through high school and on into college.

When Mike Farris asked Mike Smith to be a board member, Mike agreed and later thought, *I wish I had thought of it.* But Mike Smith readily admits that he didn't think it would really work. The odds were too great against homeschooling. After all, it would be so difficult to make homeschooling legal, and he figured few people would attempt to do it.

God was bigger than Mike Smith and Mike Farris. Little did anyone realize at the time God would grow HSLDA into a strong, vibrant organization to defend the rights of "the little guy." Tens of thousands of homeschoolers all over America would benefit.

The original board members of HSLDA were Mike and Vickie Farris and Mike and Elizabeth Smith. Soon they asked Jim and Jeannie Carden to be on it as well.

While Mike Farris was working for the Bill of Rights Legal Foundation and spending the rest of his time working for Concerned Women for America and Beverly LaHaye, Beverly indicated that she wanted Mike to come to Washington, DC, to open an office there so they could be close to the workings of our national government. In the fall of 1983, Mike and his family moved to Washington.

HSLDA was already incorporated. Mike hired Jordan Lorence, an attorney from Minnesota and a single man, to handle legal contacts for the homeschoolers for half of his time; the other half of his time, he would be working for Concerned Women for America. All membership for HSLDA was handled in Dallas by Jim Carden's secretary.

In June 1985, as HSLDA was still struggling with about twelve hundred members, Mike Farris received a résumé from a third-year law student at the O. W. Coburn School of Law in Tulsa, Oklahoma. I had heard about Mike Farris and read the Concerned Women for America newsletter. God had put a call on my life to go into constitutional law, and I thought, *There may be a glut of attorneys in this country, but there's a shortage of Christian attorneys.* I, for one, wanted to do my part to reform our legal system to help protect my brothers and sisters who were under legal attack from the government. I would consider it a privilege to work for Mike Farris at Concerned Women for America.

I was interviewed by Mike Farris and Jordan Lorence, but not for CWA. I was being considered for the new position of executive director of the Home School Legal Defense Association. The Bible says that man makes his plans, but God directs his steps (see Prov. 16:9). God had led me to apply for a job I did not know was available with an organization that I did not know existed.

I was hired and moved to Virginia with my wife, Tracy, in May 1985. I began working at HSLDA while studying for the bar exam to become a full-fledged attorney. We did not have children yet, but we were already committed to home-schooling them. I clearly felt God's call to dedicate my life's work to defending families so they could teach their children God's ways. I have been with HSLDA ever since.

I've had the privilege to grow with the homeschool movement and to work with the first state homeschool leaders and develop friendships that run deep. And in times of persecution and challenge, relationships grow far stronger with the people you work alongside.

Mike Farris's Personal Account of His Most Inspiring Case

The Robin Diegel case in Ohio is the most inspiring case ever. The day before the trial, I flew out there and went to Mrs. Diegel's home. I went out in her backyard, and we sat at the picnic table. I was getting her prepared for trial and was talking to her about her religious beliefs. It was obvious to me that she really didn't know the Lord, even though she had a high respect for the Word of God and was oriented toward Christian things. So I walked her through the steps of salvation, and she prayed to receive Christ that afternoon. The next day I walked into the trial. The judge called us into chambers and said, "Mr. Farris, I just read the Schmidt decision from the Supreme Court of Ohio. You lost that case; you're going to lose this case again today." You know, I've been in courts where I thought the judge made up his mind before we started, but I never had one openly tell me.

I went out, but I did not tell Robin what the judge said. I told her the night before that I thought God was going to do something really powerful in her case to welcome her to His family and to go home and read the Bible.

The prosecutor put his case on first. He called the superintendent. My turn to cross-examine came up, and I asked a question I never asked before and never have asked since. It's a dumb question. It's objectionable, really. I asked, "Did you get any legal advice before you decided to turn this lady down in her right to homeschool?" The superintendent should have said no. What could I have said? Rather than do that, he tried to justify himself. He said, "Well, I didn't talk to any lawyers or anything like that, but I talked to some government officials." I said, "Well, like who?" He said, "Well, like the judge here." I said, "You talked to this judge about this lady's case before this thing ever came to court?" He said, "Yeah." You should have seen the judge's face. There was a newspaper reporter in the courtroom.

The judge called recess, and he took us back into the chambers. This time he was talking to the prosecutor: "You find a way to approve this lady." We had some pow-wows in the hall, and she got approved. We went out and announced that in court. The judge was very concerned that the newspaper reporter be informed that this case had been approved and none of this discussion business made it into the press. It turns out the judge made a good-faith mistake. He wasn't being a bad guy; he was just a brand-new judge who didn't know what the rules were. It worked out. The one question that was the chink in their armor jumped into my head out of the blue. That illustrates better than anything I know who is really the Advocate here.

It's not us; it's God. That is the story of HSLDA—that God is our Advocate, and we are just the conduits.

Who Are You Going to Call?

A police officer is at your door with an arrest warrant to take your six-year-old child. Whom can you call?

The truant officer is at your door and pushes his way in. He will not leave until he can take your children to public school. What can you do?

A social worker demands entry to your home and insists on interrogating your children. What are your rights?

A local public school official insists that your homeschool arrangement is not legal and threatens you with criminal charges. Where can you get help fast?

Home School Legal Defense Association is the answer.

The above accounts all actually happened to HSLDA members in Maine, Michigan, Alabama, and Indiana. In each situation, the family called me, and I was able to resolve the conflict on behalf of our members by telephone, fax, or Federal Express. This typifies the work of HSLDA's lawyers and legal staff on a nearly daily basis. HSLDA has enabled homeschooling parents throughout the country to pool their resources in order to defend in court those families who are being legally challenged. To this day, HSLDA handles more than ten thousand negative legal contacts and scores of court cases on behalf of member families each year. HSLDA also provides legal information to thousands of homeschoolers annually.

I am convinced that God has raised up HSLDA to become a major barrier against legal attempts to infringe on the freedoms of homeschoolers.

On the Side of the "Little Guy"

HSLDA has always been on the side of the "little guy." When threats and intimidation from the state loomed large, many families in the eighties felt alone and isolated. Membership in HSLDA gave these people confidence and hope that they had a voice. Faith in God and a feeling of strength in numbers helped us all think that maybe we could win this struggle.

Here are some of the comments we received from homeschool members during those early years:

> "Thank you so much for offering this service at such a reasonable rate. We feel so much more peaceful knowing that we have godly lawyers on our side."
> (Nypomo, California)

"I was impressed with your attitude and your real concern for our local problem. Thanks for representing us." (Monroe, Michigan)

"Thanks for your help and your assurances. We feel shaky treading on new ground, and it's comforting to talk to those who have been there and know the territory." (Chicago, Illinois)

"Once again, we are grateful to you for providing invaluable legal services and encouragement to American families committed to taking full responsibility for the rearing and educating of their children. Our prayers for you will continue." (Albany, New York)

"We definitely want to renew our membership but pray that we won't have to use it. We really feel from our hearts that this money is well spent to support those who do have to use your services." (Hewitt, Texas)

"We want to thank you for the prompt, kind, and helpful attitude that HSLDA displayed in our situation. It is good to know that we have dedicated, qualified, and concerned people to go to bat for us. HSLDA makes it easier for us parents to carry out our responsibilities and convictions we feel that God has given us." (Inyokern, California)

An Investment to Protect All Homeschoolers

For twenty years membership in HSLDA cost $100 annually per family. In 2004 the annual fee was raised for the first time to $115. If you do not use your $115 to receive legal representation yourself, another family will. In fact, in one case alone

involving a member homeschool family, HSLDA expended
over $75,000 in legal services and representation.

You are making an investment in protecting homeschoolers
throughout the nation when you join HSLDA. Mark DeJonge,
whose case took eight years to finally win, said, "It was the best
investment [I] ever made." It is a way for homeschoolers in
every state to work together to protect our commonly shared
freedoms.

Although homeschooling is finally legal in every state, each
state varies as to the manner in which it restricts the right to
homeschool. Each year, families face criminal prosecution for
teaching their children at home. Generally, only a few homeschoolers in any community are selected for trouble. When
this happens, the family faces enormous legal expense, mostly
in attorney fees. Families who are not prosecuted are often
intimidated into giving up or moving by the mere threat of
prosecution.

HSLDA enables such families to have low-cost access to a
quality legal defense, should the need arise. HSLDA guarantees
experienced legal counsel and representation by qualified attorneys to every member family who is challenged in the area of
homeschooling. Attorney fees, court costs, transcript charges,
expert witnesses, and attorney transportation will be paid in
full by the association. Presently, HSLDA has more than eighty
thousand families that are members with a staff of nearly sev-
enty, including eight attorneys and seven legal assistants.

You can join HSLDA by writing the Home School Legal
Defense Association at PO Box 3000, Purcellville, VA 20134,
or calling (540) 338-5600. You can also request an application
and a free summary of your state laws or apply online at www.
hslda.org.

Since 1983, after thousands of legal battles, HSLDA has
never had a member homeschool family who was forced to stop
homeschooling by the state. If a case was lost, HSLDA was able
to win the case on appeal or find an alternative legal way for the

family to homeschool or even change the law through legislation. We do not take "no" for an answer from the government. God and God alone deserves the credit for this extraordinary record.

HSLDA reserves the right to refuse membership to anyone who is already in trouble with their school district, so join before you encounter any problems. We depend on most of our member families not to be in trouble at a given time in order for there to be adequate finances to represent any member family who is threatened or criminally charged.

In addition to legally defending homeschool families, HSLDA also goes on the offensive in the fight to protect our freedoms. As the need arises, the organization files civil rights suits against school districts or social worker agencies for violating the rights of homeschoolers. Sometimes HSLDA will meet with a department of education or with a local school district in order to convince them to change a policy.

HSLDA attorneys regularly testify before state legislatures on behalf of good legislation or opposed to bad legislation. They can testify to a proposed law's constitutionality and the need for protecting homeschoolers' rights. Scores of "e-lerts" are sent out each legislative season, prompting thousands of homeschoolers to swamp legislatures with calls to help pass or defeat legislation that would affect the homeschooling community. And homeschoolers respond! Homeschoolers per capita are much more responsive and active than regular citizens when it comes to legislative matters, so when homeschoolers speak, the legislatures listen.

Homeschoolers have captured the whole principle of "the widow at the judge's door." Like HSLDA, homeschoolers will not take "no" for an answer. They want their children to have more freedom than they do, and so they are willing to sacrifice the time and effort to make a phone call to committee members or to legislators in order to influence legislation.

Lobbying the United States Congress

In addition to monitoring all fifty states' legislation, we are strategically based in Washington, DC, which enables us to monitor federal legislation. We spend scores of hours each month on Capitol Hill meeting with and persuading congressmen to vote to protect homeschool freedoms, parental freedoms, and religious freedoms.

For five years I superintended over HSLDA's National Center for Home Education, which was established in 1990 primarily for this purpose—to have a federal presence on Capitol Hill in order to protect your rights. One law from Congress can rewrite all fifty state laws and undermine our homeschool freedoms.

Your Homeschool Advocate

Each week we also talk with at least a half dozen correspondents from newspapers, TV, and radio to help get the word out about homeschoolers and their tremendous academic success.

We provide a bimonthly magazine, the *Home School Court Report*, for member families at no charge. The magazine covers legal issues and other matters of concern to homeschool parents.

In addition, the HSLDA attorneys travel regularly around the country, speaking at homeschool conventions, helping to inspire people to keep on keeping on in the area of homeschooling, and warning home educators of important legal issues that will affect them.

Recently HSLDA launched Generation Joshua, a ministry that encourages youth to become active in political campaigns to help elect godly leaders who understand our constitutional freedoms. This program also provides civics instruction and coordinates voter registration drives.

Fighting Spiritual Battles Every Day

Week by week, month by month, year by year, the opponents of homeschooling have proven tireless. Of course, we are not naïve; we understand that this is spiritual warfare:

> For our struggle is not against flesh and blood, but against the rulers, against the powers, against the world forces of this darkness, against the spiritual forces of wickedness in the heavenly places. Therefore, take up the full armor of God, so that you will be able to resist in the evil day, and having done everything, to stand firm. (Eph. 6:12–13)

As long as the ruler of this world, Satan, is still active, until he is finally thrown into the everlasting lake of fire, we will face these battles. But God is on the throne, and we can do all things through Him who strengthens us. God has called me to stand firm until I can go no further, until He is done with me. So I intend to serve the homeschooling community as long as He gives me the breath and the ability to do so.

HSLDA Lawyers Always on Call

One of the benefits of membership in HSLDA is an emergency hotline for members to call day or night, including weekends and holidays. This way, HSLDA is able to provide defense for a family in case a social worker or truant officer comes to their door at odd hours when our office is not open.

Perhaps a few examples of the type of calls HSLDA is barraged with every day will help you appreciate the dangers to the homeschool movement that have been around since the beginning and continue to this day.

All of the HSLDA attorneys share weekend hotline duties. On this particular weekend, it was my turn to handle the calls.

Friday, 6:00 P.M.

An alarmed family in Fairfax County, Virginia, asked HSLDA for help with an urgent truancy contact. Although the family was legally operating under a religious exemption, a local truancy officer had instructed the mother to call him within twenty-four hours or he would return with a court order and a search warrant.

I helped the family draft a letter describing their religious beliefs to the school board to demonstrate that they had met all the requirements for Virginia statutory religious exemption. The family was able to avoid further harassment, and the truant officer never returned.

8:05 P.M.

A California member was being harassed by protective services. The father had cerebral palsy and was in a wheelchair. Acting on false allegations regarding the cleanliness of the home, the CPS agent gave him an ultimatum to be answered by Tuesday, February 20. If he would sign papers agreeing to six months of surveillance visits by a social worker, the CPS would drop the investigation. We were able to help resolve the situation to the family's satisfaction and remove the threat.

8:19 P.M.

A member family in New Hampshire just received a note from Health and Human Services regarding an alleged lack of supervision of their children. I counseled the family to give minimal information to the social worker and resolve the contact.

Saturday, 12:30 P.M.

In January a single mother moved from another state to Enrico County, Virginia. She had called HSLDA on Saturday, shocked to have received a letter, dated February 6, indicating the school district was filing a petition of truancy against her on February 13. The mother, who was homeschooling her special needs child, had previously notified the school district pursuant to the homeschool law in Virginia, which required her to demonstrate that her curriculum met the state standards of learning objectives for language, arts, and math. She was understandably upset by this rude welcome to Virginia.

I promised to follow up with the school district, and the following Tuesday I was able to get the petition of truancy canceled. I persuaded the school district to formally recognize the homeschool program by simply having the mother submit a copy of the table of contents for her books, covering language, arts, and math.

3:45 P.M.

A member in Ohio called after being visited by a local child welfare agency. The social worker wanted to meet with the entire family, including their eight children on the following Tuesday. The family was turned in by a neighbor—the local superintendent—on allegations pertaining to their oldest daughter. Although there was no evidence of abuse, the social worker insisted on interviewing all the children. I extensively counseled the family to postpone the scheduled meeting. The contact was later resolved.

Monday, President's Day, 8:43 A.M.

Received a call from a family in Indiana. The Department of Child Welfare Services had contacted them in regard to their homeschooling. I provided the necessary legal advice, and the situation was subsequently resolved.

11:20 A.M.

Another HSLDA member called, this time from Kansas. The mother had taken her homeschooled child to the emergency room for a slight injury. One of the nurses asked about the child's immunizations. The mother explained that she did not do immunizations and understood that was her right. The nurse immediately became upset and told her that she would turn them into the Social and Rehabilitative Services Agency. I helped the mother write a religious exemption letter concerning their immunization exemptions to provide to social services, and the situation was resolved.

5:15 P.M.

A homeschooling father in Iowa called me. His wife had taken their two children to the dentist, and the dentist discovered four cavities in the mouth of one child. The dentist wanted to work on the cavities immediately, but the mom declined, saying that she wanted to make an appointment with the local university's dental school, so she could acquire fillings for her son at a lower cost. Upset, the dentist turned the family into the child welfare service.

The father called HSLDA's emergency number when a social worker arrived at their home. Over the telephone I talked with the social worker, explaining that she could not enter the house and talk to the children, as she was insisting. I also prepared the father to have a brief conversation with her sticking to the singular subject of the dental situation.

The father handled the social worker well and with confidence. When she wanted to see their son's teeth, he asked if she was a dentist. When she said she needed to make sure "the child was healthy," the father responded, "Are you a doctor?" Again she answered no and this time stated that she needed to make sure the children were alive!

I discussed further with the social worker the situation and reminded her that she had enough evidence to prove the child was alive and healthy without conducting an invasive private interview and going on dental explorations. The social worker agreed to drop the case as unfounded.

Homeschooling Will Always Be a Target

Homeschooling will always be a target of the state as long as the state has jurisdiction over families through the compulsory attendance laws and the child welfare codes. Our job is to help families be prepared and feel confident so that they don't get caught unaware and end up letting social workers into their homes and interviewing their children. I know homeschooling is a safer choice because of HSLDA, and I believe God has raised up the organization for such a time as this.

Yet those of us who began with HSLDA in the early years had no concept of the vast influence God would give us to help shape the laws of the country to protect the rights of homeschoolers in all fifty states. This is nothing short of a miracle. God uses small beginnings to do great things.

As I struggle now with physical weakness and my inability to put my own socks on, I appreciate more and more how God uses the weak things of the world to put to shame the mighty (see 1 Cor. 1:27). This is God's way. He doesn't need a huge army; He just needs some Davids who are willing to face the Goliaths of state government to stand up for what is right and for His truth. God and God alone deserves all the credit and glory for how far we have come.

America stands as a beacon for freedom throughout the rest of the world in this area of homeschooling, and we continue to hope and pray that our influence will be used by God in America to keep homeschoolers free.

4

Homeschoolers Prove Themselves

But may it never be that I would boast, except in the cross of our Lord Jesus Christ, through which the world has been crucified to me, and I to the world.

GALATIANS 6:14

When the "new" idea of homeschooling first made the rounds in the latter years of the twentieth century, it was immediately dismissed and rejected. The education establishment was offended at the idea. After all, they demanded, how could a mere mom educate her child as well as the public school system? Who were these parents who dared to think they could provide a sufficient education for their children?

The public school system and institutional schooling had been around for a hundred years, so people had forgotten that our country was established by men who were taught by their own parents. How easily people can forget their heritage.

In my book *Home Schooling: The Right Choice*, I cite much recent evidence of the tremendous successes of millions of families teaching their own children. However, there continues to be many members of the educational establishment who still think the homeschooling "experiment" is a failure.

When I began working at HSLDA in 1985, a Gallup poll came out showing that 70 percent of Americans were of the opinion that homeschooling should not be legal. Thankfully a Gallup poll taken in the late 1990s discovered the opposite was now true: 70 percent of Americans now believed that homeschooling was a valid educational alternative.

No doubt this is because study after study has shown that homeschooling works.

This is one of the messages HSLDA routinely sends to the press: Homeschooling works. So why should the government pick on families who choose this option? It's a powerful argument to put before those who would like to stifle parental choice.

The facts are clear, homeschoolers have *earned the right* to be left alone, and they have achieved the successes summarized in this chapter *without government money*. The government has never provided a dollar to the homeschool movement, and without the government's help the homeschool movement has achieved unparalleled success.

God Uses Dr. Moore to Light the Flame

In the early 1980s, Dr. Raymond Moore and his late wife, Dorothy, discovered the truth that children learn better if they are educated later than earlier. In 1972, Dr. Moore wrote an article for *Harpers Magazine* on the dangers of early schooling. *Reader's Digest* picked up this article and distributed it to many more millions of people. Dr. Moore struck a chord. More and more people began to doubt the American education system.

Dr. Moore ended up writing a book called *Better Late than Early*, which served as one of the foundational books for the modern homeschool movement. In 1982, he was interviewed twice by James Dobson, with *Focus on the Family*. These shows on homeschooling created a spark in the Christian community. Millions of people were exposed for the first time to the thought of teaching their children themselves. And it made sense, especially in light of the failing public school system.

Dr. Moore has said, "Dr. Dobson's attention made a great deal of difference. He said he got three times as many listener letters from our appearances than he had ever gotten from any program before." Dr. Moore did further ground-breaking research on parent-directed education, which helped to fuel the homeschool movement. He was the first voice heard in the major media advocating homeschooling.

Brian Ray and the National Home Education Research Institute

Also in 1982, the Holy Spirit was stirring in the heart of a young man named Dr. Brian Ray. When he first began homeschooling, he was a doctoral student at Oregon University. He began reading studies on parental involvement in a child's education to help increase his academic performance.

Before he actually started homeschooling, Brian had formed the "Homeschool Researcher" in 1985. He began to see that the facts could not be disputed: *Homeschooling, no matter what the establishment says, really works.*

His wife, Betsy, was a student teacher and witnessed firsthand the inefficiency and ungodliness of the public schools. One day she came home from another day in pursuit of her teacher's certificate, saying, "I don't know what I'll do, but I'll never put my child in school." She was pregnant with Hallie, the Rays' first child.

Michael Farris, president of HSLDA, had met Brian while he was pursuing his doctorate and told him, "The moment you become a Ph.D, give me a call, and we will make you an expert in the courtroom." To prove our cases, HSLDA needed experts who could testify from an academic-professional vantage point that homeschooling really does work.

By 1987, Brian had attended a Gregg Harris seminar, and they began homeschooling their firstborn. In 1990, he founded the National Home Education Research Institute to report on what he and others had found in their studies of homeschoolers.

He was fully convinced of the validity of homeschooling when Hallie came home from her first day of public school. When asked what she liked about school, she said, "I like recess." When questioned about the rest of school, she said it was "kind of boring just sitting around."

Brian told me, "My goal continues to be to glorify God. That's my number one motivation for helping continue to establish the legitimacy of homeschooling in a doubting world."

Research: A Key to Establishing Legitimacy

Homeschooling has held up to scrutiny more than anyone ever imagined, as study after study has been done over the last twenty years. It is beyond dispute that homeschooling is one of the most (if not the most) successful forms of education.

In 1985, HSLDA sponsored a random sampling survey of HSLDA members by independent educational research consultant Lauri Scogin. Three hundred homeschooling families were surveyed from all over the United States. The main purpose of the survey was to compare standardized test scores with students' actual grade levels.

Approximately 63 percent of the families had been homeschooling for two or more years. In reading, 18.26 percent of the students surveyed were reading at their grade level or up to eleven months ahead, while 72.61 percent were one year or more ahead. In math, 29.46 percent were working at their grade level or up to eleven months ahead, while 49.79 percent were working one year or more ahead of their public school counterparts.

The educational background of the parents was also studied, revealing that 45 percent of the parents had a college degree or higher, while more than 50 percent of the parents teaching their children at home successfully had only a high school diploma.

This was encouraging news for everyone in the homeschool community. Of course, we knew it in our hearts already, but it was nice to see it on paper in one of our early issues of HSLDA's *Home School Court Report*.

The Trickle of Research Becomes a Flood

At this point the research began coming in faster and faster from all over the country. Local school districts were monitoring homeschooling and finding that homeschoolers were scoring above average. State departments of education were concerned about the homeschool movement and began investigating and found the same results.

This proved to be the groundwork for our work at HSLDA, proving our case in courts of law. Even though the preliminary research was coming in strongly in favor of homeschooling, most states still did not allow homeschooling or regulated it so heavily that it was near impossible to choose this option. So the research conducted by Dr. Raymond Moore, Brian Ray, and many others was useful for proving that homeschooling was a less restrictive means to "otherwise serve" the state's compelling interest that children be educated.

Nonetheless, too often the courts turned a blind eye. They were concerned more about whether the family had "bowed the knee" to the state by being a licensed certified teacher or submitting to home visits and curriculum approval than whether their children were succeeding academically. But HSLDA fought on, knowing their cause was right.

Somehow, God would find a way.

A Brief Summary of the Growing Research

Below is some of the research that came out during those early years, and even until the present day it continues to show unabated that homeschooling works.

Strengths of Their Own

In 1997 a study of 5,402 homeschool students from 1,657 families was released. It was entitled *Strengths of Their Own: Home Schoolers Across America*. The study demonstrated that homeschoolers, on average, outperformed their counterparts in the public schools by thirty to thirty-seven percentile points in all subjects. A significant finding when analyzing the data for eighth-graders was that students who are homeschooled two or more years score substantially higher than students who have been homeschooled one year or less. The new homeschoolers were scoring on average in the fifty-ninth percentile compared with students homeschooled the last two or more years, who scored between the eighty-sixth and the ninety-second percentile.[1]

This was confirmed in another study by Dr. Lawrence Rudner of 20,760 homeschooled students, which found that students who have homeschooled all their school-aged years had the highest academic achievement. This was especially apparent among students in the higher grades.[2] This should encourage families to catch a long-range vision and homeschool through high school.

Another important finding of *Strengths of Their Own* was that the race of the student does not make any difference. There was no significant difference between minority and white homeschooled students. For example, in grades K–12, both white and

minority students scored, on average, in the eighty-seventh percentile. In math, whites scored in the eighty-second percentile,
while minorities scored in the seventy-seventh percentile.

In the public schools, however, there was a sharp con-
trast among races. White public school eighth-grade students
nationally scored in the fifty-eighth percentile in math and the
fifty-seventh percentile in reading. Black eighth-grade students,
on the other hand, scored on average at the twenty-fourth percentile in math and the twenty-eighth percentile in reading.
Hispanics scored at the twenty-ninth percentile in math and
the twenty-eighth percentile in reading.[3]

These findings show that when parents, regardless of race,
commit themselves to make the necessary sacrifices and tutor
their children at home, almost all obstacles present in other
school systems disappear.

Another obstacle that seems to be overcome in homeschooling is the need to spend a great deal of money in order to obtain
a good education. In *Strengths of Their Own*, Dr. Ray found the
average cost per homeschool student is $546 annually while the
average cost per public school student is $5,325. Yet the home-
school children in this study significantly outperformed public
school students in nationally standardized achievement tests.[4]

Similarly, the 1998 study by Dr. Rudner of 20,760 students,
found that eighth-grade students whose parents spent $199 or
less per year on their home education scored, on average, in
the eightieth percentile. Eighth-grade students whose parents
spent $400 to $599 on their home education also scored, on
average, in the eightieth percentile! Once the parents spend
over $600, the students do slightly better, scoring in the eighty-
third percentile.[5]

The message is loud and clear. More money does not mean
a better education. There is no positive correlation between
money spent on education and student performance. Public
school advocates could refocus their emphasis if they learned
this lesson. The presence and attention of loving and caring

parents are what matters. Money can never replace simple hard work.

The last significant statistic from the *Strengths of Their Own* study regards the effect of government regulation on homeschooling. Dr. Brian Ray compared the impact of government regulation on the academic performance of homeschool students and found no positive correlation. In other words, whether a state had a high degree of regulation (i.e., curriculum approval, teacher qualifications, testing, home visits) or a state had no regulation of homeschoolers, the homeschooled students in both categories of states performed the same. The students all scored on average in the eighty-sixth percentile regardless of state regulation.[6]

Homeschool freedom works. Homeschoolers have earned the right to be left alone.

Riverside Publishing Study

In a study released by HSLDA's National Center for Home Education on November 10, 1994, standardized test results provided by the Riverside Publishing Company from 16,311 homeschoolers from all fifty states, K–12, showed that homeschool students tested, on average, at the seventy-seventh percentile of the basic battery of the Iowa Test of Basic Skills. In reading the homeschoolers' nationwide grand mean was at the seventy-ninth percentile. This means that homeschool students performed better in reading than 29 percent of the same population on whom the test was normed. In the area of language arts and math, the typical homeschooler scored in the seventy-third percentile.

These 16,311 homeschool students' scores were not self-selected but represented all the homeschoolers whose tests were scored through the Riverside Publishing Company. It is important to note that this summary of homeschool achievement test scores demonstrates that 54.7 percent of the students in grades

K–12 are achieving individual scores in the top quarter of the population of students in the United States.[7]

1991 HSLDA Survey

In 1991 a survey of standardized test scores was performed by the Home School Legal Defense Association in cooperation with the Psychological Corporation, which publishes the Stanford Achievement Test. The study involved the administering of the Stanford Achievement Test (8th Edition, Form J) to 5,124 homeschooled students. These K–12 students represented all fifty states. Testing was administered in spring 1991 under controlled test conditions in accordance with the test publisher's standards. All tests were machine-scored by the Psychological Corporation.

The homeschoolers' composite scores on the basic battery of tests in reading, math, and language arts ranked eighteen to twenty-eight percentile points above public school averages. For instance, 692 homeschooled fourth-graders averaged in the seventy-seventh percentile in reading, the sixty-third percentile in math, and the seventieth percentile in language arts.

The homeschooled high schoolers did even better, which goes against the trend in public schools where studies show the longer a child is in the public schools, the lower he scores on standardized tests. One hundred and eighteen tenth-grade homeschool students, as a group, scored on average in the eighty-second percentile in reading, the seventieth percentile in math, and the eighty-first percentile in language arts.

Montana Homeschoolers Score High in 1991 Study

The Bob Jones University Testing Service of South Carolina provided test results of Montana homeschoolers. Also, a survey of homeschoolers in Montana was conducted by the National Home Education Research Institute. Dr. Brian Ray evaluated the survey and test results and found that, on average, the home-educated students in this study scored above the national norm in all subject areas on standardized achievement tests. These students scored, on average, at the seventy-second percentile in terms of a combination of their reading, language, and math performance. This is well above the national average.[8]

North Dakota Study of Homeschoolers

In North Dakota, Dr. Brian Ray conducted a survey of 205 homeschoolers throughout the state. The middle reading score was the eighty-fourth percentile, language was the eighty-first percentile, science was the eighty-seventh percentile, social studies was the eighty-sixth percentile, and math was the eighty-first percentile. Further, Dr. Ray found no significant statistical differences in academic achievement between those students taught by parents with less formal education and those students taught by parents with higher formal education.

South Carolina Homeschoolers Score Significantly Higher Than Average

In South Carolina in 1990, the National Center for Home Education did a survey of sixty-five homeschool students and found that the average scores on the Comprehensive Test of Basic Skills were thirty percentile points higher than national public school averages. In math, 92 percent of the homeschool students scored above grade level, and 93 percent of the homeschool students were at or above grade level in reading. These scores were "achieved in a state where public school SAT scores are next-to-last in national rankings."[9]

Nationwide Study of 2,163 Homeschool Families

In 1990 the National Home Education Research Institute issued a report entitled "A Nationwide Study of Home

Education: Family Characteristics, Legal Matters, and Student Achievement." This was a study of 2,163 homeschooling families. The study found that the average scores of the homeschool students were at or above the eightieth percentile in all subject areas.

The research revealed that there was no positive correlation between state regulation of homeschools and the home-schooled students' performance. The study compared homeschoolers in three groups of states representing various levels of regulation. Group 1 represented the most restrictive states such as Michigan; Group 2 represented slightly less restrictive states, including North Dakota; and Group 3 represented unregulated states such as Texas and California. The institute concluded:

> *No* difference was found in the achievement scores of students between the three groups which represent various degrees of state regulation of home education. . . .
> It was found that students in all three regulation groups scored on the average at or above the seventy-sixth percentile in the three areas examined: total reading, total math, and total language. These findings, in conjunction with others described in this section, do *not* support the idea that state regulation and compliance on the part of home education families assures successful student achievement.[10]

Furthermore, this same study demonstrated that only 13.9 percent of the mothers (the primary teachers) had ever been certified teachers. The study found that there was no difference in the students' total reading, total math, and total language scores based on the teacher certification status of their parents: "The findings of this study do *not* support the idea that parents need to be trained and certified teachers to assure successful academic achievement of their children."[11]

Pennsylvania Homeschoolers Are No Exception

In Pennsylvania, 171 homeschooled students took the CTBS standardized achievement test. The tests were administered in group settings by Pennsylvania-certified teachers. The middle reading score for the students tested was the eighty-ninth percentile; math, the seventy-second percentile; science, the eighty-seventh percentile; and social studies, the eighty-first percentile. A survey conducted of the homeschool families who participated in this testing found that the average student spent only sixteen hours per week in formal schooling (i.e., structured lessons that were preplanned by either the parent or a provider of educational materials).[12]

State Department of Education Statistics on Homeschoolers

Several state departments of education or local school districts have also gathered statistics on the academic progress of homeschooled children. Although perhaps prejudiced, even the states could not argue with the facts. It is interesting to note that they all seem to have stopped conducting these studies. I guess they didn't like what they found.

Tennessee

In the spring of 1987, the Tennessee Department of Education found that homeschooled children in second grade, on average, scored in the ninety-third percentile, while their public school counterparts scored in the sixty-second percentile on the Stanford Achievement Test. Eighth-grade homeschooled students scored, on average, in the eighty-seventh percentile in reading and in the seventy-first percentile in math, while their public school counterparts scored in the seventy-fifth percentile in reading and the sixty-ninth percentile in math.[13]

Alaska and Oregon

In 1986 the State Department of Education in Alaska, which had surveyed homeschooled children's test results every other year since 1981, found homeschooled children to be scoring approximately sixteen percentage points higher, on average, than children of the same grades in conventional schools.

In Oregon, the State Department of Education compiled test score statistics for 1,658 homeschooled children in 1988 and found that 51 percent of the children scored above the seventy-first percentile and 73 percent scored above the fifty-first percentile.

North Carolina

In North Carolina, the Division of Non-Public Education compiled test results of 2,144 homeschool students in grades K–12. Of the 1,061 homeschool students taking the California Achievement Test, they scored on average at the seventy-third percentile on the total battery of tests. The 755 homeschool students who took the Iowa Test of Basic Skills scored at the eightieth percentile in the total battery of tests. The remaining students who took the Stanford scored, on average, at the seventy-third percentile in the whole battery.[14]

Arkansas

In Arkansas, for the 1987–88 school term, the Department of Education reported that homeschooled children on average scored in the seventy-fifth percentile on the Metropolitan Achievement Test 6. They outscored public school children in every subject—reading, math, language, science, and social studies—and at every grade level.[15]

Arizona

According to the Arizona State Department of Education, 1,123 homeschooled children in grades 1–9, on average, scored above grade level in reading, language arts, and math on standardized tests for the 1988–89 school year. Four grades tested scored a full grade level ahead of their peers in public school.[16]

Nebraska

The Nebraska Department of Education reported that of 259 homeschooled children who returned to public or nonpublic schools, 134 of them were automatically placed in their grade level according to their age without testing. Of the remaining who were given entrance tests, thirty-three scored above grade level, forty-three were at grade level, and twenty-nine were below grade level. Approximately 88 percent of the returning students scored at or above grade level after being home-schooled for a period of time. This survey included responses from 429 accredited schools.[17]

Early Local School District Statistics on Homeschooling

In 1988 thirty homeschooled children in Albuquerque, New Mexico, participated in the state-mandated testing program (Comprehensive Test of Basic Skills) and scored, on average, in the eighty-third percentile for third grade, the eighty-fifth percentile for fifth grade, and the eighty-ninth percentile for eighth grade. This group of homeschoolers scored twenty to twenty-five percentile points higher than the local public school students taking the CTBS in 1987.[18]

A 1980 study in Los Angeles showed homeschooled students scoring higher on standardized tests than children in the Los Angeles public schools.[19]

In South Carolina, the Greenville County School District stated, "Kids taught at home last year outscored those in public schools on basic skills tests." In that county, fifty-seven out of sixty-one homeschooled students "met or exceeded the state's minimum performance standard on the reading test" of the Comprehensive Test of Basic Skills. The homeschool students' passing rate was 93.4 while the public school counterparts passing rate was 83.9 percent. Furthermore, in math, the homeschooled students passing rate was 87.9 percent compared to the public school students' passing rate of 82.1 percent.[20]

In Nevada, according to Washoe County School District's data, homeschooled students scored higher than their public school counterparts in first through seventh grade. All children were tested with the Stanford Achievement Test, and homeschoolers consistently scored higher in reading vocabulary, reading comprehension, math concepts, math comprehension and application. The most extreme gap between the public school children and the homeschooled children showed up in the area of vocabulary. For example, fourth-graders in public school scored in the forty-ninth percentile while the homeschooled fourth-graders scored in the eightieth percentile.

Homeschool Excellence Continues Unabated

Homeschoolers continue to exhibit academic excellence when compared to public school students and national averages for college admissions tests.

ACT college admission exam scores show homeschoolers consistently performing above the national level. In both 2002 and 2003, homeschoolers scored at a national average of 22.5, while the national average overall was 20.8. The College Board, which administers the Scholastic Aptitude Test (SAT), also notes the above-average performance of homeschoolers. In 2002 homeschoolers averaged a total score of 1092, seventy-two points higher than the national average of 1020. In 2001 homeschoolers scored 1100 on the SAT, compared to the national average of 1019.

Homeschoolers are also making their presence known in the National Merit Scholarship Program. The National Merit Scholarship Program is an academic competition for recognition and scholarships that began in 1955. High school students enter the National Merit Program by taking the PSAT/NMSQT and by meeting published program entry and participation requirements. Approximately 1.3 million initial entrants are screened each year.

Each year about sixteen thousand nationwide qualify as semifinalists, and about 90 percent of these students go on to become finalists. The National Merit Scholarship Corporation has announced that 250 of the semifinalists in 2004 were homeschool students.

The National Merit Scholarship has also seen a dramatic increase of homeschoolers who place as finalists. Of the 248 homeschoolers among the 2003 semifinalists, 129 of these students advanced to finalist standing, receiving the National Merit Scholarship. As noted by Kate Grossman, a reporter with the *Chicago Sun-Times*, the number of homeschoolers receiving National Merit Scholarships has increased more than 500 percent over the past nine years.

Patrick Henry College serves as an example of the quality of homeschool students. Ninety-six percent of PHC's students have been homeschooled at some point in their education. The 2002 middle range of freshman SAT scores was 1200–1410. Compared with *U.S. News and World Report*'s 2002 college rankings report (in which PHC was not included), Patrick Henry College would rank second among Christian colleges in SAT scores.

Evidence of the academic excellence of homeschoolers is nothing new, but these statistics only reinforce the trend that homeschoolers, on average, score higher than their public school counterparts.

The statistics point to one conclusion: Homeschooling works. Even many of the state departments of education, which are generally biased toward the public school system, cannot argue with these facts. Not only does homeschooling work, but it works without the myriad state controls and accreditation standards imposed on the public schools.

5

The Relentless Opposition

Be of sober spirit, be on the alert. Your adversary, the devil,
prowls about like a roaring lion, seeking someone to devour.
But resist him, firm in your faith, knowing that the same
experiences of suffering are being accomplished by your
brethren who are in the world.

1 PETER 5:8–9

As I have traveled around the country defending home-schooling families in court, speaking at conferences, and testifying before legislatures since 1985, I have become convinced of the crucial war that is raging over the control of our children. Families trying diligently to teach their children are being harassed and intimidated by the state authorities instead of encouraged. I have seen too many families charged with criminal truancy or child neglect for simply taking an interest in educating their children and following God's call on their lives. Some families are even threatened with having their children taken away.

Every now and then during those years I wondered, *How can the right of teaching our own children, one of the most basic of all rights, ever be in jeopardy in the Land of the Free?* We don't want to believe that persecution from the state can really happen, but it has and it does. From the beginning of the modern movement, homeschoolers have been fighting on the front lines for the preservation of their basic First Amendment freedoms. If the homeschoolers had lost, the Christian schools would be lost; and, ultimately, the family would be lost. Homeschoolers back in the 1980s did not take this war lightly; homeschoolers today must continue to be vigilant.

It has become increasingly apparent to me during the course of my work that the issue was rarely whether a family's children are being educated—in virtually every case HSLDA has ever handled, the children have scored above average on standardized achievement tests. The real issue, I learned, is who has the authority to dictate how the children are educated, the parents or the public school authorities. This issue can be further divided into two underlying themes: control and money.

The Philosophy of Control

The state, in the form of the public school system and its lobbying arm, the National Education Association (NEA), believe that they alone have sufficient knowledge and ability to control the education of America's children. In my interactions over the years with public school administrators and teachers and many hundreds of local superintendents, I have found this belief to be common.

Time and again superintendents have told me that parents who have not had at least seven years of higher education couldn't possibly provide their children with an adequate education. Some superintendents personally admitted to me that to their minds "no form of homeschooling is adequate." As a result, these superintendents tried to stop homeschools from operating in their district.

Other superintendents have denied homeschools the right to exist because, they assert, children cannot be properly socialized unless they are in a large class interacting with other children. One outrageous argument was raised in a North Dakota homeschool trial handled by HSLDA's Mike Farris. The prosecutor stated that homeschooling was inadequate because the children did not have the educational advantage of being pushed around by a school bully. In other words, it is harmful for a child to be sheltered from bullies because he will miss out on an important social experience that would have prepared him for life. Of course, this is the exact kind of "negative" socialization that homeschoolers want to spare their children and replace with godly standards for personal interaction.

I have seen homeschoolers prosecuted because the superintendent did not personally like the family, and others have been prosecuted because their curriculum did not adhere close enough to the public school's curriculum.

The crux of the matter is that many school administrators actually believe that both the authority and responsibility to teach children resides with the state. They believe sincerely that they are the "guardians" of our children and that their authority surpasses that of the children's parents. They argue that the education of our children should be left to professionals who possess teaching certificates and are specially trained. As a result, many superintendents over the years have operated under the assumption that they had and should have virtually unlimited authority to control a homeschooler's program, and their pride was hurt if a homeschooler tried to resist their attempts to control the homeschool.

Unfortunately the law has often been vague or completely on their side, allowing administrators to pursue this philosophy without limit. That is why we at HSLDA have stood in the gap for the homeschoolers to protect them from prosecution.

National Education Association: Biggest Advocate for State Control

The largest union in the country was and still is the National Education Association. This organization is the single greatest factor contributing to states' mentality that demands control over homeschoolers. In 1986, the NEA published *Today's Education*, a 166-page yearbook documenting what they wanted to accomplish in the schools. Some of their agenda included pushing for mandatory kindergarten and teaching sex education, reproductive freedom, affirmative action, disarmament, and nuclear freeze in the classroom. Also, they were against teaching creation in the schools, against a federal balanced budget, against aid to freedom fighters, and against tuition tax credits.

As far as homeschooling, the NEA recommended in 1984 that its members push for laws that require homeschool teachers to be certified. They also recommended that public school teachers work toward legislation to enact laws requiring annual approval of the homeschool, monitoring by the local public school, home instruction comparable to that in public schools, mandated testing, and records of progress, attendance, and instructional time. This is all contained in the *Report on Home Schooling* by the NEA Standing Committee on Instruction and Professional Development.

To this day the NEA continues to pass resolutions stating that homeschoolers need to be licensed instructors and their curriculum must be approved by a state specialist. Their stance against homeschooling has not changed one iota since 1984. It's plain and simple, and they don't want to be confused by the facts.

In nearly every legislative battle over homeschooling I have ever witnessed, the proponents for greater regulation have always been supported by the NEA or another major educational establishment organization. They need to maintain tight controls in order to achieve their agenda. They want to turn homeschools into small public schools in the home. In fact, I have personally talked to dozens of school superintendents who have claimed that homeschools are just "extensions of the public schools," thus justifying their restrictive standards and tight monitoring they have tried to apply. The prevailing philosophy held by the public schools administrators is that homeschooling is a privilege, not a right.

The Philosophy of Money

The other issue besides the states' desire for control is one of money. Your child in 1985 was worth between $2,000 and $3,000 in tax dollars given to the school district by the state and federal government if your child was enrolled in the public school. Today that amount has increased to $7,000 per child!

It was to the advantage of public school officials back in 1985 to deny the homeschoolers' right to exist in order to get children back into public schools. With an estimated two million homeschool students in the country today, that's quite a bit of lost revenue for the schools!

Professional educators understood that the more lenient the laws and policies—which homeschoolers were pushing so hard for—the more likely large numbers of students would be removed from the public schools. The survival of the public schools and the teachers union is dependent on the number of children in the public school system. They have a vested interest in public education, and homeschooling is competing with that interest.

In the 1980s public schools officials had two choices to bring more money into the school district: they could disprove or make it impossible for homeschoolers to exist in their locale, thereby forcing children back onto the public school rolls and, subsequently, collecting the tax money for that child; or they could try to collect the money for each homeschool student anyway.

Time and time again I had parents tell me that when the truant officer came to the door to intimidate them to return their children to public school, they would indicate, "Do you know how much money the public school is losing because you have removed your children from public school?" This was a common refrain.

Today things are changing.

By God's grace and much sacrifice by many brave families, the laws have largely shifted in favor of homeschoolers. The same homeschoolers who once upon a time had the law against them now have the law with them. Homeschooling is legal in all fifty states, all thanks be to God.

The Battle Is Still Not Over

The battle has been intense these last twenty years, as homeschoolers have emerged from essentially bondage to freedom. It is easy to assume that, now that homeschooling is legal in every state, public school authorities will support homeschooling. But a recent survey by the *American School Board Journal* tells a different story.

A Xavier University research team joined the journal to conduct a national survey of nearly one thousand public school executives, including superintendents and principals. Surprisingly 55 percent of the public school officials surveyed believe that homeschoolers do not meet the academic standards set by the state, and 24 percent admit they have no idea whatsoever how homeschoolers perform academically.

When asked to rank the alternatives to public schools, 95 percent of public school officials believe *anything* is better than homeschooling. And when it comes to regulation of homeschooling, 71 percent of them believe homeschoolers are not regulated enough. Finally, a mere 1 percent of school officials believe that homeschool students perform better than their peers in public schools.

It is clear that the old prejudices still remain. The majority of public school officials are presently being held at bay by the law and court decisions favoring homeschoolers, but their hearts have not been won. At the first opportunity, they will implement methods to regulate and curtail homeschooling. Let's not give them an excuse by going back to Egypt for handouts (a.k.a. tax dollars).

※ 6

Are Parents Qualified to Teach?

He does not delight in the strength of the horse; He does not take pleasure in the legs of a man. The LORD favors those who fear Him, those who wait for His lovingkindness.

PSALM 147:10–11

Iflew to North Dakota in the dead of winter to represent two HSLDA families in 1987. The weather was as cold and nasty as the treatment homeschoolers received at the hands of the authorities.

The first family I represented was the Nelsons. They were homeschooling their only child. At the airport I was picked up by my friend Greg Lange of Hazen. He was a homeschool dad and lawyer who served as HSLDA's local counsel in all our many cases throughout North Dakota. The law said all teachers had to be licensed by the state. If a North Dakota homeschool family was discovered, they went to court!

But the principle behind HSLDA that Mike Farris had envisioned was working! We only had about forty-five members in North Dakota in the 1980s, and their membership fees together would not even be enough to finance one case! But we handled dozens of cases—and for each case: airfare, court fees, transcripts, local counsel, hotels, and more. Homeschoolers' membership fees in other safer states paid for their brothers and sisters in sparsely populated North Dakota.

On November 17 the Nelson family was tried in Sargent County. The elements of the crime were that the prosecution had to prove whether the child was school age and lived in the county and whether the parents were licensed, certified teachers.

The prosecution presented its case. The prosecutor explained that the parents were not certified and described where they lived within the county. The prosecutor stated confidently, "And, your honor, the Nelson child is definitely school age. I guess that's it!" Then the prosecutor rested his case.

I stood up and immediately made a motion to dismiss and said, "According to the state rules of procedure, the prosecution had to prove, with evidence, that the child is school age; he did not present any evidence. Therefore I ask this court to dismiss these charges against the Nelsons."

The judge looked over his glasses at the prosecutor. The prosecutor started fumbling around with his papers and then suddenly stood up and said, "Your honor, I have seen the child; he's about this big!" And he motioned with his hand the approximate height of the child. The judge just shook his head, turned back to me, and said, "Motion granted, case dismissed." It was the shortest case I had ever had, and was I thankful. The Nelsons were ecstatic.

Believe it or not, the Nelsons were never recharged. I think the school district was too embarrassed to try to prosecute them again. So they happily and successfully homeschooled without a teacher's license!

The teacher certification wars were in full swing across the states; but the worst states, which fought the hardest to preserve the unnecessary and onerous teacher requirements, were Michigan, Iowa, Alabama, and North Dakota. Let's look at how God faithfully delivered His people!

The Legal Landscape: Pretty Ugly

When I began working at HSLDA in 1985, I was somewhat familiar with the legal landscape. I had just completed a three-hundred-page analysis of the compulsory attendance laws in all fifty states for John Whitehead of the newly formed Rutherford Institute and found that there was little recognition, if any, of homeschooling throughout most of the country.

The compulsory attendance laws, in each of the fifty states, required children to attend public school between certain ages, such as seven years old and until the child turns sixteen, seventeen, or eighteen. In addition, these compulsory attendance statutes described the subjects all children have to be taught and the penalties for truants and those who did not comply with the law. Families could be criminally prosecuted if they did not send their children to school.

Each of these state statutes allowed for certain exemptions from sending your child to public schools. The most frequent exemption was the allowance that families could send their children to private school or have them taught by a certified tutor.

Back in 1925 the state of Oregon passed a compulsory attendance law requiring that all children attend the public school only. At that time they were concerned about the number of immigrants coming who weren't learning the English language, and they believed if the child came to school, they could better fit into society. Private Catholic schools fought back. Needless to say, the U.S. Supreme Court ruled in *Oregon v. Society of Sisters* that it is a fundamental right for parents to be able to choose an alternate form of education other than the public schools. The court made it clear that children are not "the mere creature of the state," but they are the parents' responsibility. This right, although not spelled out in our U.S. Constitution, was declared by the U.S. Supreme Court to be a fundamental right that needs to be protected.

Many years have gone by since that date, but the U.S. Supreme Court continues to uphold the fundamental right for parents to direct the education and upbringing of their children, which is guaranteed by the "liberty clause" in the Fourteenth Amendment. This guaranteed liberty includes parental liberty.

Homeschool Families Stay "Underground"

The families who were beginning to homeschool in 1985 were taking a step of faith. Many had to stay "underground" just to survive.

Most of the states did *not* have an exemption from sending your children to public school under the compulsory atten-dance laws for homeschooling—by 2005, thirty-seven states have homeschool laws; and it is legal to homeschool in all fifty.

Many parents thought that if they could prove their chil-dren were being taught and educated, that is all that really mat-tered. Unfortunately we learned that a different perspective was held by the school districts and judges of the land. We learned quickly that the issue wasn't whether the children were being educated but whether the children were following the require-ments and the controls placed on them by the state.

One of the earliest and toughest battles, which lasted for over ten years, was teacher certification. Thousands of non-certified teaching parents had to stay underground or suffer the wrath of the state.

The educational experts said that for an individual to be able to teach children successfully, he or she must be certified by the state. This means that an individual would have to complete four years of higher education and then be licensed specifically by the state. Many teacher colleges were established around the country that provided further education for these teachers that were to teach in the public schools.

The educational establishment convinced themselves that mere parents could not possibly teach their children! In fact, many of these homeschool parents had only a high school diploma or less! As I've said earlier, the educators were offended; but even more so, they really didn't think it could work. They just did not trust parents.

Higher Teacher Qualifications Do Not Make Better Students

However, the studies were coming showing quite the opposite. One of the most significant studies in this area was performed in 1990 by Dr. Eric Hanushek of the University of Rochester who surveyed the results of 113 studies on the impact of teachers' qualifications on their students' academic achievement; 85 percent of the studies found no positive correlation between the educational performance of the students and the teachers' educational background. Although 7 percent of the studies did find a positive correlation, 5 percent found a negative impact. The results of these 113 studies are certainly an indictment on the proponents of the necessity of certain teacher qualifications for homeschoolers.

The only problem was that in the early years this study was not available. Dr. Eric Hanushek's study did not come out till 1990. In my book *Home Schooling: The Right Choice*, I give a whole chapter on myth, "The Myth of Teacher Qualifications." In it there are scores of studies demonstrating that teacher qualifications and teacher certifications do not have any positive correlation to student performance.

In fact, Dr. Brian Ray of the National Home Education Research Institute has numerous national surveys on the academic success of homeschooling and has found that only 13.9 percent of the mothers were certified teachers. His study confirmed that there was no difference in students' total reading, total math, and total language course based on the teacher certification status of the parents. Brian Ray stated, "The findings of the study do not support the idea that parents need to be trained and certified teachers to ensure successful academic achievement of their children." The studies have *all* shown that whether the homeschool parent has a teaching certificate, a college degree, or a high school diploma or less, did not make any difference—all their children scored on the average twenty to thirty percentiles above average.

However, without these studies, it was difficult to show the courts what we knew in our heart—that parents could successfully teach their children. Michael Farris, when he began homeschooling in 1982, with his wife who was a certified teacher, has often said, "It took Vickie a few years of homeschooling to finally overcome her handicap of being a certified teacher and teach our children!" Mike was joking, of course, but his point is clear, and the studies back it up. Teacher certification is not necessary.

A Losing Battle—but Not with the Lord on Our Side!

Iowa was another state that vigorously imposed teacher certification requirements on homeschoolers. Iowa has always been proud of their educational system. As a result, they did not want to give an inch. Already the Christian schools had lost several cases before the Iowa Supreme Court. They, too, had to use only certified, licensed teachers to teach the students in the Christian schools. The Christian schools raised all of the right arguments, including the First and Fourteenth Amendments.

Nonetheless, the court upheld the teacher certification require-ment, even though they improperly applied the compelling interest test.

To me, winning the right to homeschool for most parents looked impossible. But soon I learned once again with God all things are possible.

HSLDA had an uphill battle in Iowa since the case prec-edent was stacked against us. In the mid-80s, I would get calls from homeschoolers who were frantic because they had been discovered by the school district. Many of the families were homeschooling underground. Others had tried to hire a certi-fied teacher to help with the homeschooling on a consultant basis. Others used a certified teacher for a couple of hours a week.

Unfortunately this was not even good enough! The unrea-sonable Iowa Department of Education was insisting that a certified teacher had to be used for all classes, all of the time.

As a good attorney, always trying to find a loophole, I was able to convince many school districts to allow the home-schoolers to operate if they just had a certified teacher as a consultant.

But this was not always the case. The Trucke family was homeschooling and using a certified teacher minimally. When the school district discovered that they did not have a certified teacher teaching all subjects, they brought a criminal complaint against them with multiple charges. We hired Iowa attorney Dave Siegrist, and he was able to get all charges dropped except those charges concerning the certified teacher. The judge quickly ruled against them on those grounds, even though afterwards he said, "I have doubts about the correctness of my decision."

One thing I have learned in my work at HSLDA is that you can be completely right with all your legal arguments and have the Constitution supporting you, but that does not mean that you are going to win the case. I think that what the judge ate for breakfast is going to have the greater influence on how the decision is finally decided!

Even though the family lost, we enabled them to continue to homeschool after obtaining a stay on the Trucke sentence that they had to either put their children in public school or hire a full-time certified teacher.

"We Do Not Need the State's Permission— Only God's"

Karen Trucke epitomized what many parents believed at that time. "What the superintendent wants is a certified teacher to teach all of the time," Karen Trucke said, "but that is against our religious beliefs. God told us in the Bible that we are responsible for our children." Karen and her husband provide 90 percent of the instruction and believed that God called them to be the primary instructors. The certified teacher they hired only taught four hours a week.

Superintendent Dennis Webner said he had filed charges against the Truckes originally because they did not report that they used a certified teacher at all on the forms they submitted to the school district. Karen Trucke's response was, "The reason we didn't include the certified teacher on the form is that we feel that we do not need permission from the state to do what God commanded us to do. We wanted to spare our certified teacher. We knew the battle with the superintendent was coming." The Truckes were right since the judge ruled that the certified teacher had to teach all of the time.

Meanwhile, another family, the Paulsrud family, was also homeschooling and using a certified teacher only four hours a week. They were approved by the local school board for 1984 and 1985, but as school districts often do, an arbitrary decision was made in 1985–1986 that they were illegal.

Attorney Siegrist, however, was able to persuade the prosecuting attorney to drop the charge against the Paulsruds. He used an argument that we provided him that the Iowa law was unconstitutionally void for vagueness because an earlier federal district court, the *Fellowship Baptist Church* case, had indicated that the requirement that parents provide "equivalent instruction" was "vague." This was a big encouragement to all of us.

Department of Public Education to the Rescue?

Hopeful, I flew to Des Moines and testified at a public hearing before the Department of Instruction. Maybe they would listen to reason and voluntarily work to remove this onerous requirement from homeschooling parents! I presented documentation showing that few states still required homeschool teachers to be certified and that certification was not necessary for children to be educated. I pointed out that the requirements violate both the Fourteenth and Fifteenth Amendments. Homeschooling was clearly working. What could be the problem with allowing it?

Unfortunately, it fell on deaf ears with the Department of Instruction. Homeschoolers would receive no relief here. I have learned since then that most education bureaucrats have a deep-seated prejudice against homeschooling—so they continued to urge prosecution of homeschoolers in Iowa.

I have discovered in my many years working at the Home School Legal Defense Association that Departments of Education are the last places to go in order to gain help, or even accurate information, for homeschoolers. The state departments of education seem to be entrenched in the education establishment and tend not to be supportive of homeschooling. Therefore, we continue to this day to urge people who are beginning homeschooling or who have questions not to go to the department of education in their state but rather to contact the Home School Legal Defense Association or statewide homeschool association.

A Hint from the Supreme Court

Meanwhile we took the *Trucke* case up the appellate ladder. The court of appeals bypassed the *Trucke* case and sent it straight to the Iowa Supreme Court.

Remember: the Christian schools had lost all of their cases and still had to operate with certified teachers. We would only be raising the same argument before the Iowa Supreme Court. The outlook was bleak, but God was teaching me that He is the God of miracles, and He was about to perform one with the *Trucke* case.

The president of HSLDA, Michael Farris, prepared a brief where he challenged the teacher certification requirement as violating parents' right to direct the education and upbringing of their children and their right to freely exercise their religious belief. The court, however, elected not to address these issues in its opinion, stating, "We recognize the duty to avoid constitutional questions when the merits of the case may be fairly decided without facing them."

Amazingly, after oral arguments, the court requested that HSLDA submit a supplemental brief on the issue of possible premature charges being filed before an offense had been actually committed by the Truckes. Now HSLDA had not raised this argument at the trial level. The normal protocol is that if you do not raise an issue at the trial level, you cannot raise a legal issue at some other point as you climb the appellate ladder to the higher courts.

However, there is one exception. That exception is that if the state supreme court tells you to brief and argue another issue, then you better brief the new argument!

Little did we know what God was doing here. He was moving the hearts of the justices who always ruled in favor of teacher certification by providing the homeschoolers in the state of Iowa with the winning argument. As a result, Mike Farris briefed the issue and sent it in to the supreme court.

We argued that since the Iowa compulsory attendance law only requires children to attend school for 120 days, rather than the traditional 180 days like most states (even though all school districts in Iowa met for 180 days), the charges were premature. We explained that if the family began homeschooling some-time in May and used a full-time certified teacher, they would be able to meet for 120 days before the beginning of the new school year in September and thus comply with the law that they use a full-time certified teacher. To charge the Trucke family back in September was premature. Sounds crazy, doesn't it? How could this argument win?

In an unbelievable turn of events, what looked like an impossible case, became a victory, and the charges were dis-missed against the Trucke family. Not only was it a victory for the Trucke family, but it was a victory for all homeschoolers in the state. As homeschoolers were discovered in school dis-trict after school district or notified the school district of their homeschooling, virtually no one was charged with criminal truancy anymore for not using a certified teacher.

The superintendents, ever since the *Trucke* decision, had no idea when to have the family charged for violating the compul-sory attendance law for not having a certified teacher so they did not bring any charges.

Lesson of the *Trucke* Case

What is the lesson from the *Trucke* case? To God and God alone be all the glory. God is our Champion. He promises us that He will protect us and keep us and defend us. He is our Deliverer.

The victory did not come about by our clever arguments or slick lawyering. God, in His mercy, made the supreme court tell us the winning argument!

I was learning a lesson little by little that even though the legal atmosphere was completely impossible across the country, with God all things are possible. This valuable lesson learned enabled me to take heart to keep on fighting the good fight even though the odds were daunting in our work to win the right to homeschool in all fifty states.

But that isn't the only miracle that happened on behalf of Iowa homeschoolers!

The Case of the Missing Senator, or Where's Waldo?

Within a few years the Iowa legislature tried to pass a law that would allow homeschoolers to operate, but they would have to have a college degree. This was still anathema to us and the homeschoolers.

Homeschooling is not for everybody, but it is for anybody. Any parent who wants to take the time to homeschool should have the right regardless of their qualifications. We sincerely believe that parents are qualified to teach their own children simply because they are the parents and were given these children by God. We have the studies cited above to support our position.

Michael Smith and Michael Farris flew to Iowa the day of the Iowa legislature's vote, lobbying members to urge them to vote against this restrictive bill. After the homeschoolers had counted the votes, it looked as if there would be a twenty-five–twenty-five tie in the Senate, and then the lieutenant governor would provide the twenty-sixth vote causing this bad bill to pass.

We wanted the bill defeated. It turns out that God wanted the bill defeated, as well.

The Iowa law requires that a bill has to pass by at least twenty-six votes. One of the senators who opposed this bad homeschool bill had stepped out because the session dragged on into the evening. He left because he wanted to attend a Newt Gingrich meeting.

When it was time for the vote, the conservatives were looking for this missing senator and couldn't find him. But then they suddenly realized that if he didn't come, they would win and the homeschool bill would be defeated.

So now the pro-NEA supporters of the restrictive homeschool bill started to look for their missing opponent.

It was the most confusing game of "Where's Waldo?" you ever saw!

The anti-homeschool legislators couldn't find him, either. (Pre-cell phone days!)

Therefore, the vote was taken, and it was twenty-four opposed, twenty-five in support, and the supporters never got their twenty-sixth vote because the lieutenant governor was not allowed to vote unless there was a tie. The restrictive homeschool bill was defeated as the legislative session ended.

Once again God and God alone provided the victory. He conveniently removed one of the senators in order to give us the victory.

It wasn't long before a new homeschool law was introduced and passed that is still the law today and requires no teacher certifications or any qualifications of any kind! Praise God!

Homeschoolers: Just a Bunch of Illiterates?

In 1987, Etowah County, Alabamam, the director of student services contacted two families because they had been reported by their neighbors that their children were not in school. The families explained their connection with the local church school.

Later that day a probation officer told the family that they were illegal and explained that charges against them would be filed that same day.

The families immediately contacted me at HSLDA, and I called the director of student services who stated that since the children were not actually in attendance in a church school, they were illegal—this is what the state superintendent had already said. He said that the probation officer was already meeting with one of the local judges to press charges.

I immediately called the number that the officer gave me, and to my surprise the judge answered the phone!

The judge disagreed entirely with homeschooling and felt it was illegal. When I explained to him that other counties had recognized homeschools operating as ministries of the local churches, he stated in a southern drawl, "I dawn't care. I'm not gonna recognize them as ministries of the local church."

Then the judge went on and stated that, "These home-schooled child'ern are a bunch of illiterates—the jails are filled with illiterates." Then he paused and stated, "What asylum did these families escape from?"

When I confronted him with the high illiteracy rate among the public schools, the judge admitted, "The public schools aren't what they used to be."

How can you argue with that brilliant reasoning? I hung up after our brief conversation and prepared our member for the worst.

As God would have it, we never had to go before that judge, and we were able to resolve the situation with the school district. I talked with the assistant superintendent and convinced him to stop all proceedings immediately and to contact some of the neighboring counties to find out how they were interpreting the law and recognizing church satellite schools.

They finally recognized the families' "church school" status. God just did not want them to go to court.

"Homeschooling Not Allowed Unless the Parent Is a Certified Tutor"

Homeschoolers across Alabama had troubles through the 1980s because of the requirement for a certified instructor. The Department of Education insisted repeatedly that homeschoolers, in order to operate freely, had to be certified tutors. In fact, if you called them in 2005, they would still say the same thing. Not much has changed.

Wayne Teague was a state superintendent in 1987. He declared that homeschoolers could not operate as satellites of church schools, which is what we had been arguing. He said that to operate legally they had to meet the standards of a certified tutor.

Already there had been a number of homeschool cases before we came onto the scene where homeschoolers lost big. In fact one family, the Pangelians, ended up fleeing the state of Alabama when the court tried to snatch their kids. Alabama was a mess. As homeschool families began calling me to determine what their rights were, I searched the code and discovered a church school exemption that had been passed recently in Alabama. The church schools had recently fought hard to win the right to enact this legislation that exempted Christian and religious schools from all teacher certification requirements and state accreditation.

The definition of a church school was "a school that operates as a ministry of a church denomination or group of churches," and it could not receive any state or federal funds. Furthermore, the church school had "to offer a curriculum between grades K–12 or any combination thereof."

Aha! I thought, *That sounds like a perfect definition for the average Christian homeschool.* I immediately set my mind to writing a legal memorandum explaining the legalities of these church school exemptions so that it could be proven that it fit homeschools.

We began spreading the memorandum to superintendent after superintendent—mostly by Federal Express—as members were challenged by the authorities. Many of the superintendents originally scoffed at the idea. We were willing to back it up in court, if necessary, but we were nervous. Thankfully, most of the school districts ended up opting not to fight us.

The Thousand-Foot Rule

Another family was homeschooling in Fort Payne City. The Johnsons had filed under the church school exemption as a ministry of a local church, and they were not using a certified teacher. The local prosecutor decided that he would take this family to court. The prosecutor wanted to have a "test case."

I had been praying that God would protect us from a test case because I didn't know how we would do in court. I knew that the legal argument was sound, but the atmosphere in Alabama was so negative and the court precedent was so stacked against the homeschoolers, I was not sure how a judge would rule.

I called Mr. Johnson and explained to him for approximately two hours what he would have to prepare for to get ready for the trial. We discussed his religious convictions and the success of his homeschool program and many other details.

Finally, at the end of our long conversation, Mr. Johnson stated hesitantly, "This is probably not important, but I think we live outside the county."

"What? Are you sure?" I asked doubtfully.

He continued saying that he thought that they lived just a little bit outside of the school district and the county line.

I asked him to go down to the local government administration building to look at the maps.

The next day he called back excitedly. "Yes, I think that we're outside the boundaries of the county!"

Any good lawyer knows that the elements of the "crime" of homeschooling which must be successfully proven by the prosecution with evidence are: (1) the child is of compulsory school age, (2) the family is not in compliance with the compulsory attendance law requirements for the education of their child, and (3) the family lives within the boundaries of the county where the court has jurisdiction. I quickly called up the prosecutor and told him that he had no jurisdiction and had to drop his case because the family was outside of the county.

He stated, quite adamantly in his heavy southern accent, "I have lived here all my life. I know the boundaries of this county. I am sure that this family is within our jurisdiction." But he said that he would check to make absolutely certain.

He called back in a couple days on June 22, 1990, and explained, "I sent a survey team out to the Johnson's house. They reported that the family is approximately one thousand feet outside of the school district and the county. We will drop the case."

God had delivered His people once again through no fancy footwork of myself or any other legal mind. God had let me know once again that it wasn't by my might, nor by my wisdom, that we would win these cases, but it was His will and His sovereign power.

I called the family and gave them the good report and told them that we had made a motion to dismiss based on the new "thousand-foot rule!" The case was dismissed.

Alabama proved the adage to be true: "If you say something long enough and loud enough, a great many superintendents will come to believe you." That was an adage that I had made up and had seen played out time and time again.

Sabotaged in the Legislature

We never did change the law in Alabama, although we tried.

On February 24, I had flown out to the capitol and testified for a homeschool bill, HB 69. Homeschoolers had introduced legislation that would officially recognize homeschoolers. On February 24 I testified before a joint education committee.

More than six hundred homeschoolers packed the hearing rooms, spilling out into the halls. Many families lined up to testify. Only the Alabama Department of Education and Alabama Education Association testified against the bill. The AEA representative, when he testified, pointed at me and said, "What does this outsider know about homeschooling? Homeschooling does not allow children to be educated thoroughly or be properly socialized." He had no facts to support his prejudice against homeschooling.

When I stood up to testify later, I explained my constitutional law experience and gave much evidence to the academic success of homeschoolers and the constitutionally protected right of parents to direct the education of their children, completely contradicting the AEA representative before the committee.

The legislators present were not swayed by the AEA, and it seemed like we would win the day.

However, fourteen legislators were absent at the time of the hearing so the vote had to be postponed. It was clear that these fourteen people were absent to prevent a quorum in order to postpone the vote until a substitute bill could be introduced. If the quorum had not been required for a vote, the bill would have easily passed, for it had complete support from the members present.

But postponing the vote worked for the anti-homeschoolers, for at the next Senate Education meeting on March 2, a substitute bill was submitted for consideration. Among the worst of the bill's mandates were the submission and approval of curriculum by local superintendents, the specification that the parents have at least a bachelor's degree, and a requirement that homeschoolers take all competency, achievement, and other graduation examinations and other reference tests required of students attending the public school.

The bill was completely unacceptable. When they met again on March 2, not many homeschoolers were present. James Hart, the president of the Alabama Home Educators, spoke in opposition to the substitute bill. He found out that the Department of Education officials had written the bill. It was to no effect. The bill went forward, and the homeschoolers had to withdraw their support, which effectively killed the bill, and the matter was tabled.

But in hindsight we can see God meant it for good, even though AEA thought they were hurting homeschooling.

It is true homeschoolers were never successful in changing the law in Alabama, but it turns out we never needed to! Homeschools have more freedom operating under the church school law than they would have ever had under a homeschool law with mandatory testing!

We changed the interpretation of the present law without changing the law. God superintended over Alabama without the courts and without the legislature's help. It was each brave family taking a stand and refusing to be moved. It was a gradual reeducation of the educators.

The People's Republic of North Dakota

The other state where we had the most problem with a certified instructor mandate for homeschool teachers was the state of North Dakota. We called it "The People's Republic of North Dakota" because homeschoolers had no freedom. In fact, if a homeschool family was discovered, they would go to court—no options, no reasonable negotiations, no mercy.

Family after family lost their case, and we appealed to the North Dakota Supreme Court. In North Dakota because of its sparse population, there is no court of appeals, so individuals have a statutory right to appeal their local court cases straight to the state supreme court.

So we took every homeschool case to the North Dakota Supreme Court. Michael Farris, Michael Smith, and I took turns going to argue before the North Dakota Supreme Court. Everyone was getting a little tired of losing cases because the Court would not budge.

God was testing us all, though, and He was planning for a great deliverance. The biblical principle we followed in North Dakota was once again the "widow at the judge's door principle." We were going to keep on trying and wear them out until we finally got the justice that the homeschool families deserved in North Dakota.

We were tempted with the thought—only once—to exclude membership from North Dakota, since by far per capita, it was the most expensive state for us legally to represent people. Of course, for HSLDA, it was always "all for one and one for all" so we never gave in to the temptation. The families in the safer states were supporting the families once again in more difficult states. The families in North Dakota could not have supported their own legal defense by themselves.

The Andersons, the Dagleys, the Lunds, the Remches, the Melins, the Vanwagens, the Nelsons, the Brewers, and many others were dragged through the North Dakota courts. Michael Farris, president of HSLDA at the time, carried the majority of these cases. He was almost made an "honorary citizen" of North Dakota since he traveled there so many times to help homeschoolers. Mike, like all of us, was not going to give up.

Our position was, for homeschoolers in North Dakota and everywhere, that we would not take "no" for an answer. This was a constitutional right.

Double Jeopardy and Sleeping Judges

After many losses HSLDA was able to win one important case for the Melines. We were successful in proving that the family had a First Amendment right to exercise freely religious beliefs that were being violated by the law that required teacher certification.

At the office we were ecstatic. There was new hope.

However, the victory was short-lived. The state appealed, and the North Dakota Supreme Court ruled that the Melines were never formally declared "not guilty" by the local judge who found the family's constitutional rights were violated! Therefore, they sent the case back down for a retrial. This we believed was double jeopardy. Our American jurisprudence given to us by the Framers of our Constitution requires that someone can be tried only once for a crime.

I guess this principle applies everywhere in America except North Dakota.

In another instance I had the opportunity to go with Michael Smith to represent the Anderson homeschool family in court. We had a great trial prepared with witnesses, experts, trial notebook, test scores, arguments, prepared questions—we were going to prove their First and Fourteenth Amendment rights were violated.

But the judge, it was clear, was completely bored. He had already made up his mind before we got there!

He kept leaning back in his chair until you could not see him, and we knew that he had fallen asleep through much of the proceedings. We sometimes heard him snoring.

Every now and then, we'd make objections to the prosecutor or vice versa. In those instances the judge would suddenly start stammering and stuttering and then explain that he would reserve the right to consider that objection later on in the trial. He said this because he never heard what our objection was—he was sleeping!

In this way we were able to get everything we wanted into evidence, no matter what the prosecution's objection, because the judge never ruled on it. Unfortunately, at the end of the day, the judge did rule against us and upheld the teacher certification law against the Anderson family. At least we had a good record as we appealed it on up to the Supreme Court.

The Blizzard

I flew to Barnes County to represent the Brewer family. Their case was going to be difficult. The prosecution was ready. I spent a long time with the Brewers preparing them for testifying. I laid forth the case when the prosecution rested. I brought Mr. Brewer to the stand in order to have him explain his religious convictions so that they could see that we had the right under the First Amendment to have religious exemption. Mr. Brewer was nowhere in sight. The court had to recess briefly while we looked for Mr. Brewer.

Soon he stumbled back into the room, white as a sheet, and got on the stand in time for the court to reconvene. I discovered later that Mr. Brewer was so nervous that he had physically become sick in the restroom. The type of pressure that families had to go through back then was incredible. At the end of the case, the judge ruled against us and upheld the teacher certification law.

Mr. Brewer then drove me on to the airport so I could fly out of Fargo and return home. Well, it turned out that weather got so bad that pretty soon his small car was driving slower and slower right in the middle of this great blizzard out in the North Dakota plains—with not a house in sight!

We drove on until we were going only fifteen miles per hour, and it was only a matter of time before the car would no longer work. It was freezing to a halt. I briefly prayed, and then a miracle happened. Suddenly, on the horizon, was a lonely gas station. We turned in, Mr. Brewer put a couple cans of Heat into his gas tank, and we were able to make the rest of the trip to the airport. Praise God for even caring about the little things.

God's Protection in Spite of the Legal Climate

Time and time again I saw God's hand working in North Dakota. All the families were able to continue homeschooling. If they lost their appeal at the North Dakota Supreme Court level, we simply had them start again the next year.

Finally, Judge Meschke, one of the five supreme court justices, changed his vote and ruled in our favor and found that the family was exempt based on the First Amendment and that the teacher certification law was unconstitutionally restrictive.

Wow! We figured back at the office that maybe five or six more years and we'd finally convince two more of the judges to change their vote and we'd win.

Homeschool Leader Overhears of the Future Victory

There had been attempts on a number of occasions to get legislation through, by Clinton Birst, who was the leader of the North Dakota Home School Association. He was a sweet Christian man who loved the Lord with all his heart and homeschooled his children. He was committed to seeing homeschooling finally legalized.

Clinton told me this story later, which explains God's miraculous deliverance ultimately of the families in North Dakota. He was at a party, and he overheard the supreme court chief justice talking to the majority leader and saying, "I am tired of all of these homeschool cases coming before our court. When are you going to change the law?"

And wouldn't you know it, within that next year, a homeschool law was passed in North Dakota, and Governor George

Sinner (what a name for a ND governor!), on April 7, 1989, signed HB 1421 into law. It repealed the state's former teacher certification requirements for all teachers, which had effectively prevented all but a dozen North Dakota homeschool families from legally operating.

Once again God was letting us know that it was going to be Him and Him alone that delivers us. Just as Gideon overheard the Midianites talking about their defeat, Clinton Birst got to overhear those who were opposed to homeschooling discussing what was going to be the ultimate victory for the homeschoolers in North Dakota.

Michigan: The Last Holdout

Michigan families were harassed by truant officers who wore guns. They would often come to a family's house in an intimidating manner.

It was certainly one of the roughest states to homeschool during my tenure at HSLDA. Homeschoolers faced intense persecution under the restricted teacher certification law and hostile Department of Education. Since 1985 I have handled scores of successful cases on behalf of member families who were prosecuted by the state each year. On the average, over an eight-year span, from 1985 to 1993, I had approximately five hundred families that were threatened with prosecution *annually* by the school districts when the families were discovered to be homeschoolers. What was difficult in Michigan was that often the truant officers carried guns. Police officers had the opportunity to be part-time truant officers. This made for scary receptions when they came knocking at the door.

One such family in the state of Michigan was happily homeschooling their children in 1985. Mark and Chris DeJonge were farmers. Neither of them had education beyond high school.

When they were contacted by the local school district, they were told that in order to homeschool legally, they had to use a certified teacher or be certified themselves. Because of their strong religious convictions that God called them to homeschool their children and because they believed, as Mark said, "It is a sin for us to be certified teachers," the family informed the school district that they could not comply with the teacher certification requirement.

As a consequence, the family was charged with criminal truancy.

The Issue for the State Is Not Education

We hired Dave Kallman, an attorney in Lansing, to handle the trial initially. During the trial the judge explained that he was impressed with the "very, very favorable report of the education of the children." He also found the DeJonges religious beliefs to be completely sincere.

However, when Dave Kallman tried to introduce into evidence the children's test scores (their two school-age children were scoring above the ninetieth percentile in standardized achievement tests), the court would not allow it.

There was no question that these children were being well educated, even though the parents weren't certified. But the court did not want to hear it and found the DeJonges guilty. The question wasn't whether the children would be educated. The question was whether the family would bow the knee to the state, and the family would not.

Therefore, they were convicted and sentenced to two years probation for instructing their children without state certified teachers. They were fined $200, required to test their children for academic achievement, and ordered to arrange for certified instruction. If they did not hire a certified teacher, they would have to send their children to public school.

Circuit Court Upholds the Conviction

After we obtained a stay on the sentence so that the family could continue homeschooling according to their religious convictions without a certified teacher, I handled the case on the appeal before the circuit court. I thought, *Certainly the circuit court would understand the constitutional rights that were being violated by Michigan's teacher certification law.*

However, to my surprise and disappointment, the circuit court judge ruled against the DeJonges and upheld the conviction. I had presented clearly that the parents were standing on two fundamental rights; they had the right to exercise their religious belief, pursuant to the First Amendment, and they had the right to direct the education and upbringing of their children pursuant to the Fourteenth Amendment.

I had explained to the court that there is a "compelling state interest test" that the U.S. Supreme Court has established whenever fundamental rights are being challenged by a state law. The compelling interest test requires the state to prove, with evidence, that their particular state requirement, like teacher certification, is necessary or essential for children to be educated, and that is the least restrictive way for children to be educated. I had showed the court that the teacher certification law flunked on both accounts.

Nonetheless, the court upheld the state law.

God Miraculously Confounds Authorities in Michigan

The law was bad—no ifs, ands, or buts—all teachers had to be certified. The Christian schools had lost all their cases. The homeschoolers were losing at the lower level courts.

Homeschoolers should have been crushed by the state. But God was hearing the cries of His people pleading for relief.

On June 7, 1986, God handed HSLDA a major victory. Our local counsel, Dave Kallman, handled the *Haines, Smolls, and Gibson v. Runkel* case in the Circuit Court for the County of Ingham.

When the Haines family, an HSLDA member, was charged with violating the compulsory attendance law, we hired Dave Kallman to defend the family. Incredibly, all charges were dismissed. But why if they were not certified?

God moved the heart of the assistant attorney general to stipulate (what Dave and I wrote), and the court ended up ruling:

> There is no approval or licensing procedure pursuant to any state statute or administrative rule, that requires a private homeschool or a private nonpublic school of any kind, to be approved or licensed by the Department of Education prior to the school's opening for operation, or during the school's ongoing operation. The Michigan Department of Education's authority is limited to the disapproval of private nonpublic schools, pursuant to administrative procedures under the code.

Remember, the requirement in Michigan was clear that all teachers needed to be certified. Nearly every homeschool family in the state of Michigan did *not* have a teaching certificate. Technically, every homeschool family, therefore, was in violation of the compulsory attendance law and could be prosecuted.

We should have lost all of the cases over the eight-year period until the DeJonge case was finally decided at the Michigan Supreme Court level, which struck down teacher certification as unconstitutional. As God would have it, this was not the case. He wanted supernaturally to protect His people as they cried out to Him day and night for relief from this onerous teacher certification law that prohibited them from fulfilling the calling that God placed on their hearts.

So God used this technicality to help protect homeschoolers until they could get the complete relief through the DeJonge decision at the Michigan Supreme Court level in 1993.

With the *Haines* ruling I was able to write more than five hundred letters a year during the eight-year period of the DeJonge case, to convince school districts and prosecutors to leave homeschoolers alone. I demonstrated to school districts that the homeschool families they had located in their school district could not be prosecuted because the State Department of Education had to exhaust their administrative remedies (required by never used law) and disapprove of a homeschool as not meeting the standards of a private school, *before any criminal charges could be brought against a family.*

Confused yet? Since the Department did not want to hold five hundred administrative hearings a year, only about twelve were charged each year—the rest kept homeschooling without a hitch!

"You Can Ask but We Won't Tell" Policy

The State Department of Education tried a new tactic. They began sending out a form to all the homeschool families asking them if they were certified.

Would you tell them if they were just going to try to prosecute you?

We advised our member families not to answer the certified teacher question in the form because there was no law or authority requiring them to fill out the form.

Even though the families were not certified teachers, we did not tell the state or the school districts that fact. Even the Fifth Amendment protects citizens from self-incrimination. The state not only wanted them to be certified teachers but also to be certified in every single subject they taught! This made it impossible even for the few families where the mother was certified to teach.

Even though twelve or so families went to court each year after the *Haines* case, we were able to get the cases dismissed without ever getting to the issue of whether the parents were certified. We simply argued that we did not have an administrative hearing by the Department of Education and that the family did not break any law by not filling out the form from the Department of Education because no form is required by law.

Now are you confused? This is how God confounded those who thought themselves wise in Michigan. He made them foolish. In spite of the hostility from the state, God allowed the homeschool movement in Michigan to grow and grow. I literally ended up writing thousands of letters to school districts on behalf of families until every school district knew about HSLDA.

God again prevailed and protected His people so that not a single HSLDA Michigan family had to stop homeschooling.

Once Is Not Enough

I appealed the DeJonge case, meanwhile, to the Michigan Court of Appeals. I submitted a brief to three judges, explaining these legal and constitutional issues. The court of appeals agreed to accept the case, which they didn't have to do. *Wow,* I thought, *we are going to win!*

When I traveled to Lansing to argue the case a few months later, I found that three different judges were presiding. Two of those three judges had affiliation with the NEA, who, as I have explained in an earlier chapter, are opposed to home education except by a certified teacher. As you can imagine, the court of appeals ruled against the DeJonges once again. In fact, they said that "teacher certification was one of the backbones" of the education system in the state. The court didn't want to be confused by the facts.

I asked the court then for a rehearing. I was told that they never grant rehearings in the court of appeals. Again, to my surprise, they granted a rehearing. I excitedly called up the DeJonges and said, "They never grant rehearings. God must be moving on their hearts to give us the victory in this case!"

I submitted the brief to the court of appeals for a second time with some additional arguments. Once again the court of appeals ruled against the DeJonges, upholding teacher certification for homeschoolers across the whole state.

I appealed the case to the Michigan Supreme Court, which only takes approximately 8 percent of their cases. It was a long shot. Much prayer was going up among families across Michigan because the persecution was continuing every year. Somehow families were being protected, and the homeschool movement was growing.

I found time and time again that with persecution comes strong faith. The families in Michigan who were homeschooling had developed strong faith. They leaned hard on God. As a result, God was answering their prayers and protecting them while the *DeJonge* case continued to drag on over eight years!

The Michigan Supreme Court finally ruled: they were not going to take the case, but they were going to remand the case to the court of appeals for a third decision! There had been a case on religious freedom that they handed down in the meantime, and they wanted the court of appeals to review that case, in light of the DeJonges, to determine if they would change their decision.

The Michigan Court of Appeals dug their heels in hard. All three judges ruled against the DeJonges for a third time. Boy, was I doing a good job for homeschoolers in the state of Michigan! I had just lost three statewide precedent-setting cases condemning homeschooling in the state of Michigan—all with the same case! This case wasn't going to be won by "lawyering." This case would have to be won by the mighty power of God.

Going on the Offensive

In December 1991 four HSLDA families were visited by a local principal and police officer and threatened with arrest in Saint Joseph's County. In one instance the family was threatened with removal of their children from the home. They also received intimidating letters from the intermediate school district threatening criminal prosecution if they did not enroll the children within one day of receiving the notice.

Immediately I contacted the school officials and prosecutor to try to attempt to avoid prosecution. The prosecutor did not care. He insisted on filing charges against the families. However, he did concede that he would not arrest the parents or remove any of the children from their homes. What a nice guy.

The families were beside themselves with the pressure. All the families spent much intense time in prayer.

A few weeks later the local newspaper printed an article based on the interview with the prosecutor, in which he announced that approximately seven homeschool families would be criminally prosecuted. I immediately contacted the prosecutor to try once again to stop him from filing more charges.

As a result of the prosecutor's persistent and unfounded harassment of these families, Mike Farris and I filed a civil rights suit in the circuit court in January 1992, *Arnett v. Middleton*. We sued the prosecutor, the superintendent, and the school district for violating the civil rights of homeschool families. We figured that we needed to get their attention!

We listed five causes of action, including threatening to prosecute the families under an unconstitutionally vague law, attempting to require illegal reporting procedures, threatening to prosecute while intentionally disregarding the law requiring the families to have a due process hearing with the Department of Education, and others.

Within a week, lo and behold, HSLDA was contacted by the school district and the prosecutor, both of whom had a change of heart. They both wanted to settle the suit. Both of them promised that they would no longer pursue or prosecute homeschoolers.

The prosecutor wrote, "The opinion across the state seems to be that the law is presently too vague and confusing."

The school district had "seen the light," and God's people were once again protected. I prepared a consent decree that would put this promise of the prosecutor and the school district in the form of a court order.

The response of the school district and the prosecutor to the civil rights suit was an answer to prayer. We praised God for working in the hearts of the authorities in protecting His people once again.

A Lesson in Perseverance

Once again I appealed the decision to the Michigan Supreme Court and submitted my eighth brief. Praise God, the supreme court accepted the case as one of their few cases they accept each year. (They only accept for review about 8 percent of the cases that are appealed to them.)

Michael Farris had the honor of arguing the case before the Michigan Supreme Court. But it took eight months before the Michigan Supreme Court came down with a decision in the *DeJonge* case.

To everyone's joy, the case was won! The court summarized its wonderful decision by stating:

> In summary, we conclude that the historical under-
> pinnings of the First Amendment to the U.S.
> Constitution, and the case law in support of it, compels

the conclusion that the imposition of the certification requirement upon the DeJonges violates the free
exercise clause. We so conclude because we find that
the certification requirement is not essential to, nor
is it the least restrictive means of achieving the state's
claimed interest. Thus, we reaffirm the sphere of envi-
able conscious and belief, which is the mark of a free
people. We hold that teacher certification requirement
is an unconstitutional violation of the free exercise
clause of the First Amendment as applied to families
whose religious convictions prohibit the use of certified
instructors. Such families, therefore, are exempt from
the dictates of the teacher certification requirement.

The results of the *DeJonge* case are truly a miracle, but just
winning the case is not the real miracle.

God Turns the Heart of a Judge

A miracle had happened behind the scenes, we found out later.
A *Detroit Free Press* news reporter was talking to Chief Justice
Cavanaugh, who mentioned to him that the decision was actually a four to three decision against the homeschoolers for that
eight-month period after the oral arguments.

The one day before the printed decision was to be released,
Justice Levin came up to Chief Justice Cavanaugh and said,
"I want to change my vote."

The chief justice simply asked, "Why?"

Justice Levin replied, "I don't know. I just want to change
my vote."

Then this fourth justice joined the other three justices in
support of the DeJonges giving homeschoolers the victory! The
printers had to scramble and change the majority opinion to the
dissenting opinion and the dissenting opinion to the majority
opinion.

When you look at the written DeJonge decision, you see three judges all agreeing in the majority opinion supporting the DeJonges. Then you see Justice Levin's concurring opinion—just a paragraph—that isn't real clear, but he sides with the three pro-homeschool judges giving them the majority!

We know what happened—even if Justice Levin did not. The Bible tells us in Proverbs 21:1, "The king's heart is like channels of water in the hand of the LORD; He turns it wherever He wishes." That is what God did. He turned Justice Levin's heart.

Certainly God deserves all the glory.

7

Each Superintendent Did What Was Right in His Own Eyes

In those days there was no king in Israel;
everyone did what was right in his own eyes.

JUDGES 21:25

In 1987 the French family in Crown Point, New York, was successfully homeschooling for their fourth year. However, they received a letter from the local superintendent stating that he had decided *they could no longer homeschool.*

He stated no reason. He merely evoked his arbitrary power to approve or disapprove a homeschool program, pursuant to New York law.

Mrs. French was certified, and the children had scored above the ninetieth percentile on standardized achievement tests for the last three years in a row. Their curriculum included all of the required subjects in New York.

To pressure the family more, the superintendent turned the family over to the child protection agency for investigation.

The French family were beside themselves with concern. They were feeling the full brunt of the state's power against them. They turned to the Lord in this trying time crying out for His mercy. As the word spread, God's people began to pray.

The Frenches called me and explained their situation. I immediately contacted the child welfare agency and convinced them to drop the investigation since no child neglect was involved. Then I sent a letter describing the French family's constitutional rights under the First and Fourteenth Amendments. At that time the homeschool law in New York was vague, since it simply required that homeschool programs be "equivalent" to the public schools. No one really knew what this meant.

The Frenches received my letter and went to a board meeting of the local school district where they were planning on making this decision to bring criminal charges against the family. Mr. French delivered a copy of my letter to all of the members of the board, and they went into executive session.

Within a short time the board adjourned, and the superintendent put his arm around Mr. French, laughing and joking. He acted as if he was Mr. French's friend and stated, "Your attorney really knows that constitutional law. We are not going to have any further problems."

Mr. French quickly learned that the board had not only decided not to prosecute the family, but it had reversed the disapproval and were now praising the Frenches' homeschool program!

What happened here? The New York law gave the school district power to approve or disapprove instruction "elsewhere than at school." How could one letter reverse the disapproval? We did not even need to fight in court.

The answer is simple—God delivered His people in spite of the bad law.

He delivered thousands more homeschool families in all the states that required approval for years until the laws were finally repealed. I am convinced God wanted homeschooling to grow so His children could be trained in the Lord.

The Eastern Bloc: Homeschoolers Face Arbitrary Disapproval

In the early 1980s and into the 1990s, many states had archaic compulsory attendance laws that did not specifically include protections for homeschoolers. Many of these states required educational programs other than attendance at school to be "approved" by the local school authorities. The only problem was that there were no guidelines or requirements for the school districts to follow. As a result, there were many arbitrary decisions.

Back then I often liked to refer to the states that allowed arbitrary approval to be the states that made up the "Eastern Bloc." Most of the eastern states were far more regulated in the area of education than the western and southern states. It also seemed that the states in the East had copied one another in their enactment of compulsory attendance laws many years ago.

The rules in Maine, New York, Pennsylvania, Ohio, Connecticut, and Massachusetts were essentially like the time of the judges, where "everyone did that which was right in his own eyes." We definitely had that situation in these states as superintendents did whatever they pleased, regardless of the constitutional rights that were threatened or trampled.

Superintendent Disapproves of Successful Effort

The Smeltzer family was successfully homeschooling their daughter for three years who had been labeled learning disabled by the public school. The parents were so successful that when they showed the superintendent her progress and high test scores, she was relabeled to be gifted and talented!

One problem though—the superintendent and his committee disapproved the family from continuing to homeschool for the fall of 1986.

Completely shocked, Mrs. Smeltzer asked, "How could this be? Our child has improved so much through our homeschooling her!"

The response from the superintendent was matter-of-fact. "Since your child is now gifted and talented, my staff and I believe that you cannot handle her anymore. You need to send her to school."

After three years of successfully homeschooling their child, the Smeltzers were incredulous. "How could the superintendent arbitrarily decide that we couldn't homeschool anymore? We couldn't teach our child anymore because our child was gifted!"

They objected to the superintendent but to no avail. So the family refused to put their child into public school and continued homeschooling. Unbelievably, *the superintendent had criminal charges of truancy brought against them!*

When the Smeltzers called me, my mouth dropped open. I knew it was difficult to get approved for new homeschoolers in Pennsylvania but not three-year veterans—especially when the family had such a proven track record! I thought, *This shows how absolute power corrupts—biased bureaucrats should never be given the authority to determine whether someone can exercise their constitutional rights.*

I immediately informed Michael Farris of the situation. He was indignant for the family and leaped into action. As I watched him start preparing a civil rights complaint, I was so glad he was on our side!

Working at lightning speed, as usual, Mike asserted that the family's constitutional rights under the First and Fourteenth

Amendments were being violated. He also made sure to explain that *the superintendent himself would be personally liable for damages!*

We sent a copy of the complaint overnight to the school board's lawyer. By 10:30 the next day, when Federal Express arrived, we received a phone call that the superintendent and his staff reconvened and decided to approve the Smeltzer's homeschool program after all. Of course, they would drop the charges too!

Their attitude was simply, "Oops. Sorry for the inconvenience."

We won. The family then was able to homeschool without any further problems. I learned we needed to be a dogged warrior on behalf of the homeschoolers; otherwise the public schools would push them around.

Sometimes threats need to be made and HSLDA puts their money where their mouth is. This was one of those instances, and it worked.

The law was not changed, however, leaving homeschoolers everywhere still under siege in Pennsylvania.

Pennsylvania Districts: 501 Different Rules for Homeschoolers

The Pennsylvania compulsory attendance law simply stated that people who were not sending their children to school had to use a "properly qualified private tutor," and each family's curriculum was subject to the local superintendent's approval. There were 501 school districts in the state of Pennsylvania, so you can imagine the patchwork quilt, application, and implementation of the law.

This nebulous Pennsylvania statute was misapplied almost daily as I scrambled to help families throughout the state. In fact, at one time between 1987 and 1989, I had an average of eighteen cases per year. The families were dragged into court simply because their programs were not satisfactory to the superintendent. Some school districts in Pennsylvania required the parents to be certified tutors. Others would require a college degree. Still others were satisfied if the parents had a high school diploma. As far as standards for approving curriculum, there were so many different variations that it would fill another book just to describe them!

By June 1986 at least eighteen homeschool families that were members of Home School Legal Defense were in various stages of litigation. As a young lawyer, I was getting my feet wet pretty fast as I juggled these cases.

The Steudler family, for example, was contacted in 1986 by the school district superintendent. He sent them, as was typical of many school districts throughout the state, a massive form that needed to be filled out if the family was *possibly* going to be allowed to homeschool. I helped the family substantially amend the application to homeschool.

After a tug-of-war of negotiations, the superintendent finally agreed to most of our changes. One snag—he wanted the children to be tested in the public school. We politely refused. Then I brought to the superintendent's attention a recent study that was done by the American Psychological Testing Association, which concluded that children do best on the standardized test when the child is tested in familiar surroundings. The superintendent finally relented and allowed the family to homeschool and be tested at home.

Bringing Charges . . . and More Charges . . . and More Charges

The Hull family in Butler, Pennsylvania, were successfully homeschooling their children. They both had bachelor of science degrees, and Mrs. Hull was even a certified teacher.

They learned quickly the superintendent did not care if their children were being educated. He just did not like homeschoolers!

In spite of my letter and explanation of the family's tremendous qualifications and excellent homeschooling program, the superintendent still brought criminal charges against the family. Then, to add more pressure, as was all too often the custom with other superintendents in Pennsylvania, he had a "dependency action" filed against the family in order to get social workers snooping around.

Working with a lawyer friend, Vic Vouga, we were able to get the dependency action dismissed. Nonetheless, the superintendent refused to back down and began refiling charges against the family every week!

Upon some further investigating, I discovered that the Pennsylvania statute allowed all of the money collected for truancy fines to go to the school district! Week after week, as the case was pending, the superintendent filed new charges against the family, building up the fines into the thousands of dollars.

This superintendent just wouldn't give up. He believed he was right, and he wasn't going to be confused with the facts. The facts were that the family was qualified far beyond necessary, and their children were academically excelling. That didn't matter to this superintendent.

When we went to court to represent the family, I worked with John Sparks, a former professor of mine from Grove City College. We were able to convince the judge to dismiss most of the charges on various technicalities and postpone the final trial until the recently filed federal suit was decided.

Since so many families were going to court in Pennsylvania, the caseload was becoming unmanageable. So Mike Farris decided to file a federal lawsuit to challenge the law as being void for vagueness. I began working on the case, gathering homeschool policies from dozens of counties around the state to prove to the court that no county had the same policy, evidencing vagueness in the law.

For a law to be unconstitutionally vague, the reasonable superintendent or government official must not know specifically what the law means. Furthermore, the reasonable citizen, who has to obey the law, has to have no clear understanding of what the law means from reading it. This was truly the case in Pennsylvania. No one knew what the term "properly qualified tutor" meant, and no one knew what "approval" meant. Therefore, the law was completely confusing to all.

"Let the Record Show that the Superintendent Is Ready to Hit Me"

We added the Hull family into our lawsuit and had convinced the judge to put the criminal case on hold pending this action. We set up a deposition with the Hulls and the superintendent in order to gather evidence before trial. A deposition is essentially a sworn statement from witnesses that will be called to the trial to avoid bringing those witnesses to the trial. If we gathered more evidence concerning the vagueness of the law, we were hoping to get a summary judgment from the court and not have to go through a lengthy trial.

We arrived at the appointed meeting place with the Hulls. The Butler superintendent was there with his attorney. I started by questioning Mr. and Mrs. Hull about their homeschooling and treatment by the school official. I could tell that the superintendent was getting hot under his collar. Soon it was his turn to be questioned.

Mike Farris questioned him with the stenographer typing away everything that was said. Mike asked the superintendent many questions showing that his answers clearly demonstrated how arbitrary he was acting toward the Hulls and how much he didn't really like homeschooling.

Finally, as the superintendent was beginning to get redder and redder, Mike asked him, "You really hate homeschooling, don't you?" The superintendent stood on his feet and began to lunge at Mike Farris, who quickly leaned as far back as he could in his chair. Mike, always with a quick wit about him, frantically shouted, "Let the record reflect that the superintendent is standing over me ready to hit me!" Well, needless to say, the lawyer on the other side grabbed the shoulders of the superintendent to sit him down and began to calm him so that a major incident didn't occur.

But it was too late. The stenographer faithfully took Mike's words down for the record. The federal judge would understand and be able to visualize the hostile actions of the superintendent and thereby ruin his credibility.

The Bible says that "a gentle answer turns away wrath." We saw this principle work as we finished the deposition.

"Not Under Any Circumstances"

The Metcalfs in Coraopolis, Pennsylvania, at the same time, were contacted by their superintendent and told that his school district "does not permit home instruction under any circumstances." I did not have much "wiggle room" to negotiate. To further demonstrate his obstinacy, the superintendent even refused to receive any information on the curriculum, excellent test results, or the Metcalfs' qualifications.

Instead, he simply filed charges against the family. So we added them as defendants in our federal suit thereby halting the court proceedings until the federal court ruled.

In the Jeffrey case, we also asserted that since the superintendents have a financial stake in the outcome of the criminal action, they could not be a "neutral decision maker" as required by the federal and state constitutions under the due process clauses. If they disapprove of a family's homeschool program, they will more than likely end up back in the public school system, which meant, at that time, an additional $2,000 to $3,000 for that local school district in state and federal tax money.

Furthermore, we discovered the school districts receive all of the criminal truancy fine money, and it directly goes into the public school coffers! The financial incentives to bring charges against homeschoolers were obvious.

As was often the case, when we filed the federal lawsuit and started including various school districts as defendants for this civil rights case, we began to see a change of heart. Two school districts involving five families immediately changed their local policies and made them constitutional—just as I had been asking nicely all along.

In the meantime I scrambled to keep families afloat. We had various families file and establish themselves as a non-licensed private school. Private schools were routinely denied, and we had to appeal to the State Department of Education. This allowed for more time to keep families out of court. Also, a law was passed by the legislature in regards to church schools, and we argued that homeschoolers could establish themselves as a church school, provided they were operated by "a bona fide church, or other religious body."

Needless to say, I learned "the more options, the better," in order to avoid families going to court.

By March 1988, Pennsylvania earned the reputation in our "Home School Court Report" as the *worst state of the year.* More than sixty-four HSLDA families had been threatened and contacted by the school districts. Amazingly, by simply standing my ground, I was able to resolve all of those contacts and negotiate solutions in favor of the families outside of court.

"You're Wasting Your Breath Talking about the Constitution"

In Wellsboro, the Yarian and Brown families were convicted of violating the compulsory attendance law. The previous year they had both had their homeschool programs approved by the superintendent without any difficulty. The families even sent in their test scores at the end of the year, proving their children were progressing adequately. During the 1987–1988 school year, the superintendent decided to add a new requirement, even though the law had not changed. He wanted the parents to have college degrees and submit to home visits. After extensive negotiations I was not able to persuade him to waive any of his requirements. I flew up to Wellsboro to represent the families in court. As I began presenting the case to the judge, explaining the important First and Fourteenth Amendment rights that were at stake here, the judge leaned forward and said, "Counsel, I'm not a constitutional lawyer. You're wasting your breath talking to me about that. Just stick to the statute."

I couldn't believe my ears. A judge didn't even care about the Constitution of the United States of America, which he was sworn to uphold. I quickly responded to the judge that we have our "right to a day in court" and proceeded to lay out the constitutional arguments anyway, knowing that I was talking to a "brick wall."

In the Blackhawk school district, the Whitmoyer family was charged even though they had been approved for the last three years. The change was that a new superintendent had taken office. He decided to add a college degree requirement, which the Whitmoyers did not have. In spite of the fact that Mrs. Whitmoyer was qualified and was involved in teaching reading and writing to adult illiterates, and had scads of proof that the Whitmoyer child was progressing well, the school district still brought charges!

The Stow-Rox school district convicted a homeschool family because the mom was not a certified teacher. The Sudas of Dallas, the DiGerlandos of Nazarath, and the Arseneaus of Waynesboro were all charged within a few weeks of each other.

Meanwhile I went to the legislature because we were trying to pass a bill, HB 1364, that would eliminate all of these requirements. Unfortunately, the bill did not pass that year.

Deliverance at Last

Finally the long-awaited decision came down from Judge Kosik of the Federal Court in the *Jeffrey* case. He held that the Pennsylvania Compulsory Attendance law was unconstitutionally void for vagueness. He declared in his ruling that since certain fundamental rights were at stake, there was even stricter scrutiny that had to be used in judging vagueness of the statute.

We didn't even have to have a long, drawn-out trial. He made this ruling on summary judgment—based on the evidence we gathered in the depositions and the arguments in our brief.

Praise God! Pennsylvania was delivered after several years and much fear and stress on the families. Nonetheless, during this whole time every member homeschool family in Pennsylvania was able to keep homeschooling. God enabled us to help these homeschoolers keep on going in the midst of the intense persecution.

Concern about Socialization

Connecticut was another one of those states where the law just allowed for attending public school or have "equivalent instruction." No one knew exactly what that term meant.

For example, the Dionne family was faithfully homeschooling their children; and as required by the school district, they presented their homeschool program to the local school board. In 1985 homeschooling was not common in Connecticut, so not very many of the school districts were even familiar with the concept.

I communicated with the school district to explain the right of the families to homeschool. Nonetheless, the family was rejected by the school board. When I contacted the school board to discover on what basis the families were rejected, the official explained that it was over a concern about "socialization" of the children.

Socialization was a big issue in those days. School officials really believed that children would be social misfits if they were not institutionalized in the public schools. They would hold their nose over a private or Christian school but not allow the isolation of children in homeschool families.

This, of course, could not be further from the truth.

Knowing that the assumption that the children were not being properly socialized would never stand up in court, I requested a rehearing before the school board. The rehearing was granted, and I hired a good friend of mine, Joseph Secola, whom I knew as a fellow student at O. W. Coburn School of Law in Tulsa, Oklahoma. He attended the rehearing with the Dionne family before the school board. I told him to allow only the family to answer certain questions that were relevant. All the way I had been explaining to the school district the family's constitutional rights.

Many of the Dionne family's friends were praying fervently. Then, as God would have it, the school board reversed its earlier decision and recognized the Dionnes' right to homeschool their children.

Over and over again throughout Connecticut, I worked with local school districts to try to persuade them to allow homeschooling, while never actually seeking approval.

Requesting Approval without Requesting Approval

The families represented that were members of HSLDA were nearly all Christian families. They felt strongly that they were called by God to homeschool their children. As I discussed the beliefs with many of these families, I realized early on that we could not have the families request approval from the school districts to homeschool.

Homeschooling is not a privilege granted by the state. Homeschooling is a right that is guaranteed by a higher law: the Constitution of the United States through the First and Fourteenth Amendments.

Furthermore, there is even a higher law than our Constitution that we were appealing to—God's law. The right to teach our children is a right granted by God Himself.

Therefore, when I had families write to the school district, I had the family state specifically in their letter:

> This letter is an assurance that our children are being thoroughly educated. We are not seeking approval of the school district to homeschool because we believe it is a God-given right. Nonetheless, we are willing to assure you that our children are being thoroughly educated. Therefore, we are willing to give you certain information for informational purposes only. In our homeschool we teach our children for at least 180 days a year and teach the same basic subjects that are required in public school.

I also had them explain that they were homeschooling for religious reasons and thus were protected by the First Amendment. These religious beliefs made it a sin for them not to educate their children. Therefore, they would teach their children diligently.

God blessed this faithful witness before the authorities. We were able to persuade school district after school district to "recognize" the families because they felt comfortable that the families were in fact educating their children.

We were not giving the school districts the snub by refusing to communicate with them, as some religious homeschoolers before us had unsuccessfully tried to do with the school districts. These families had asserted that the school district had no jurisdiction. Although it is true that God has granted families the right to teach their own children, the issue of jurisdiction is determined by geography. In other words, if a family was in a particular school district, that school district by state law had authority over them and could compel them to attend school. The local judge in the county had authority over the family as well to enforce the compulsory attendance law. The state legislature had authority over them as well because they lived within the boundaries of the state. There was no question in the state's eyes or the judge's eyes of jurisdiction. Any family who asserted that the state or the school district had no jurisdiction over their family's educational program and that only God had such authority, lost their cases and sometimes their kids.

I wasn't going to go down that path, and so God gave me wisdom to seek approval without seeking approval. This way, in court, we would have a stronger position because we were standing on the First Amendment's right to exercise freely our religious belief and our Fourteenth Amendment right that gives parents the fundamental right to direct the education of their children. This may seem like semantics, but this is actually an important distinction—not only for the family's own conscience before God but to preserve certain fundamental rights in the courtroom and not simply to lay ourselves at the whim of the school districts.

As far as I was concerned, I was not going to take "no" for an answer.

Our position at HSLDA was and always will be that home-schoolers have the right to homeschool, and we were going to push it until we finally won.

The Ohio Approval Wars

When I came on board HSLDA in 1985, I was hit in the face with an out-of-control situation in the state of Ohio. Approximately 615 superintendents were in Ohio, and each superintendent established his own personal requirements with which homeschoolers in the district had to comply. This dis-cretionary power of the superintendent tended to be exerted arbitrarily, often to the detriment of the homeschoolers' con-stitutional rights.

For example, some superintendents only recognized parents as qualified to teach their children if they were certified by the state, and others were satisfied if the parents had a bachelor's degree or possibly only a high school diploma. This was similar to the situation we faced in other states.

The Schmidt family was faithfully teaching their children at home when they were charged and convicted at trial with violating the compulsory attendance law. The Schmidts had strong religious beliefs.

Mr. Schmidt explained, "We do not believe the state has the right to approve our homeschool so that is why we had not sought the superintendent's approval."

When they were discovered, they were criminally charged. One mishap after another happened as the state pursued the Schmidt family. The prosecution was almost a month late in filing the appellate brief, and the transcript of the lower trial court was destroyed.

Meanwhile two other families were charged at the same time. In the case of the Svoboda family, both parents even had college degrees, but it did not make any difference with the superintendent. We appealed the cases to the juvenile judge within the statutory ten-day limit and secured Robert Melnick of Youngstown and Steve Lieby to serve as local counsels. The family's case, however, was dismissed on a technicality because although a $35 check was filed by the local counsel, which is required for appeal, the court stated that it had to be a $35 bond, not a check. God nonetheless was with us, and we continued to appeal the case while the family was able to homeschool in the midst of the challenge.

The Cline family of Jefferson County was the other family at that time who was denied the right to teach their children because they only had high school diplomas. I was amazed that the families were being charged when the children were tested and found to be two to three grades ahead of their age groups. Of course, this was normal. At that time school districts didn't care about whether children were being educated but whether or not the family bowed the knee to the school district's demands.

However, by God's grace, after many dealings with the school district, we finally were able to convince the superintendent to withdraw his denial, and the family avoided court.

The Carrikers of Cleveland, under my direction, met with the school district officer who determined that their academic program was more than adequate and that their religious convictions were sincere. Nonetheless, without ever personally meeting the family, the superintendent sent the family a letter denying their right to homeschool because they were not certified teachers. He completely disregarded their right to a religious exemption, which I had argued for based on an attorney general opinion. We hired attorney Bob Lynch to appeal the case to the Cuyahoga County Court of Common Pleas within the ten-day limit.

This was happening all over the state as families were arbitrarily denied by superintendents, and we would immediately issue an administrative appeal through the courts.

In Ada, Ohio, two families were denied the right to home-school without a hearing. We sent a letter via Federal Express and explained to the school official that the families' religious beliefs were sincere and the program was thorough. I requested that the superintendent withdraw his denial and grant the families a hearing. He did so, and the families were exempted. Every school district was different.

Meanwhile, on December 4, 1986, the court of appeals ordered the *Svoboda* case to be reversed and remanded in favor of our position. The court stated that the lower court had improperly denied the Svobodas their due process right to be heard because they were trying to enforce a ridiculous technicality. As a result, the case was remanded back to the superintendent for a rehearing.

I flew to Ohio to represent the family and stayed with them that night. After I stayed some time with them, the family mentioned that one of their children had chicken pox.

I instantly froze. I had never had chicken pox. Needless to say, I prayed fervently that God would protect me—and He did. In fact, He didn't give me chicken pox until over ten years later.

The next day I went before the superintendent, and I presented the thoroughness of the family's program and their constitutional right to exercise freely their religious belief that was not only recognized by the U.S. Constitution but also by an attorney general opinion in Ohio. The family was finally granted the right to homeschool. It was a long, drawn-out process, but God prevailed. There were many more cases, and the climate only got worse.

Michael Smith took over Ohio and continued working with school district after school district.

The *Schmidt* case, meanwhile, was working its way up in the court process. We had figured out that the Schmidts could continue to homeschool under the auspices of a Christian satellite program with a private school, but that had not worked because they were charged nonetheless. The State Board of Education had earlier given the Christian satellite school permission to approve homeschool programs, and a Christian school had even approved the Schmidts' homeschool program. After several conferences with the superintendent, the superintendent still decided to bring charges against them.

I mentioned earlier that the record of the trial was destroyed. Mike Farris, who appealed the decision raising several constitutional arguments, explained to the court the loss of the trial record. Nevertheless, it was HSLDA's word against the prosecution's word as to what the facts actually were that brought the situation to court.

The court of appeals arbitrarily decided to rely on the prosecutor's version of the facts, which were very different from the actual truth. Finally, on March 25, 1987, the Ohio Supreme Court decided the *Schmidt* case, upholding the conviction of the Schmidts. The court held that because the Schmidt family did not exhaust their administrative remedies, that is, they did not request approval and be denied by the superintendent and appeal to the juvenile court, the court would not rule on HSLDA's constitutional arguments.

The Ohio Supreme Court also relied on the prosecutor's version of the facts, which stated the family did not meet with the superintendent but blatantly ignored the law. On the contrary, the Schmidts had in fact met with the superintendent several times, and the superintendent made clear to them that they must be certified teachers. Instead of denying them the right to homeschool and follow administrative procedure, he had charges brought against them.

But God was still in control even though prospects looked dim.

I remember after the *Schmidt* decision was handed down being so depressed I just left the office and walked through the fields for a couple of hours, crying out to God. We were so right. The family was so right. The Constitution allowed the family to homeschool. The facts were improperly represented by the prosecution. The prosecution had violated time limits and deadlines.

The Schmidts should have won. Why, God, did they lose? I had put so many late hours into writing briefs for that case. Mike Farris and I had put much time and effort and prayer into this case, yet it was still lost.

Well, God was not worried about a loss!

He just enabled us to continue to have the Schmidt family operate as a homeschool by establishing them under a chapter that allowed for them to be largely religiously exempt from most approval requirements; it was called an "08 school."

God always promises He will provide a way of escape, and He did once again!

More and more families established themselves as "08 schools" all across the state, and fewer and fewer families went to court.

Finally some new guidelines were established by the Department of Education allowing for homeschooling with nothing more than notification. We praise God for His final deliverance of Ohio, but it took many years. Looking back, I remember that just between the 1986 and 1987 school year, we had more than forty-four legal conflicts with homeschoolers and school districts, and we had resolved them all favorably while the *Schmidt* case was preparing.

"If You Take Those Kids . . ."

In Maine in the 1980s, the law required that all instruction be "equivalent" to the public schools and "approved by the commissioner." The commissioner had enacted "Guidelines for Equivalent Instruction Through Home Schooling" which provided extensive procedures for homeschoolers that they had to follow in order to be approved. These guidelines required

detailed information concerning the curriculum and the qualifications of the teacher. In addition, often the homeschooler
would be subject by the local school district to the arbitrary and
restrictive standards of the local school committee.

One example in 1986 involved the Dionne family. This
family had been successfully homeschooling in another state
for the last two years. Now they lived far north in Maine in the
town of Frenchville.

Two weeks after they moved to Maine, they were visited
by a welcoming committee—the friendly neighborhood school
attendance officer! This was followed by a "friendly" phone
call by the local superintendent telling them that their children were truant and had to be enrolled in the public school
immediately.

The Dionnes were a kindly family and tried to make peace
with the school district, but they could not change their convictions that God had called them to homeschool. The superintendent would not budge.

Quickly the Dionnes contacted me, and I called the superintendent and explained that the family was not truant unless he
had evidence that the children were not being educated. I had
the family partially fill out an application for home instruction,
explaining that they were not seeking approval but only providing information to assure the school district that their children
were being educated.

The local school committee, however, rejected their application and gave them ten days to remedy the problem. I called
the school district several times, but my calls were never
returned. The school district was acting in a very unprofes-
sional manner.

Then without warning a truant officer appeared on the
Dionnes' doorstep. He said, "I will not leave until I can take
the children away to the public school." Mrs. Dionne called me,
frantic because this truant officer was threatening to take her
children away. I told her to hand the phone out the door to the

truant officer. I told the truant officer that he was overstepping his authority and that he would be held personally liable under the 1983 Civil Rights Act. I put him on hold for a moment and filled Mike Farris in, who was in the next office, about what was happening.

Mike quickly got on the line and yelled, "If you take those kids, then we're going to see kidnapping charges brought against you!"

Needless to say, the truant officer left without the children. I then tried to call the superintendent to come to an understanding, but the superintendent abruptly hung up on me.

I ended up flying to Augusta, the state capitol, to meet with the commissioner of education since I had appealed the Dionnes' case pursuant to the administrative appeal procedures. To my amazement the snow was so deep that it was past my waist. It was extremely cold, and the sky was dark. It did not seem that we would ever see the light of day in Maine.

But with God nothing is impossible. After I explained the family's constitutional rights and described their solid homeschool program, the commissioner, on April 27, 1987, handed down a ruling allowing the Dionnes to homeschool.

There was some light getting brighter in Maine. Throughout the next several years we struggled, negotiated, and battled with school districts. During that time not one Maine HSLDA family was prevented by the state to homeschool.

And so it was with all the other "approval states." Gradually, we worked side by side with the statewide homeschool associations and amended those onerous approval laws in the legislatures or by state school board regulations.

The homeschoolers, meanwhile, marched on, standing firm on the principle that homeschooling is a God-given right—not a privilege granted by the state.

8

A School Is a School, No Matter How Small

We are afflicted in every way, but not crushed;
perplexed, but not despairing; persecuted, but not
forsaken; struck down, but not destroyed.

2 CORINTHIANS 4:8–9

The young Texas homeschool family was excited. It was 1987, and a class-action suit had just been won recognizing homeschools as legal private schools. The family had heard so much about the positive benefits of homeschooling, and now they had their curriculum and were ready to go.

They lived in a small Texas town, so the word got around fast since they were the only family doing this "strange" home-schooling. One day the new homeschool father happened to meet the local justice of the peace at a coffee shop. The judge was sitting around with his cronies and then asked the father, "Why don't you have your kids in school?" Of course, he already had heard.

The father explained about his homeschool. The judge frowned and shook his head. He impatiently told the father, "You need to put your children in school now!" When the father responded weakly, "Why? It is legal."

The judge responded with arrogance, "We just don't allow homeschooling in our town."

Through intimidation he sought to deter the family. The father called HSLDA, and I counseled them on their rights and also wrote to the judge explaining that he had no authority to shut down their school because it was a legal private school in the home. He backed off, and the family was left alone.

Homeschools are private schools—that is what we argued from school district to school district. In fact, there are more than one thousand school districts in Texas! And the courts finally agreed. In this chapter you will see how God delivered.

Homeschools Masquerading as Private Schools?

In the early 1980s homeschool laws were nearly nonexistent. A student had to be in either a public school or a private school. When I wrote my three-hundred-page analysis of the fifty state compulsory attendance statutes in 1984, I realized that in some states private schools weren't regulated. Homeschools could, therefore, be really small private schools and practically meet the law's requirements for a private school. I began to think small.

Others I discovered had already tried this argument successfully in the 1950s. Back then, both the court of appeals in Indiana (*Peterson* case) and the state supreme court in Illinois (*Levison* case) had found that a homeschool was a private school. It didn't matter what the size of the school was as long as an education was taking place. The Illinois Supreme Court said that "the object is that all shall be educated, not that they shall be educated in any particular manner or place."

On the other hand, the argument did not always win. In several cases like the *Edington* case in New Mexico and the *Buckner* case in Florida, state courts had ruled against homeschools and said they could not be a private school. A school, they reasoned, had to be "an institution"; otherwise it did not meet the intent of the law.

Not willing to allow parental liberty to be trampled, I set to working at trying to figure out how homeschools could meet the requirements of private schools in various states. This was not just stubbornness, however, because I was standing on a basic rule of statutory construction. The statutes should be interpreted to protect the constitutional rights rather than to denigrate them. We were convinced that parents had the right to direct the education and upbringing of their children, guaranteed by the Fourteenth Amendment. Therefore, state statutes requiring compulsory attendance had to be interpreted to find a way to allow for that option.

Here are some of the stories of how God provided "a way of escape" in certain tough states.

Kansas Homeschooling Starts Out on Shaky Ground

In Kansas we were faced with a compulsory attendance law that allowed for public schools and private schools only. There was no homeschool statute. The private schools had a separate category of nonaccredited private schools. These nonaccredited private schools had almost no regulations or controls, except filing with the state department of education and having an equivalent instructional program. The instructor also had to be "competent."

We believed homeschools could legitimately operate as non-accredited private schools. But the Kansas homeschoolers faced a few hurdles since the public school authorities were dead set against us. In fact, as you will see, the Department of Education and Kansas Supreme Court both declared homeschools illegal.

But when you are called by God to homeschool, you have no choice—you have to homeschool!

Witness Ends Up Siding with Homeschool Family

In the first few years of HSLDA's existence, we needed to find good Christian lawyers in particular states to help carry our litigation load. We were small, and the cases were many. Through referrals from members, lawyer friends from law school days, and hosting two homeschool seminars to train lawyers around the country, we built up our internal list of attorneys that HSLDA paid to defend our members.

In 1985 criminal charges were filed against an HSLDA member family, the Josts. Kim Jost was a pilot with a major U.S. airline. He and his wife Constance were homeschooling their three children in Hillsboro, Kansas. They were called by God to homeschool their children—come what may, God would provide.

In early January 1985 the test of the Josts' faith began. The Josts were served with court papers, which included a temporary restraining order against them requiring them to stop their homeschooling entirely. Temporary restraining orders were extreme legal measures and rare in homeschool situations, but this school district was vehement in wanting to stop the homeschooling of the Jost children.

The school district's attitude was indignant—how dare these parents not send their children to the public school!

We hired Richard Peckham, a Christian lawyer, who was eager to help. In court Mr. Peckham argued that the Jost school was a bona fide nonpublic school, which is legal under Kansas law. He called as defense witnesses the local banker and dentist to attest to the quality of the Jost school as well as a former child welfare worker, who happened to be Mrs. Jost's sister.

The prosecutor, on the other hand, only called one witness, the local newspaper editor. He thought this would be an open-and-shut case! The Kansas Supreme Court had already condemned homeschooling in the 1983 *Sawyer* case.

On the stand the editor said that he began his two-hour interview with the Josts very much opposed to homeschooling. However, by the end he had become convinced that it was a valid form of education. So much for the prosecution's witness! God had turned his heart.

As a result, the judge declared the Jost school legal, dismissed all charges against them, and dissolved the temporary restraining order that he had signed earlier. Once again God had delivered His people against incredible odds.

The miracle of the story is that the Jost case, a little unreported case, was just the beginning of freedom to homeschool in Kansas. One family stood firm and followed God's call to obey and teach their children His ways. God used this little case to help me convince scores of superintendents around the state that homeschooling was legal even though the Kansas Supreme Court, in the 1983 *Sawyer* case, essentially declared homeschooling illegal in the state of Kansas.

To this day the law in Kansas has never changed! Thousands of homeschoolers operate freely as private schools. But it took about ten years to educate the educators throughout the state, and God did it little by little.

If You Say It Loud Enough
and Long Enough . . .

Over the next decade I spent many late nights writing letters to prosecutors and school superintendents trying to convince them not to prosecute, using the Jost case and copies of a few other local court cases that had been won. For instance, in the *Ahmand* homeschool case, the county judge stated:

> The statute does not authorize independent evaluation of the competency of the *prima facie* private school by local public school officials or local law enforcement authorities, absent clear evidence of a sham or subterfuge involving educational neglect. Children found to be participating in a *prima facie* private school are not truant under the law notwithstanding the fact that such a school operates in a private residence.

I placed these rulings, along with various logical arguments of how homeschools satisfied the nonaccredited school law, into a legal memorandum. I distinguished our homeschools operating as nonaccredited schools from the negative Kansas Supreme Court cases. This legal memorandum was sent far and wide across Kansas to school district after school district over the years, educating the educators.

We were not going to take "no" for an answer, and one by one the school districts came to realize that we were serious. So they began to concede that homeschoolers were operating legal schools.

I was beginning to realize and practice that if you say something loud enough and long enough, a great amount of superintendents will come to believe you!

God made this strategy really work for Kansas and many other difficult states.

Creative Solutions

The main problem in Kansas was that when superintendents ran up against a homeschool family, they would simply turn them over as truant and have the Social Rehabilitative Services agent take care of it. Of course, the SRS workers were mostly trained as social workers although they wore a truant officer's hat. When they came to your door, they didn't simply want to talk to you; they wanted to enter the home and talk to all the members of the family. It was a scary situation for these families to face.

Below are examples of this common treatment Kansas families received in the 1980s.

Let's start with the Garretson family. They had been discovered by the local school district as not having their child in public school. The superintendent contacted the SRS worker, and the SRS worker contacted the prosecutor; the prosecutor contacted the Garretsons and told them that what they were doing was illegal. I immediately sent a letter by Federal Express and my Kansas legal memorandum overnight, as was my custom, to try to stop cases from being filed.

The prosecutor reviewed the memorandum and became convinced that a homeschool was a private school under state law—in spite of the negative Supreme Court precedent condemning homeschooling.

In one court case in Topeka, the Wilms family was charged with criminal truancy and faced with a prosecutor bent on prosecuting. We hired attorney and homeschool dad Kent Vincent and presented the argument that they were operating as a satellite of a private school. The school was made up of individual homeschoolers with certain accountability requirements. There was no building, and each family taught their own children. The prosecutor accepted the arrangement, and the criminals charges were dropped against the Wilms.

So now we had two options in Kansas; homeschoolers could be private schools, or they could operate as a satellite with a group of homeschools.

I learned to be creative, and God was providing various ways to victory.

Power of Prayer

In another tense situation a family faced a frightening contact from an SRS agent, which once again proved to me the power of prayer. The family prayed for God's mercy and deliverance when the SRS workers came to the door.

Then an unusual thing happened.

The SRS workers found no problems whatsoever with their homeschool even though they refused to let them in the house. In fact, the SRS agent was so impressed with the member family's homeschool that she wrote the mother saying, "My supervisor said they are not going to do anything. I think homeschooled children are probably getting a better education than public school children. Relax and enjoy your job."

This was a huge relief to the family. Once again God showed He was bigger than the state.

In Kingham County the Melrose family was charged with not having their child in attendance at school. The SRS found that schooling was taking place in the home. Nonetheless, the local public school principal pushed for prosecution, apparently because he did not believe that homeschooling was legal since it was not state accredited.

I contacted the prosecutor and the court and was able to get the court date postponed. I sent my legal memorandum to the prosecutor and requested dismissal. A few months later the prosecutor finally capitulated and dismissed the case. We had given them enough legal arguments so he had an excuse to drop it.

Department of Education Declares War on Homeschoolers

In another development in 1990, the Kansas legislative department, which was a branch of the Department of Education, wrote up a memo that was distributed throughout the state. The memorandum did not mince any words about their opposition to homeschooling.

"Is home instruction permitted in Kansas as an alternative to attendance at a public school? Is home instruction in essence the same thing as a private denomination parochial school? The answer to both these questions has been no."

The memorandum summarized the three homeschool cases that had at this time been ruled on by the Supreme Court of Kansas, all against homeschooling. This was sent to all the school districts.

It looked like it was all over for homeschooling in Kansas!

But they were too late. HSLDA, Jim Farthing, and the Teaching Parents Association of Wichita as well as brave homeschoolers throughout the state had already educated the educators—district by district.

Because many families joined HSLDA, we were able to "put our money where our mouth was," and the school districts knew it.

No school districts listened to the "declaration of war" handed down from the Department of Education!

Most Aggressive School District Gives Up without a Fight

Although many families had cases filed against them over the next ten years, we were able to dismiss them all without trials. Amazingly, the Jost case was the last trial we had in Kansas.

Again, all the glory goes to God.

In fact, in Johnson County where the *Sawyer* case originated (which condemned homeschooling), an HSLDA family received a lengthy form requiring them to give information on how much time a psychologist was involved in their homeschool. They also wanted the daily schedule, the lesson plans for the last two weeks, regular testing, accreditation of the homeschool program, a list of textbooks, and more. The accompanying letter from the prosecutor stated that he "wanted all this information in order to determine if I should bring charges."

I wrote back to the prosecutor telling him we would not self-incriminate the family and demonstrated that the family met all the minimal requirements of a nonaccredited school by filing with the Department of Education as one.

The prosecutor responded by saying that he would prosecute the family in thirty days unless they completed the school district's forms. The full pressure of the state was bearing down without mercy on the poor family.

I stood my ground repeating that all the questions exceeded the state's authority. I explained, "Since the prosecutor does not know what a legitimate school is, we would not give him the family's information since it might possibly incriminate them."

Miraculously the prosecutor gave in and left the family alone. Why did he give in when he had all the case law on his side? God intervened.

In spite of this volatile atmosphere, God protected His people. Homeschoolers continued to be able to operate, based on local court decisions that we used again and again.

The Worst Bill of the Year

The Kansas Association of School Boards was so miffed at the proliferation of homeschooling that they had House Bill 2392 introduced in 1991. It was the worst homeschool bill of the year in all fifty states, and it would have outlawed virtually all homeschooling.

The two main provisions of the bill required that home-schools "be taught only by certified teachers" and that "all students had to participate in the minimum competency program administered by the state board of education."

HSLDA unleashed the homeschoolers on the bill, and they flooded the legislature. It wasn't long before the chairman of the education committee indicated that the bill would not "see the light of day." Homeschoolers had won again.

Every single family in Kansas that we represented was able to homeschool even though the highest levels of the state government prohibited it. No one was forced to stop home-schooling by the state.

How was this possible? Simply by God's grace alone. There is no other explanation.

Texas: 150 Homeschool Families Prosecuted at the Same Time

Texas was another one of the major battlegrounds for HSLDA. When I came on board in 1985, cases were being filed against Texas homeschoolers all over the state. I hardly knew where to begin.

What made it particularly difficult is that there are more than one thousand school districts; and each school district did, like at the time of the judges, that which was right in their own eyes. Few school districts were sympathetic to homeschoolers, and most were simply turning them over to prosecution. Why? They had the full support of the Texas Education Agency (TEA) behind them who said homeschooling was illegal.

In 1981, the Texas Education Agency had issued a policy that stated, "Educating a child at home is not the same as private school instruction and therefore is not an acceptable substitute." This, in effect, outlawed homeschooling in Texas. It was "open season" on homeschool families. Many brave families, nonetheless, remained obedient to the call of God. By March 1985, approximately one hundred fifty innocent home-schooling parents were being prosecuted across the state.

The thought going through my mind was, *When will God deliver His people?* It looked so hopeless. God was teaching all of us patience and endurance.

Soon HSLDA decided to go on the offense rather than just wait for the next prosecution.

We joined with several Texas homeschool families as plain-tiffs to bring a class-action civil rights suit against the 1,060 school districts in the state and the Texas Education Agency for violating homeschoolers' civil rights. The homeschool plain-tiffs retained attorney Shelby Sharpe of Fort Worth, Texas, to handle the case.

"You Can Teach at the Public School but Not at Home"

Meanwhile one particular hot spot was Katy, Texas, where five HSLDA member families were facing charges for homeschool-ing their children. Negotiations between the Katy officials and HSLDA proved fruitless since the Katy official insisted that homeschooling was illegal under Texas law.

This extreme position was taken one step further by the school officials when they prosecuted the fifth family, who clearly was qualified to teach by public school standards. The wife held a valid teacher's certificate for the state of Texas. We were asking ourselves, *What more can they want?*

The Katy attendance officer even told Mrs. Davis, "You are qualified to teach children in the public schools, but you cannot teach your own children at home!"

The group of cases was soon dubbed "the Katy Five," and the homeschool cause received a sympathetic ear from the press. *USA Today* wrote a story about them, and one of the families appeared on the CBS morning news.

The class-action suit filed by Shelby Sharp was called the *Leeper* case, and Christian Liberty Academy Satellite Schools (CLASS), and Calvert schools all joined HSLDA as plaintiffs in the case. The goal was to declare homeschooling legal under present Texas law by defining it as a private school. The secondary argument was that the law be ruled void for vagueness. Also the case asked for $4 million in damages.

Meanwhile, in spite of the overwhelming odds, two of the Houston area families won at trial!

The Scene of the Crime

In May 1985, Mark and Erma Davis were amazingly acquitted of criminal charges of violating the Texas compulsory attendance law. Mrs. Davis was the mother with a valid Texas teaching certificate. HSLDA had hired attorney and homeschool dad Tom Sanders to represent the Davis family in court.

One court observer reported favorably on Sanders's creative and sometimes humorous defense tactics. Sanders used a diagram of the Davis's house to demonstrate where the children were homeschooled. After he had the mother identify the various rooms on the diagram, Tom Sanders referred to the diagram and the homeschool as "the scene of the crime"!

The justice of the peace, who presided over the trial, was so impressed with homeschooling that he told Sanders that he would dismiss the charges against all homeschoolers unless the parents were clearly abusing or neglecting their children.

Praise God for giving us all hope!

The second outright court victory came in a case against Don and Ginger Haluzan. The Haluzans' trial was postponed because Mrs. Haluzan was in a late stage of pregnancy.

When their trial was rescheduled, God arranged for HSLDA local attorney Mike Edwards to argue the case before the same judge who had presided over the Davis trial. As you can imagine, the charges were quickly dismissed. Meanwhile, we at HSLDA were successful in postponing many of the other cases across the state, pointing to the class-action suit. The TEA continued to fight homeschooling by trying to "nip it in the bud," but God had other plans.

The TEA made many attempts in 1986 to thwart the *Leeper* lawsuit by various means. They tried to enact various regulations even though the legislature did not give the authority to regulate private education. The first time they got the message when they were swamped with five or six thousand letters from homeschoolers telling them to back off!

Hundreds of homeschoolers also attended a rally in Austin protesting the new "regulations" of the TEA that essentially outlawed homeschooling. The public protest safely put the regulations to rest.

Local Court Hands Down Injunction Halting Prosecution

Finally, in April 1987 the Tarrant County District Court, in the *Leeper* class-action suit, ruled in favor of the homeschoolers. Subsequently the state school districts appealed.

The Semone, LeTourneau, and Galbraith families had their cases quickly dismissed in Katy by Tom Sanders and Mike Edwards, the HSLDA attorneys. I worked with Beaumont school officials to convince them to hold off litigation against targeted homeschool families while the *Leeper* case was on appeal.

In *Leeper*, the trial court established that homeschools are completely legal as a small private school and described the proper activity at home that constitutes a school under Texas law. If a school has a written curriculum, is operated in a bonafide manner by covering the subjects of reading, spelling, grammar, math, and good citizenship, it is considered a private school.

Immediately an injunction was instituted that prohibited any further litigation while the case was pending. This was fantastic news for the beleaguered homeschoolers in Texas that had been facing outlaw status for homeschooling. God once again delivered the victory.

But the TEA and many school districts did want to give up or give in. In spite of the injunction, they were going to make life miserable for homeschoolers.

Now the battle was not for the right to exist, but rather for the right of the school district to approve or disapprove the homeschoolers' curriculum under the *Leeper* decision. Our work was just beginning!

"If Anyone Can Teach, Teaching Will No Longer Be a Profession"

During those days in the late 80s and early 90s, I talked to many superintendents, two of whom had told me that they had to prosecute the homeschoolers, or the "TEA will jerk my public school's accreditation and my certification."

It was apparent that the TEA remained prejudiced against homeschooling.

John Cole, president of the Texas Federation of Teachers, said his organization was seeking to intervene on behalf of the public school districts in the *Leeper* case. A brief that the TFD prepared stated, "If as a result of this case anyone can teach children in the homeschool, that will have the natural and inevitable effect of devaluing teaching as a profession. If anyone can teach, teaching will, indeed, no longer be a profession."

That sums up what most of our opposition was about across the state: *protecting turf, not children!*

The homeschool parents were showing the public school teachers up with the effectiveness of the teaching of their children, and the public schools weren't going to take it lying down.

The School Districts Do Not Get the Message

When the Leeper victory came down, the pressure began to let up. Nonetheless, many superintendents throughout the state continued to intimidate and harass homeschool families. I handled hundreds of incidents where homeschoolers were threatened with various tactics of superintendents: the sending of forms demanding information that exceeded the law, having truant officers make threatening visits, or just referring them to social services.

For instance, in September 1990, during the first two months of the school year, over sixty HSLDA members were contacted by social workers, truant officers, and various other school officials. Here are a few examples:

In Richardson, Texas, several families received negative contacts. One family received a demand for a curriculum review and a home visit. Another family was told that school district officials had the authority to come into their home at any time and review their curriculum to ensure that it met the state standards. I advised both families on their rights and contacted the school district. I explained that they had no such authority, and they subsequently backed off.

However, another family, after assuring the school district that they were in full compliance of the law, received a letter demanding that they allow the truant officer to enter the home to inspect the following: a copy of their curriculum, textbooks, school calendar, and appropriate space for teaching. The letter to the family ended by stating, "Failure to comply will result in immediate legal action as provided by the school laws in Texas."

When the family refused to allow the home visit, the school official contacted them and told them that a criminal action was being filed against them. I immediately called the school district and was told by the school official to "see us in court."

I then prepared a letter, as I have done hundreds of times, that was more like a mini brief. It explained the unconstitutionally of home visits, the violation of the *Leeper* court precedent, and the statutory limitations. Finally the school district gave up.

Then, on November 27, 1991, the Texas Court of Appeals completely affirmed the lower court's ruling, and even found that the Texas Education Agency had "deprived the homeschool parents of equal protection under the law" since their private schools in the home were unfairly discriminated against "on the sole basis of location within the home."

The final victory came when the *Leeper* case was upheld by the Texas Supreme Court on June 15, 1994, with a unanimous decision in favor of the homeschoolers.

Needless to say, God reigned in Texas. Even though the Texas legislature never had the opportunity to pass a homeschool law, homeschooling is alive and well due to these key court decisions.

The threats, illegal requirements, and social worker harassment never ends. Texas, believe it or not, is still one of our most litigious states. In 2003 seven homeschool families were taken to court!

As long as there are compulsory attendance statutes in every state that are enforced by the prejudiced public schools, homeschoolers will continue to be harassed and intimidated.

California: A Powder Keg Ready to Blow

By the end of 1985, 1,041 members had joined from the state of California, more than any other state. We counseled most of the homeschoolers to file "private school affidavits" with the State Board of Education because there was and still is no homeschool law.

Michael Smith was our California attorney. Although he was on the HSLDA Board, he lived in California at that time. (In 1987 he came to work full-time as a staff attorney at the HSLDA offices in northern Virginia. Now he is president of HSLDA.)

In the early years he and I worked together contacting school districts on behalf of the families who were being harassed. We argued that homeschools were private schools, although very small private schools, located in the home; they nonetheless met the requirements of a private school.

Several school districts wrote threatening letters to anyone who requested a private school affidavit. The letters warned that if someone filled out the private school affidavit but was actually teaching their children at home, those parents had to be certified under the private tutor statute or else suffer the consequences of violating the compulsory attendance law.

One thing we learned in California and most states was that school districts tend to bluff. Their biggest weapon is intimidation. It is costly to pursue truants for the school district because they have to convene a SARB (Student Attendance Review Board) hearing and then pursue criminal truancy charges.

Although homeschools were in a precarious situation in California, God had His protection on the homeschoolers. The numbers of families turning to homeschooling was growing steadily. Yet the California Supreme Court ruled twice, starting in the 1950s, that homeschools were basically illegal. The *Turner* and *Shinn* cases seemed straightforward enough, and the Department of Education agreed. In fact, the California Department of Education believed a parent could only homeschool if they qualified as a certified tutor.

We knew that at any moment the powder keg could go off because homeschoolers in some other states had been losing the "private school argument." Courts were determining that to be a school you had to be an institution; in their eyes a home did not cut it. Of course, California already had its own bad legal precedent where homeschools lost.

Things looked pretty bleak for homeschooling.

The Miracle Case

Then a miracle happened on March 10, 1986. Michael Smith and attorney Jerry Crowe, who was also a homeschool father, argued the case of *People v. Darrah and Black* in Santa Barbara County. The Darrah family was faithfully homeschooling their children, and they were excelling. The Black family was seeing the same excellent academic results. But the school district did not care that the children were successfully learning; that apparently was not the goal. The school officials were upset that the Blacks and Darrahs were not qualified to teach their children because they were not certified.

To everyone's surprise the court sided with Mike Smith and found that the statute for compulsory attendance failed to "establish minimum guidelines to the local officials as to what constitutes a person capable of teaching, and what constitutes a private, full time, day school." As a result, the court held that the compulsory attendance law violates the state and federal constitutions and, therefore, is unconstitutionally vague and unenforceable.

Normally the influence and effect of a municipal court decision is almost nonexistent except for the immediate county in which it is located, but God had bigger plans for this little court decision as you will see in a moment.

A couple of miraculous things happened in this case.

First of all, Michael Smith had filed the demur, which normally is only an opportunity to deal with the facts of the case, not the constitutionality. Nonetheless, Mike argued in his brief that the law was unconstitutionally vague.

The judge should not have even heard this case, but we know that "the king's heart is like channels of water in the hand of the LORD; He turns it wherever He wishes" (Prov. 21:1). And God opened the heart of the judge to allow the issues to be presented in this unique and unusual procedure.

Second, the case was a municipal court case. It should not have had widespread impact in the state of California. It should have only applied to the local county. Nonetheless, Michael Smith was able to use this case a thousand times over to convince local school districts that the law was vague and that homeschools can legally operate as private schools.

Of course, the California homeschoolers did not sit by idle. They educated many school districts one by one. They did not flinch.

Also Roy Hanson and his right-hand man, Jim Davis, founded and faithfully ran Family Protection Ministries. The FPM has monitored and lobbied the California legislature preventing *every* negative bill that would have harmed homeschoolers' rights in any way. Praise God for His goodness.

Weak and Foolish Things Confound the Wise

God, once again, proved to all of us that He uses the weak and foolish things of the world to confound the strong and the wise. He did not need a Supreme Court victory in order to change the atmosphere in California.

This is particularly phenomenal in light of the fact that there had been two California Supreme Court decisions, the *Turner* and *Shinn* cases, where homeschools lost. The California Supreme Court condemned homeschooling and upheld the convictions against those two families. How could a lower court case by one little municipal judge change the whole legal atmosphere in a large state? Why didn't liberal California simply squash homeschoolers because they had the Supreme Court on their side, all the public school districts, and the department of education?

Once again God was showing Himself faithful and strong on behalf of homeschoolers. Many parents and children were praying for protection, and God answered.

Little County Court Decision Protects Families Everywhere

In 1987 two HSLDA families, the Bairds and the Allisons, were harassed by both the child welfare agency and the attendance officers for the school district. Michael Smith and local attorney Al Cunningham were able to convince the school district not to send them over for prosecution. Instead, as is allowed by California law, a Student Attendance Review Board (SARB) hearing was set up on February 12.

Even though this was set up, the child welfare officer continued to write letters threatening prosecution of the family and possible juvenile court action, should the parents not enroll their children in a public school or a private school "as recognized by the attendance officer."

At the student attendance review board, Mike Smith argued the point that the families had a constitutional right to homeschool under the First Amendment and, furthermore, were in compliance with the private school law since both had filed private school affidavits.

In a short opinion the board indicated that it did not believe that it could take any action or refer the matter any further. The cases were won, and the families were allowed to continue to homeschool.

This is just one example of the many ways Michael Smith of HSLDA was able to use the *Darren and Black* decision to hold off prosecution of homeschoolers.

Another miracle of the story of California is that no legislation was ever passed recognizing homeschooling, and no case was won above a municipal court judge's decision. Yet now, at the writing of this book, homeschooling is readily accepted by school districts throughout the state, and tens of thousands of homeschoolers are prospering.

Of course, school districts still abuse the law and try to intimidate families. But it is obvious that homeschooling is being protected in California by God's almighty hand.

Many other states faced these same battles, and we used the same private-school defense with eventual success.

God has truly protected the homeschool movement all these years.

9

The Home Invasion

Let us therefore draw near with confidence to the
throne of grace, that we may receive mercy and may
find grace to help in time of need.

HEBREWS 4:16

A school official comes to your door. She explains that in order for you to continue to homeschool, you have to let her in so she can observe the instruction of your children.

Against your better judgment, you decide to let her in. She is an official from the school district, so you feel somewhat intimidated. She walks around your house looking at the curtains and carpet, making comments like, "These are ugly and don't really match." She then sits down at your table and asks to see your books. You bring in your books one by one, and she frowns as she looks at them, taking notes furiously.

Then she asks to see your child. Now you are getting a little more nervous!

Your seven-year-old comes and sits at the table, and she begins to quiz him to determine his knowledge. All of this occurs within fifteen minutes. She asks your son, "Use the word *professional* in a sentence."

Your son thinks and then says, "My father, who is a plumber, is a professional." She then responds, "Plumbers aren't professionals. Don't you know that?"

You feel violated. The school official insists on looking through the rest of your books before she goes, and then she abruptly leaves.

This is what a home visit was like in the early 80s and early 90s. This was one family's experience in South Dakota at that time. In fact, school districts across America were trying to intimidate homeschoolers by demanding home visits.

As recently as a few years ago in Illinois, a school district sent letters to homeschoolers insisting on inspecting their "private schools." Many of the other private school states, even to this day, like Texas, Indiana, Kansas, California, and others, are visited by truant officers or school officials who try to come into the home.

Of course, social workers are most known for trying to gain entrance. I have handled more than a thousand social worker contacts over the years, and there was not one who did not insist on entering. It is part of their protocol that they are required to follow through whenever they get an allegation, whether it is from an anonymous tipster or not. Their job is to get into the home and interrogate the children separately.

The Unconstitutionality of Home Visits

Home visits are unconstitutional because they violate a family's Fourth Amendment rights to privacy and freedom from searches and seizures. In other words, the government official cannot come into your home, whether he is a social worker, school officials, police officer, or whatever, unless he has a warrant signed by a judge. The only way he can acquire a warrant signed by a judge or court order to gain entrance into your home is if he provides that judge with a probable cause. This means it must be credible evidence, more than mere suspicion or an anonymous tip.

Thus, this was the battle for home visits that we were engaged in and continue to be engaged in across the country. But in the mid 80s and 90s, it was fearsome because the law was still unsettled.

The Battle for Freedom from Home Invasion in South Dakota

South Dakota had a statute that gave the local school officials the authority to do home visits. Charles and Susan Davis of Newell, South Dakota, lived in a district where the officials chose to exercise their "right" to do a home visit. In October 1992 they were notified by the school district that a school official would be contacting them to arrange for a home visit.

The Davises were opposed to this invasive policy and informed the school district, under my counsel, that they would not allow a school official into their home. I explained in a letter that the Fourth Amendment protects the right of privacy and the right to be free from unreasonable searches and seizures. Therefore, the family would not allow the home visit. I also asked the county to waive their statutory right to do a home visit in light of the Davises proof of test scores showing that the children were academically excelling.

The state would not back off so I counseled with Mike Farris, and he and I filed a federal civil rights suit in February 1993, challenging South Dakota's home visit provision as being unconstitutional. We argued in the complaint that the South Dakota legislature exceeded their authority to give state officials the unconstitutional right to come into the homes of homeschoolers.

Shortly after the civil rights suit was filed, we learned that several other member families were being threatened with prosecution for refusing home visits. We contacted the school districts and kindly offered to include them in the civil rights suits. Whereupon they agreed not to conduct any home visits or proceed with any prosecution while the lawsuit was pending.

Legislation Introduced to Repeal Home-Visit Requirement

I contacted Barbara West, from the Weston South Dakota Home Educators, and Mary Sayler, a homeschool support group leader in Pierre, South Dakota, and suggested introducing legislation to repeal the home-visit requirement. I worked with the South Dakota homeschool leaders to draft the legislation, and Mary Sayler was able to find a sponsor for the bill; the sponsor was also the chairman of the House Education Committee, which always helps!

In early February I traveled to Pierre to testify in front of the House Education Committee. Barbara West and I along with others presented testimony, and it was well received. The committee voted nine to four to pass HB 1260. The legislators had been swamped with phone calls from the homeschoolers. Two weeks later the bill was considered before the Senate Education Committee. We knew this would not be easy but just gave it to God.

A Gentle Answer Turns Away Wrath

Once again I boarded the plane and went out to testify along with Barbara West and Bernie Schock of Sioux Falls. The response by the Senate Education Committee was frosty and very different from the friendly atmosphere we had experienced in the House.

I was grilled unmercifully on the legislation for nearly an hour. One of the committee members was a public school teacher, and he would not let go. He stated that home visits are necessary in order to know if children are being educated— "You can't just trust parents!" When I explained that they were unconstitutional because they violated the Fourth Amendment, his temper flared hotter and hotter. In fact, for ten minutes he grilled me, and his voice grew louder and his comments got nastier as he made accusations against homeschool moms and my work.

Finally, the committee chairman, in a rare move, had to chastise him publicly and tell him to be quiet since he was losing his temper. "You are finished questioning him!" she declared forcefully as she hit her gavel. After that, the other unsupportive committee members started to look more favorably on the legislation. God's Word in Proverbs rang true that "a gentle answer turns away wrath."

During a recess I met with the chairman of the committee, and she said: "I am very open to some alternative to home visits. However, I am still concerned about children and the need to check on them halfway through the school year to make sure they are getting an education." I said, "I have some language for you, and I believe we can work out a good compromise like we did in the state of Colorado."

In a nail-biter three to three tie that day, the committee deferred the vote until Saturday.

This gave me opportunity to write up the amendment. In exchange for deleting the statutory right of the state to do home visits, I offered an amendment that the school district can, within fourteen days of written notice, inspect the records of the homeschool if they "have probable cause to believe that the program is not in compliance with the law." The language, of course, carried with it the weight of the Constitution. It also gave the impression to the committee members that they would be able to check the records of families during the school year.

By God's grace the language passed, and the bill was eventually passed through the whole legislature and signed by the governor.

To this day not a single family has had their records reviewed or inspected by the school district. This is because they need to have the records in order to have sufficient probable cause to inspect the records! God had delivered South Dakotans, and we dismissed our civil rights lawsuit with never reaching trial.

Massachusetts: Home Is Where the School District Official Is

Massachusetts continued the home-visit battle. The home-schoolers in Massachusetts have one of the oldest approval laws in the country, and they still have it to this day. In order for a homeschool to operate legally, the law says they have to be approved by the local school district. One of the means of approval public school districts used was to conduct home visits. The Brunelles and the Pustells were two families that knew God did not want them to submit to such invasion of their home. They said "no" to Lynn public schools.

The Pustells notified Lynn public school officials in 1991 of their intention to home educate. The Brunelles also notified the same school district that they would be teaching their five school-age children at home. The school district reviewed both their curriculum qualifications and found them to be completely satisfactory.

So the problem was not the education of the children; the problem was control. The school district wanted the Pustells and Brunelles to "bow the knee."

They insisted the families must "allow the superintendent to periodically observe and evaluate the instructional process and to verify that the home instruction plan is being implemented in the home." So much for trusting the parents.

So Mike Farris and our legal team at HSLDA ended up challenging this by filing a civil rights suit in federal court. The federal circuit court abstained from making a ruling, declaring that state issues need to be solved in the state court first. Mike Farris then filed for declaratory judgment, asking that the home-visit requirement be a violation of the homeschool families' rights under Massachusetts's law and constitution.

Finally, after several years, on December 16, 1998, the Massachusetts Supreme Judicial Court handed down the *Brunelle* decision, recognizing that the home-visit requirement was not constitutional. The court said that since this case involved the "fundamental right" of parental liberty, the court needed to apply the "compelling interest test," which requires the court to determine whether the state regulation or policy, like home visits, is "essential" to fulfill the state's compelling interest in education.

The court ruled on the side of the Brunelles (and Pustells), stating:

> Both the U.S. Supreme Court and this court have emphasized in connection with the fundamental right of parents to raise their children that government not intrude unnecessarily on familiar privacy. This concern, as well as others, dictates that home education proposals can be made subject only to essential and reasonable requirements. Nonconsensual home visits are dead in Massachusetts.

Praise God. God had delivered the Massachusetts homeschoolers through much patience and long-suffering. God had delivered His people once again. "Many are the afflictions of the righteous; But the LORD delivers him out of them all" (Ps. 34:19).

Ever since the Brunelle decision, we have been able to use that to send to school districts around the country to keep home visits at bay to this very day.

10

Homeschoolers Flood the Legislatures

But one thing I do: forgetting what lies behind and reaching forward to what lies ahead, I press on toward the goal for the prize of the upward call of God in Christ Jesus.

PHILIPPIANS 3:13–14

In 1993 Virginia homeschoolers had trouble on their hands. Senate bill 913 was the "baby" of the Department of Education. It would lower the compulsory attendance age from six to five. This meant that families who operated under the homeschool law would have to test their five-year-old! The department figured passage would be easy with a completely democratically controlled house, senate, and governor's office.

However, they underestimated the power of God working through homeschoolers!

Upon the bills passage in the Senate, HSLDA and the Home Education Association of Virginia (HEAV) got busy. We mailed out several alerts to thousands of homeschoolers three or four times during the course of the battle, and the "phone trees" were humming. (The Internet was still in its infancy.) Homeschoolers were able to convince House member Jay O'Brien to introduce an amendment that would allow a parent to choose to wait a full year before formally starting school until this child was six years old.

Due to the pressure of the homeschoolers, the amendment was passed in the House after the Senate had already passed the original bad version. It went back to the Senate for a revote and miraculously passed.

It then went to Governor Wilder, and he predictably vetoed it with his line-item veto power.

We bombarded the legislature once more with phone calls, and the Senate voted thirty-nine to one and the House voted eighty-seven to zero to override the governor and restore the O'Brien amendment.

As a result, the bill finally was passed, and we now have *a mandatory kindergarten law in Virginia, which is not mandatory!*

One senator commented on the floor of the Senate, "Based on the number of phone calls and visits and letters that came in concerning the bill, I can only assume that every other person in Virginia is homeschooling!"

The teacher's union was fuming.

Homeschoolers' Voice Is Bigger Than Their Size

In the middle 1980s and on, homeschoolers were blessed with having a much bigger voice than anyone would have ever expected. In relation to the organizations and other lobbying forces in the United States, homeschoolers were miniscule in comparison. But homeschoolers cared about the future. They thought generational. Homeschoolers wanted more freedom to teach their children God's ways, and also, to preserve that freedom for future generations.

As a result, the homeschoolers responded when a phone tree sent out alerts concerning pending legislation that would affect their freedoms. Homeschoolers, almost to the man, were faithful in calling committee members, their legislators, writing to the editor of various newspapers, attending rallies at the capitol, and jamming hearing rooms on legislation before legislative committees.

Besides, attending a hearing, or rally, or writing a letter or phone call, is just another part of their civics curriculum. Being involved in the legislative process is a natural aspect of the overall home education of their children.

In 1985, when I began working at HSLDA, seven states had recently passed homeschool laws: Arizona and Mississippi in 1982; Wisconsin and Montana in 1983; and Georgia, Virginia, and Louisiana in 1984. This happened all with tiny homeschool populations, but somehow these homeschool laws passed. Of course, we know the real power and where it came from.

Of those seven states, Mississippi, Wisconsin, and Montana, against the odds, had passed unbelievably excellent homeschool laws. None of those states required more than just simply a notice of intent to homeschool and a promise that certain subjects for a certain amount of days would be taught. It was an honor system, which protected and maximized parental freedom.

These laws loudly proclaimed, "We trust the parents." They stood for the principle that even the U.S. Supreme Court has recognized—parents act in the best interest of their children. Arizona's law was a little bit more problematic in that it required homeschool parents to take a "teacher's test" of basic literacy, and the students had to take an annual standardized achievement test.

It was clear for all to see that the homeschool movement had as its foundation Jesus Christ. These were largely parents who love the Lord and desire to train their children according to the Word of God. This is why I believe blessings of legislative victories came on the homeschoolers.

In 1985 seven more states passed homeschool laws. Over the next ten years, most of the states passed homeschool laws or won cases that recognize the right of homeschools to operate as private schools. Once again, the odds were clearly against the homeschoolers, but God gave them the victory.

We at HSLDA crisscrossed the country, testifying on behalf of good bills and opposition to bad bills for homeschool freedoms. For example, during 1991, Mike Farris testified in Connecticut and Montana; Michael Smith testified in Arizona, Maryland, and Oregon legislatures; and I testified in Maine and North Dakota legislatures. We were also involved in the drafting of favorable amendments to legislation affecting home-schooling.

Of course, HSLDA has always been in the business of keeping members informed. In the 1980s when we were small, we utilized "snail mail." It was hard to inform families at a moment's notice, but nonetheless, we always seemed to be able to get out the notification about the legislation in time.

In this chapter I will give you just a few examples of how God miraculously delivered homeschool families and enabled us to win legislative battles when the education elite with all the millions of dollars was arrayed against us.

"God and God alone"—that has been the homeschoolers theme. He deserves all the credit and the glory for the true stories you are about to read.

"We Won't Be Needing These Anymore"

In 1991 we received a plea from military homeschoolers that were stationed in Washington, DC. To our dismay we discovered that Washington, DC, had implemented one of the worst homeschool policies in the nation.

It required homeschoolers not only to be certified teachers, but also required unannounced home visits! I sent a letter to the DC school superintendent not really expecting an answer, but then within a few weeks the superintendent indicated that he wanted to set up a meeting to discuss this issue.

It was just a few days before the appointed meeting that we had a clandestine gathering of homeschoolers in Washington, DC, at Bollings Air Force Base. Everyone was concerned; all were operating underground. It was "homeschool suicide" to contact the DC Public School authorities. After my talk, we committed the future school district meeting to prayer, and the prayers continued throughout the time that we were there.

I went to the meeting with a homeschool military couple, Rich and Linda Geel, and provided two legal memoranda proving the unconstitutionality of both home visits and teacher certification.

Meanwhile the homeschooling support group was praying.

I, still being of little faith, again expected that any forthcoming decision would be weeks if not months of deliberation among the DC school administration and school board.

But was I surprised!

At the end of the meeting, the vice superintendent picked up the DC homeschool guidelines and ripped them in half right in front of us saying, "I guess we won't be needing these anymore."

As a result, all requirements for homeschoolers were suspended, and they asked me to help draft new guidelines. The prayers of DC homeschoolers were answered in a mighty way that day.

By 1999 there were *still no requirements* for homeschoolers in DC.

Then, without warning, a slightly adjusted old version of the DC guidelines resurfaced. Certain school officials were quietly working to have the DC School Board enact these restrictive guidelines into more permanent regulations. This time we had the ear of the Majority Leader of the Senate, Trent Lott, and the Majority Leader of the House, Dick Armey. I contacted the staffers of both these offices and explained our dilemma.

Both leaders immediately issued a letter to the DC Public Schools expressing a desire that the school board "work with the Home School Legal Defense Association to ensure that the proposed changes to the city rules concerning access to education will not have adverse impact on homeschool families in the District." Needless to say the guidelines once again disappeared, and homeschoolers to this day continue to enjoy having no policy, rule, or regulation for homeschooling.

They have complete freedom in a potentially hostile climate. Only God can make Washington, DC, the best legal atmosphere in the country.

Michigan Case Derails Legislation in South Dakota

In January 1994 State Representative Barbara Everist introduced House Bill 1262, which would have required all homeschoolers in the state of South Dakota to be state-certified teachers in order to comply with the law by the year 2000.

When homeschoolers contacted Representative Everist, they were surprised to learn that she felt she was being particularly understanding by giving them six years to obtain a teacher's certificate. Mary Sayler, a homeschool mom from Pierre, explained to Representative Everist that there was constitutional concern, and she indicated she would at least talk to me.

As a routine safeguard, I sent out an alert to South Dakota members explaining the dilemma and the need to call the Senate and the House. Meanwhile, I sent overnight by Federal Express to Representative Everist a copy of the *DeJonge* decision that the Michigan Supreme Court had had decided the year before. (Chapter 6 gives the full story of this eight-year HSLDA case that resulted in teacher certification being struck down in Michigan.) I explained in an accompanying letter that teacher certification was unconstitutional since it violated the free exercise rights of many families. I further demonstrated that certification wasn't even necessary for children to be educated as demonstrated through many studies.

Not wanting to introduce any unconstitutional legislation, Representative Everist, convinced by the outcome in the *DeJonge* decision by the Michigan Supreme Court, agreed to withdraw her bill. For a sponsor to withdraw her own bill voluntarily is rare.

The DeJonge family's faithfulness in Michigan blessed even the South Dakota homeschoolers.

All we could do was praise God for once again protecting His people without us hardly having to fire a shot.

Colorado Homeschoolers Overcome the Odds

In the spring of 1988, homeschoolers in Colorado were still faced with difficult restrictions. Homeschooling had to be "approved" by local school districts, which were often arbitrary. Families who were disapproved could appeal to the Department of Education, which generally rubber-stamped the denial. I was involved in intervening on behalf of dozens of families in various school districts who were having difficulty. Some of the families were already in court.

Bill Moritz, a lawyer and homeschool father, sent me a draft of the "ideal homeschool law," which would simply give homeschools the same status as the private schools. Private schools weren't regulated in Colorado. Under this bill home-schoolers would merely have to notify the school district, and there would be no approval by the school district. The passage of such a bill in Colorado was virtually hopeless, considering the strength of the public school lobbying organizations and the makeup of the legislature at that time. The Senate was Republican, but the House was Democratic, and Governor Romer was as liberal as he could be.

Two legislators agreed to sponsor the bill.

The House sponsor, Dick Bond, was a Democrat, but the Senate sponsor, Senator Meiklejohn, was very conserva-tive. I learned early on, do not promote a bill as either being Republican or Democrat. Homeschool issues crossed party lines. "Any parent should have the right to homeschool" has been our refrain since the beginning of HSLDA.

I talked at length with the House sponsor and referred to the homeschoolers as a "minority" who were getting "picked on" by the government. Being a liberal Democrat, he loved the idea of helping a "minority." I then wrote up a letter that sup-ported the bill and demonstrated that homeschoolers were a minority protected by the First and Fourteenth Amendments. He gave a copy of this letter to all the legislators in the House. And it worked.

In fact, he carried the banner so well for the homeschool-ers that he was able to get the bill passed unanimously in the House. Meanwhile, Rory Schneeberger, a homeschool mother and leader, "camped out" at the Capitol for about a week. Many homeschoolers wrote and supported the bill, and others testi-fied at key hearings.

Rory constantly kept up with the various committees and with the amendments legislators were trying to get attached. She had never done this type of work before and was simply called to do it because she believed in protecting the freedom of homeschoolers. The two sponsors of the bill regularly called me over a two-week period to get my view on various language changes and my suggestions on countering bad amendments.

First, the opposing side wanted some sort of record keeping that could be inspected by a local superintendent. We ended up adding language that only allowed the superintendent to inspect records "if he had probable cause that the family was not complying with the law." This language looked tough on homeschoolers, but in reality, it was a paper tiger. Nonetheless, liberals could not argue against it because the probable cause standard came from the Constitution. Application of this standard meant it can only be used if the superintendent has actual evidence that the family is not educating the child. The language was miraculously adopted.

Strategy: Much Verbiage, Little Bite

Ever since this law was passed, HSLDA has not had a single family who has ever had to have their records inspected. In other words, a superintendent would have to have a copy of the records in the first place to prove he had probable cause to inspect the records. "Probable cause" means that the school district can't, only on mere suspicion or a whim, demand to see the records. There has to be some credible evidence supporting the assertion.

Second, the Department of Education wanted accountability in the form of annual testing of the homeschool. I explained that the homeschoolers would allow it if they could start testing in the third grade and if the test was administered every three years thereafter. The department agreed. Homeschoolers would be tested beginning in third grade and every other year thereafter.

I told the sponsors there needed to be a standard so that families could not be arbitrarily shut down by a superintendent who didn't like the test scores.

In a conference call I asked the department of education official what was the standard cut off for children in the public school to be able to progress to the next grade. He mumbled, "Thirteenth percentile." I said, "What was that?" making him repeat it louder. Reluctantly he stammered, "The thirteenth percentile!" Then I exclaimed, "Perfect. That's what we will use for the homeschoolers. It's only fair." The thirteenth percentile passed and became law without objection.

Finally I explained that some homeschool families were opposed to sending their scores to the public schools and suggested that they send them to a private school of their choice. It was agreed. We also made sure that the offer was still available for homeschoolers who did not want anything to do with the school district to be able to enroll in a private school but to do their teaching at home.

By the end of all this, a short, ideal bill became a long and wordy bill.

In fact, *The Denver Post*, which had been against the original bill wanting extensive restrictions on homeschoolers, changed its position and came out in support of the final wordy bill, thinking it was more restrictive.

However, in the final analysis, the bill was mostly unenforceable, and hardly restrictive at all. In effect, homeschoolers only have to communicate once a year with the public schools in the form of a short notice of intent. This is comparable to some of the better homeschool laws that we mentioned earlier, like Wisconsin, Montana, and Mississippi.

The strategy worked—heavy on the verbiage but little bite.

The inspection of homeschooler records never has happened to this day because of the probable cause protection.

"This Bill Will Give Parents a Choice, and That Is Not Acceptable"

In January 1994, we were able successfully to amend the Colorado homeschool law again, making it even better. Working closely with the Christian Home Educators of Colorado and the Concerned Parents of Colorado, we did several statewide e-lerts, and I flew out twice to testify before the House and Senate Committees. The bill passed thirty-three to two in the Senate and the House by a vote of fifty-three to nine. But it was not that easy.

The Department of Education had introduced in the Senate several amendments that would have made the homeschool law even worse. Hundreds of families came to the January 27 hearing whom I testified before the Colorado Senate Education Committee. They had to give us a big hearing room.

During the second reading in the Senate, Senator Mendez, who was opposed to our legislation, said, "This bill will give parents a choice concerning testing or evaluation, and that is not acceptable." She was further heard to say that "children do not belong to the public school, but they certainly do not belong to the parents either." She attempted to introduce a sunset clause, which was defeated.

On third reading Senator Mendez began publicly accusing homeschoolers of abusing children. Senator Meiklejohn rebuked her saying, "Stop harassing these people. I'm much more concerned, and you should be too, about the growing number of illiterates graduating from public schools and not about a few possible incidences of parents not testing their children according to the law." Believe it or not, the Senate passed our homeschool improvement bill, SB 4, by a vote of thirty-three to two and no amendments. This was God and God alone.

Homeschoolers a Burden to Public Schools?

The Colorado House was going to be a little bit more difficult, but we kept the phone calls pouring into the members and gave each of the members copies of studies, showing the success of homeschoolers. Before testifying, Treon Goossen and I met with Representative Foster, who was the majority leader. He couldn't believe how organized and effective the homeschoolers were.

Foster reported that the senators and house members were literally "flooded with calls and letters from homeschoolers."

Upon contacting the Department of Education, he had been told, "We don't want to mess with homeschoolers!" The Department of Education did not even attempt to reintroduce the amendments that they had proposed in the senate.

At the committee hearing, I was grilled for over a half hour. Representative Wayne Knox led the opposition stating that "SB 4 eliminates accountability for homeschoolers, and there must be some comparison with the public school children."

Representative Benavidez spoke up, saying she worried that homeschoolers would burden the public schools because the public schools would have to "instruct them socially as well." Of the four major provisions where we changed the law, the liberals only noticed one concerning the evaluation, which we successfully preserved over their objection.

As God would have it, the other three provisions slid by without a whimper. Ultimately, the bill was passed, making Colorado's one of the best laws in the country.

The most important element of the victory was the prayers of God's people and the protection of our Heavenly Father.

Yes, God Works in Mysterious Ways

In 1995 an omnibus child-welfare bill was on the fast track through the legislature. This bill would recodify the entire child-welfare code and remove many of the protections and due process procedures that parents had enjoyed. In other words, this bill would take away freedoms of homeschoolers and give more power to the child-welfare workers.

Treon Goossen of Concerned Parents of Colorado and the Christian Home Educator's Coalition representative, Earl Hall, spent many hours and time sending out e-lerts, doing radio spots, and lobbying representatives. From my desk at HSLDA back in Virginia, I was sending out e-lerts regularly to our membership causing hundreds of calls to pour in. Nonetheless, this bill was on the fast track.

The bill had passed the House and was all but guaranteed to pass the Senate. We knew the vote was close, but it seemed unstoppable. Of course, we know that with God all things are possible.

Then we learned of the "mysterious way" that God would be working. The vote was expected to come down to the Senate and we would lose. One of the senators who supported the child-welfare expansion bill had gotten drunk and was found sitting on the ledge of a window by the Capitol police. They ushered her back into her room. Soon she stumbled down the hall and walked into the Senate chambers during the vote.

The majority leader called for a floor vote where all those opposed to the bill would stand and be counted, and if it was less than the majority present, the bill would pass. If it was a tie, or more votes against the bill, the bill would fail. The pro-child's rights contingency had counted heads and determined that they had the votes. But when this drunken woman senator stepped into the chambers right during the vote, she remained standing even though she supported the bill because at the time she did "not know which way was up"!

Heads were counted, and it was determined that it was a tie. The bill came down in a defeat, which was incredulous to the proponents who expected this to be passed. Once again God proved that He and He alone was going to deliver us from bad legislation—even using a drunken senator.

Homeschoolers Set Records at Texas Rally

On January 26, 1993, the Texas Supreme Court heard oral arguments on the important case of *Texas Education Agency v. Leeper*. We talked about this case in detail in chapter 8. Inside the state supreme court building, the justices closely questioned both parties regarding the state's authority to regulate homeschoolers. Attorney Shelby Sharpe, representing the homeschoolers, stated the statute did not give the Texas Education Agency any authority to regulate private schools and that homeschools were simply small private schools. The lawyers for the state, on the other hand, complained about the earlier rulings in Leeper that limited the school districts' authority to monitor and control homeschools.

Meanwhile, outside the courtroom a pro-homeschool family rally was in progress. More than five thousand people gathered at the south steps of the state capitol in Austin to demonstrate their support for parental rights and family values. During the rally a show of hands showed that a majority of the attendees were homeschool families. God had the sun shining and the temperature moderate—good rally weather.

I had the privilege to give the rally's keynote speech. It was such a blessing to stand on the stage and behold the sea of concerned parents and families. As I explained the value of homeschooling and the importance of the government keeping their hands off, the people cheered—echoing across the capitol grounds.

I declared that "homeschoolers have earned the right to be left alone" and all the state representatives that were on the stage sat up and listened to the roar of the audience.

It seemed clear that God used this rally to make a huge impression on the Texas legislature and has helped keep the legislature sensitive and respectful of the needs of the home-school community ever since.

Homeschoolers Make Their Voices Heard in Maryland

In March 1987 the Maryland Department of Education drafted and tried to enact a regulation that would require homeschoolers to submit to unannounced home visits.

I always wondered why educational bureaucrats liked home visits so much. All I can think is that they just do not trust parents. I traveled to testify before the legislative committee that has oversight over the department of education.

Normally the department of education issues regulations, and the legislature simply nods the affirmative. This time God had stirred up the hearts of the legislature to go to the trouble of convening a committee hearing to discuss the merits of the new regulations. After I testified on the unconstitutionality of home visits and hundreds of homeschoolers packed the hearing room showing their opposition, the new regulations were soundly rejected by the committee, stopping home visits to homeschoolers by school officials.

Bismarck "Tea Party"

On February 20, 1989, a rally was held in Bismarck, the North Dakota state capital. Homeschoolers were still suffering under the chains of teacher certification. The Supreme Court of North Dakota was stubbornly refusing to grant constitutional protection to the homeschoolers, ruling against them. The legislature wouldn't move to "let my people go."

Clinton Birst, the homeschool leader in North Dakota, frustrated by the lack of change, sent out a national plea for help to attend a "Bismarck Tea Party." Mike Farris and one hundred fifty homeschoolers from eleven states flooded the offices of the legislature with hundreds of tea bags with the attached message, "The consent of the governed for homeschooling too!" By April 7, Governor George A. Sinner signed into law HB 1421 that repealed the state's homeschool law requiring teacher certification. (See chapter 6 for "the rest of the story.")

"Seek and Destroy" Mission against Homeschoolers

In 1988 Illinois homeschoolers received quite a scare. A 1950 Illinois Supreme Court case declared homeschools to be private schools. The court did not provide much more guidance giving the school district "wiggle room" to abuse homeschoolers by creating restrictions out of thin air. Like my experience in many other "private school states," I simply drafted legal memoranda that gave all the legal arguments establishing our position, and I would not give an inch.

If the Illinois Code did not require a particular restriction, we would not cooperate with the school districts' demands. School districts throughout Illinois would try to require home visits, curriculum approval, completion of lengthy forms, registration, and sometimes even teacher qualifications. We would respond by "sticking to our guns" and sending the school district my legal memorandum and a short letter of "assurance" that the children were being educated in a private school in the home. We refused to do anything else because it was not specifically required in the code.

Here is one example of how an active grassroots response made a difference.

Regional Superintendent, Richard Martwick of Cook County, the largest county in Illinois, right outside of Chicago, boldly declared, "The school code of Illinois does *not authorize what is commonly called homeschool.*" He was not only trying to restrict homeschooling but to outlaw it. He threatened to prosecute all homeschool families.

Mr. Martwick put his "money where his mouth was" and subsequently initiated truancy proceedings against several homeschooling families. The homeschoolers throughout the area were frightened. Martwick meant business. He boldly proclaimed in the newspapers his plan to "seek and destroy" homeschoolers.

I wrote him a letter explaining that he was violating both civil and constitutional rights of families in his district. The *Levisen* case from 1950 was the Illinois Supreme Court decision finding that homeschooling was legal. The argument then, and the argument I continued to present to school district after school district in Illinois who challenged the right of homeschoolers, was that homeschools are private schools. Private schools are not regulated in Illinois. Beyond having a requirement to teach the same branches of instruction as the public schools and the English language, it didn't matter if the school met in the home or a building. We were prepared to file a lawsuit if Martwick would continue this course of action.

Meanwhile, the homeschoolers in the area organized a picket; and dozens of families picketed in front of his office, catching the news media's attention. We sent out an alert, and families were writing to the school district from all over the State of Illinois, protesting his position.

Finally after much prayer and protest by the homeschoolers, Martwick recanted and withdrew his policy that essentially outlawed homeschooling. There had been no litigation in Illinois since 1950, and once again we avoided going to the unpredictable courts. Homeschoolers were able to continue to operate peaceably in the county.

"Homeschoolers Are Child Abusers— I Have Proof!"

The year 1991 was certainly one for negative pieces of legislation to be filed against homeschooling. The National Education Association was usually discovered to be behind the legislation. In Wisconsin, the "land of the free," a bill had slid by the previous year by one vote, which resulted in the activation of a legislative study committee to research and recommend changes in Wisconsin's homeschool statute. So the Special Committee on Home Based Private Educational Programs was convened in 1991, comprised of eighteen appointed members: eight legislators, five public school officials, four homeschoolers, and one private school representative. From August to September the committee met.

The state superintendent of Wisconsin, Herbert Grover, was completely opposed to homeschooling—*and I mean completely opposed!* He seemed to be obsessed with clamping down on them. One thing standing in his way was the law, so he was hoping to convince the legislature to change it. After all, they would listen to him as the top education expert in the state.

Grover appeared before the eighteen-member committee and stated brazenly, "Many homeschoolers are child abusers. I have proof right here in my hands," as he held a folder and waved it before the committee. When asked by a committee member to see the folder, he indicated, "Because of privacy requirements, I can't let anybody see these homeschooling child abusers." Other of Grover's Department of Public Instruction (DPI) officials came, and all recommended that homeschoolers take standardized achievement tests, have a truant officer monitor attendance and curriculum records of homeschoolers, and other unacceptable requirements.

Ever since 1984 Wisconsin had had one of the best laws in the country, with the only requirement that homeschoolers file an annual notice of intent by October 15.

Wisconsin Attacks Fall on Deaf Ears

I organized a letter-writing campaign to the committee members, causing hundreds of letters to swamp the committee. I also supplied Steve Rovics, Dave DeYoung, and other members of the committee with objective statistics that showed that homeschoolers were academically successful and reliably above average. Every time one of the department of education officials would spout off at one of the committee's hearings, Steve Rovics would quietly pass around the statistics and documentation to the other about the academic track record of homeschoolers; their acceptance to majority universities and their constitutional right to homeschool. This information particularly discredited the DPI representatives, who made numerous spurious claims that homeschoolers were failing academically and being rejected for admission into colleges. Their unsupported whining instantly fell on deaf ears!

The normal course of a legislative study committee in Wisconsin is to recommend legislation. Such legislation has a 65 percent chance of ultimate passage compared to the normal 20 percent chance of passage of a bill that doesn't originate in a legislative study committee.

To the memory of legislators that we knew, there had been no study committee that didn't send out a proposed piece of legislation, so we were certainly working uphill.

The newly formed Wisconsin Christian Home Educators Association, led by Jan Gnacinski, followed up our alert for letters by sending cards to hundreds of homeschoolers and urging them to write the committee members too. I had an opportunity to speak in Wisconsin at the same time to a Gregg Harris

Home School Workshop and again urged families to contact the committee.

I submitted written testimony to the committee, stating:

> Therefore, since the present homeschool law is functioning fine, and parents continue to successfully homeschool their children, the proper finding of this Committee would be to conclude that there is no need to change the homeschool law.
>
> Let this Committee uphold Wisconsin's homeschool law, which firmly protects and upholds the fundamental right of parents to direct the education and upbringing of their children, which is guaranteed by the First and Fourteenth Amendments.

Study Committee Votes for No Changes to the Law

I talked personally to Chairman Volk toward the end of the committee's hearings. The chairman stated, "I and many of the members of the committee, have received hundreds of letters, and it seems that the public consensus is that they do not want the law to be changed." When homeschoolers let their voices be heard, they are recognized as a "public consensus."

He said he was sure the letters had influenced many of the committee members. When questioned, he also admitted there is no "real documentation of abuse" among homeschoolers. And he expressed discouragement to me that the committee had "come up with nothing."

Finally, at the conclusion of the study committee on January 4, 1991, Chairman John Volk sent a letter to all committee members with this statement, "I am proposing that the committee terminate its work by adjourning permanently and making no recommendations."

Then the miracle happened on January 14, 1992. The entire committee voted, and to everyone's surprise they *voted unanimously* to accept the chairman's proposal and *make no recommendations for the law to be changed.*

God worked in a mighty way with this committee through the prayers, letters, and efforts of hundreds of Wisconsin homeschool families. This united effort at the grassroots level, as homeschoolers worked with the committee to stop legislation before it even started, avoided a much more difficult and dangerous battle later in the legislature.

Maine Homeschoolers Stop Home Visit Bill

In Maine, LD 888 was introduced, which required homeschoolers to submit to monthly home visits by state officials. This bill was on a fast track to be rammed through the legislature. The homeschoolers, however, were not going to take this "sitting down." There is no way they would allow public school officials into their home every month to check up on them and decide if they could continue. This was a case of "Big Brother" at its worst.

On March 26, 1981, a hearing was held before the Maine Joint Committee on Education. "Home Schoolers of Maine (HOME)," led by Ed and Cathy Green, and HSLDA had sent mailings to homeschoolers throughout the state, urging them to write letters opposing the bill and to attend the hearing.

When I arrived at the hearing after flying in from Virginia, I found the capitol covered with homeschoolers—homeschoolers everywhere. Actually, there were so many homeschoolers that the security officials moved the scheduled hearing room to a *room that was four times as large!* In my testimony I documented how home visits violate the parents' right of privacy and the right to be free from unreasonable searches and seizures and their due process rights.

All the while, the committee members sat there and stared at the crowd in the packed hearing room. The legislators had never seen anything like this before!

Few questions were asked of the numerous homeschoolers who testified with me. The committee could see the "writing on the wall."

At the conclusion of the hearing, the vote was taken, and they voted unanimously to defeat the bill. God is good.

South Carolina Homeschoolers Rally

On February 4, 1987, South Carolina homeschoolers packed out the hearing room in the state capitol as the legislature debated whether or not the department of education's onerous regulations to require homeschoolers to have a bachelor's degree would pass muster.

Zan Tyler, leading the South Carolina homeschoolers, had successfully drawn hundreds of families to attend the rally. I testified that day and provided evidence of the lack of any support for the theory that a teacher with a college degree causes students to perform any better. The legislature was impressed with the huge crowd and amazingly ended up rejecting the requirements.

However, homeschoolers were still facing arbitrary "approval" as required by law. More and more families were ending up in court in the late 1980s and early 1990s. I was scrambling to help family after family with legal contacts. Dee Black and our office were juggling many cases at once. I had filed several appeals administratively with the department of education—all to no avail. The department was a bit biased.

Mike Farris filed legislation to challenge the Education Entrance Examination (EEE), which is a test developed by the state of South Carolina to screen professional teachers. By December 9, 1991, the South Carolina Supreme Court had rendered its ruling on the EEE case that Michael Farris had filed. The Supreme Court reversed the lower court's decision and stated that the EEE had not been properly validated for use with homeschooling parents. This was a wonderful victory for the South Carolina homeschoolers.

Nonetheless, the law still had many flaws, and families were eager to get out from under the troublesome homeschool law.

In the meantime, Zan Tyler had gotten a piece of legislation introduced that would recognize her newly established organization, the South Carolina Association of Independent Home Schools (SCAIHS). This would allow homeschoolers to get help under the onerous compulsory attendance law and be protected by the independent homeschool umbrella that she had established.

Many phone calls, much lobbying and testifying was done, and God miraculously had the bill pass against great objection. Zan Tyler recounts God's hand,

> During this process, the one event that stands above all others in our memories is the March 18 meeting of the Senate Education Committee. We had received word from very reliable inside sources that there was no way we could pass our bill through our committee in the version we were supporting. That weekend we sent out a letter to our members and support group leaders, calling for fasting and prayer on March 17. We knew how God had delivered the Jews in the days of Esther and believed that God honored the fastings and prayers of the Jews and Susa with deliverance. Although our physical lives weren't at stake, we firmly believed that the spiritual and emotional lives of our children were. We saw God's deliverance during that Senate Education Committee meeting and I believe it is the result of answered prayer.

You might think that legislative battles have ended since those early days. But I have seen over and over again that the forces that want to "do homeschooling in" are never at rest. As long as the public schools have authority over homeschools and there are compulsory attendance laws in all fifty states, there are going to be attempts in the legislature to "turn back the clock."

"Against My Normal Judgment"

This last story simply illustrates that not much has changed. The prejudices still remain. The enemies still have homeschoolers in their sights.

Homeschoolers, therefore, need to stay vigilant by remaining members of HSLDA and their statewide homeschool association. The good news is that by 2001 homeschoolers proved they are still organized and ready to take action to protect their liberties at a moment's notice.

In 2001, fourteen years after Minnesota's original homeschool law was enacted, the educational elite forces that wanted to restrict homeschoolers made their first attempt to change the law. Senate File 866 made numerous technical changes to Minnesota's education code, including two particular onerous requirements for homeschoolers.

The Minnesota Association of Christian Home Educators mobilized their membership along with HSLDA to oppose this bill. The key "make it or break it" committee hearing was held March 21 in the Senate Education Committee.

Everyone was a bit nervous that homeschoolers might be getting "apathetic" and not as concerned like they were in the old days to turn out for a hearing. Any doubts we had were completely dispersed when we arrived at the capitol of Minnesota.

As I walked through the halls of the capitol, I met homeschoolers congregated around every corner and down every hall. We held a short rally. It looked like six hundred to eight hundred homeschoolers were in attendance.

When the hearing convened, only about a third of the homeschoolers could fit in the hearing room; but as the room was set up, they surrounded the legislators. They were sitting in the front, back, and all sides of the committee members who were sitting in a semicircle at the table.

The testimony began with the proponents of the restrictive homeschool legislation, making statements like, "Homeschoolers need accountability. Right now we don't know what they are doing."

My response when I testified was simply, "Homeschoolers have proved themselves time and time again in fifteen years or more of studies. Homeschoolers on the average score above average in standardized achievement tests. And besides, there was no evidence of anything broken that needed to be fixed."

Another public school teacher stood up and explained, "We just want to help these homeschool families. If we can receive their test scores each year, we can render them assistance." Some of the homeschoolers who testified after said plain and clear, "We don't want your help, and we don't need your help."

Meanwhile, every time I testified and made a good point, the people in the hearing room were required to be completely silent. But the other two-thirds of the families were outside in the halls at two or three different levels of the rotunda, looking on video screens, watching the proceedings. Every time I made a good point, there were cheers and claps, whoops and hollers, out in the hallways and in the rotunda, echoing throughout the chambers.

The senators could hear through the closed doors these people clamoring for the bill to be defeated. As they heard the cheers, they realized the huge number of families against this bill.

Finally, the committee members had a discussion about the bill before their vote. The most vocal opponent made a startling comment, "I am usually on the side of child's rights. You all know me, and that's where I vote. However, this time, I'm going to go against my normal judgment and vote in favor of the parents. I'm hearing from this testimony that the homeschoolers are doing just fine and don't want the state's help."

When she gave that little speech, it was like a wave went over the rest of the majority of the liberals on the committee, and the bill was voted down.

Praise God once again for working on behalf of His people. I believe God will continue to bless the efforts of homeschoolers in the legislatures of this land, even though we are a small minority. I believe this to be true because the homeschool movement is making Christ the center and foundation. The lesson is clear: As soon as Jesus is moved into second place, we will begin losing these legislative battles.

✸ 11

The Battle for Religious Freedom

For I am not ashamed of the gospel,
for it is the power of God for salvation.

ROMANS 1:16

Chris and Kim Landrum were finally brought before the Henrico County School Board to defend their faith on July 23, 1992. We had been wrangling with the board attorney Phyllis Errico all school year and fending off the school district's threats. They had sent a letter and various affidavits describing their sincerely held religious convictions to the board declaring a statutory religious exemption which made their homeschool exempt from Virginia's compulsory attendance law.

As I objected to irrelevant and improper questions, Chris Landrum patiently explained his and his wife's convictions—which were shared by many Christian homeschoolers. He told the board members, "I believe God called us to be the primary instructors of our children."

He said firmly, "It would be sin to send our children to public school. God wants us to apply biblical principles to every subject, and we cannot do that in the public schools. The Holy Spirit convicted us through Ephesians 6:4 and Deuteronomy 6."

The chairman interrogated the father unmercifully. He tried to cajole him and make fun of his religious convictions.

The father adamantly stated, "I believe in the Bible, and I believe the Bible tells me that I have to teach my own children at home."

The superintendent hotly said, "The Bible was written down by men, so it is not God's Word!"

In fulfillment of the Scripture that the Holy Spirit will give us the words to say before the authorities, Chris Landrum simply turned toward the school board chairman and said, "Do you see this stenographer here? She is writing down everything that I say, word for word. That is how the inspiration of the Word of God works. The men who wrote the Bible wrote down word for word everything that God said. The Bible *is the Word of God!*"

This dumbfounded the chairman of the board, and by the end of the night, the once hostile school board narrowly approved the Landrums' religious exemption.

Homeschool Movement: A Christian Revival

Most homeschooling parents in America embarked on this dangerous course at loggerheads with the mighty state because of strongly held religious convictions. As you have seen in previous chapters, the evidence is overwhelming that the majority of the homeschool movement felt they were called by God and motivated by the Holy Spirit to teach their children a biblical form of education.

Early surveys by Dr. Brian Ray and others show that as many as 85 percent of the homeschoolers declared that they were homeschooling because of religious convictions. Therefore, it was natural for us at HSLDA to use the First Amendment as our primary constitutional defense for homeschoolers in court and in negotiations with the school districts.

When I was in law school at the O. W. Coburn Law School in Tulsa, Oklahoma, affiliated with Oral Roberts University, I felt the clear call of God to become a lawyer so that I could fight for the free exercise of religion of Christians in our country. While I was in law school, I was awarded with the privilege of being on the law review for the law school. I wrote an extensive article and analysis of how the free exercise of religion intersects with the right of parents to educate. I exhaustively analyzed and summarized the U.S. Supreme Court precedent where the First Amendment's Free Exercise of Religion clause was applied to various education cases involving compulsory attendance.

Little did I know how valuable that research would be to me immediately at HSLDA. In fact, the contents of my law review article became the "centerpiece" of my briefs as I defended families in court and of my letters to the authorities to fend off prosecution.

"The mind of man plans his way, But the LORD directs his steps" (Prov. 16:9).

Supreme Court Test for Protecting Religious Freedom

The U.S. Supreme Court has made it clear through a series of religious freedom cases that a particular test has to be applied whenever religious convictions come into conflict with a state's regulation. That test is called the "compelling interest test" or "strict scrutiny standard." The compelling interest test embodies four burdens of proof.

To win a religious exemption from a restrictive state regulation, a family must prove the first two burdens. To override a family's religious convictions, the state must carry the last two burdens of proof.

First, the family or individual has to prove that they have religious beliefs that motivate their particular conduct that is in conflict with the state's law. Over time the court has stated that as long as it is not simply philosophical but relates to some higher power, it is religious, and the courts will not question the truth of that religion.

Second, the individual or family has to prove that their religious beliefs are sincere. In other words, show that they "walk their talk" and are consistent with the application of their religious convictions.

Third, the burden shifts to the state, and the state has to prove with evidence that the regulation is essential to fulfill a compelling interest (i.e., that children be educated). Teacher certification, for instance, is not essential for children to be educated. In earlier chapters we discussed many studies and evidences and anecdotal stories that demonstrate that teacher certification is not necessary for children to be educated.

Fourth, the state has to prove with evidence that its regulation is the "least restrictive means" of fulfilling its interest that children be educated. In the case of teacher certification again, or some other restrictive requirement, we often point to other states with less restrictive requirements to show that children can be well educated without restrictive government regulations such as certification.

It sounds simple, doesn't it? The test is straightforward, and any judge could easily rule in favor of homeschoolers when they require the state to carry these burdens.

Courts Pay Lip Service to the Test

My bubble was burst soon after I began working in this area. I had a hopeful, idealistic view that the First Amendment would be upheld in these homeschool cases.

Of course, I soon settled into my realistic view when I saw from all of the cases that I had researched already that the courts do not properly apply the compelling interest test. In fact, time and time again, the courts would ignore the requirement that the state prove its regulation was "essential." When it came to the "least restrictive means" part of the test, the courts would often merely pay lip service. In my book *The Right to Home School*, I extensively review the free exercise cases in education, demonstrating the misapplication of the compelling interest test repeatedly.

This was the atmosphere that Home School Legal Defense was entering into in defending the religious liberty of homeschoolers. The precedent was stacked up against us in state after state. Christian schools had already lost many of their cases, and also many of the initial homeschool cases had been lost.

The Meline Case: A Short-Lived Victory

One of the first cases we won in the area of religious freedom was in North Dakota. Jonathan and Diane Meline were charged with truancy in North Dakota because they refused to enroll their children in the public or private school and homeschooled without a certified teacher. Michael Farris and Michael Smith prepared and filed a trial brief explaining the principles of the First Amendment and the compelling interest test. The Melines were subsequently brought to trial in Dickey County, North Dakota, and were represented by our local HSLDA attorney, Greg Lange, of Hazen.

Incredibly, on September 3, 1987, Judge Neuharth dismissed the complaint against the Melines, stating that the family proved "the depth, quality, and sincerity of their religious beliefs, proved the literacy of Teddy [their son], and proved nothing harmful occurred in the public safety, health, or welfare." He further found, "teacher certification not to be the least restrictive means in achieving the state's education goal when applied to the Melines' Constitutional rights."

He stated, "It remains the legislative task and prerogative to fashion a remedy that does not unreasonably interfere with the liberty of parents in the education of their children, in the expression of Constitutional rights." He also mentioned, "Teacher certification does not correlate well to teaching ability. The Melines have proved that by Teddy's being educated with them, he is becoming a viable citizen."

This was good news. A judge had correctly analyzed and ruled according to the First Amendment, in favor of homeschooling.

HSLDA actually convinced another board to grant a religious exemption for the Evans family. They had ruled this because the child had never been in public school. The same board ruled against the VanInwagns because they had had a child in public school, and the child was "not so inculcated with Christian doctrine that their mind was unredeemable through public instruction"! So the Hazen School Board was even applying a patchwork quilt in the area of religious exemption.

Nonetheless, the victory was won. Unfortunately, the state appealed to the State Supreme Court, and they reversed the ruling, stating on a technicality that the judge had not officially dismissed the convictions.

Family Wins Religious Exemption in Colorado

In Lake City, the Hinsdale County School District brought charges against the Main family for violating the compulsory attendance law because they refused to seek approval for their homeschool as required by Colorado law. In those days families had to be approved by the school board—or else.

Almost always the school board, who was hardly neutral, denied the family's right. When the family appealed to the Department of Education, which was also prejudiced, the Department affirmed the denial.

Seeking approval of the school board was a senseless act.

Besides, the Mains, like most homeschool families, believed that God had called them to homeschool, and they did not need the approval of the school district.

I contacted a young attorney named Bruce Lorenzen, of Gunnison, and we hired him to defend the family.

From my office in Virginia, I provided him with the brief and worked closely with him on the legal arguments.

Meanwhile, the Mains, their church, and friends were all praying. "The effective prayer of a righteous man can accomplish much" (James 5:16).

God heard and God delivered the Main family on May 6, 1987.

The District Court of Gunnison County ruled in favor of the Mains. The court found that the parents had "sincerely held religious convictions."

The court recognized, "Like the Amish, the Mains' religion pervades and virtually determines their entire way of life." The court made it clear that the Mains' religious convictions require them to teach their children at home and that they could not be questioned because "in our society, public officials may not prescribe what is and is not orthodox."

The judge rejected what other courts unfortunately fall for, which is the prosecution's claim that the Mains had to be part of a "church-oriented community with century-old tradition like the fabled Amish of Pennsylvania" in order to have their religious freedom protected by the First Amendment.

The court even properly applied the compelling interest test and said that the state had to "find the least intrusive means available to accomplish its interest." The court made accurate factual findings that "the Mains are complying with the purpose of the attendance law, even if they have not obtained approval of the home-study program." The family had proved by standardized test scores that their daughter was being educated far above average.

God had given us a victory in Colorado in a small, seemingly insignificant county, but as always, His plans were bigger. The *Main* case helped me persuade many other counties to hold back their disapproval of other homeschoolers and to voluntarily grant religious exemptions or postpone their decisions while our homeschool legislation or court cases were pending.

"Enroll" versus "Attend"

One of the pending cases was *Widefield School District v. Bohl*, where my law school buddy, Bill Moritz, of Woodland Park, had won a case for a homeschooler on technical grounds that the family was operating under the private school law in Colorado. The rationale was that the family had "enrolled" their children in an "independent school" but was teaching their own children at home. The compulsory attendance statute in Colorado only requires "enrollment" in an independent school, not actual "attendance." That is what the Bohl children were doing.

There was no definition of an "independent school" in the Colorado statutes. They only had to teach reading, writing, math, history, civics, literature, science, and our Constitution. No particular size, place, testing, teachers, or approval by the public school authorities.

Sounds like a homeschool could fit into this nicely with a little creativity.

The independent school the Bohls children were enrolled in was a school on paper with no building and comprised of other homeschool families teaching their children at home. One parent was the administrator who kept the records.

The public school district was not happy.

They appealed the case. The school district did not want their unbridled discretionary power over homeschoolers to slip away because of some silly technicality.

I filed an amicus brief (friend of the court brief) on behalf of the Bohls to support their position.

The Court of Appeals of Colorado subsequently ruled in the Bohls' favor and thereby opened up a tremendous option for homeschoolers in Colorado, enabling them to escape the onerous and useless approval process in their school districts.

The Court reasoned, "Since the district has not challenged the adequacy of the education provided by the academy, the matter of the sufficiency of the children's attendance is between the Bohls and the independent school in which they are enrolled."

What does God say in the Scripture? He "will provide the way of escape" for His people. That is what He did in Colorado, provided the way of escape while the legislation could be worked on and eventually passed, to provide freedom for all.

Pennsylvania Federal Court Recognizes Religious Beliefs

In chapter 7 I told many stories of states that required homeschoolers to be "approved" by the school district. This arbitrary discretion usually resulted in the denial of the family's constitutional rights.

We filed a federal civil rights suit in Pennsylvania, called the *Jeffery* case, on behalf of several Christian homeschool families threatened with prosecution. The defendant school district superintendents entered a motion in February 1987, asking the court to appoint "guardians" for the children of our member families in the case on the grounds that the children may not want to be homeschooled or held different religious beliefs than their parents.

The superintendent's attorney stated in his motion, "A conflict inherent between the parents and the children exists in this case because the religious beliefs of the parents may not be what is best for the children in terms of the children's rights to an education."

All of us at the HSLDA felt this was a low blow. This of course could not be further from the truth. The public school districts were drawing straws and just trying to harass the families.

By God's grace, Judge Kosik didn't buy their argument. In fact, in his final ruling, he stated, "The threat to sensitive religious freedoms mandate judicial intrusion in the form of declaring the particular provision in the law as applied to home-schools, unconstitutional for vagueness." He stated further, "When First Amendment rights are affected by the enforcement of the statute, the state law will be held to a higher standard of specificity than might be the case if purely economic regulation was at issue."

The court placed an injunction on the defendant school districts from prosecuting the homeschoolers. It was a significant victory for the protection of religious freedom!

The bottom line was that when you have religious freedom at stake, the state's law needs to be specific. In Pennsylvania, as I mentioned before in chapter 7, the law simply required home-schoolers to have "satisfactory" instruction and have a "qualified" person teaching. There were no definitions. Those terms were too vague, and school districts were violating families' rights left and right by denying them the right to homeschool.

More Than One Way to Win the Battle

Even though not every court case was won on the issue of the Free Exercise of Religion, as it should have been, God's will still prevailed.

If a case was not won in court, God always provided "the way of escape."

If we could not win a case for the homeschoolers on religious freedom grounds, we would try to win the case on other technical or procedural grounds, and often we did win home-school cases on technical grounds.

If we couldn't win a decision in court on other technical grounds, we would try to get introduced and pass a favorable homeschool bill in the legislature that expanded parental freedoms.

If we could not win in the legislature, we would just practice "noncompliance" and follow God's call and obey the higher law. We would try to pass the bill again the next year in the legislature—and the next year if necessary.

We learned to be "wise as serpents and harmless as doves" (Matt. 10:16 KJV).

If God commands you to homeschool, you have no other choice than to homeschool—no matter what the public school superintendent says. We would not give up or give in.

Mike Smith and I and others in our office can testify how we have evoked the First Amendment's Free Exercise of Religion clause as we have written and argued with school districts all across this country on behalf of homeschoolers during the first ten years. At that time we were faced with teacher certification laws, home visits, and arbitrary and discretionary approval by local school districts, and we have little to argue except the First Amendment. We wrote letter after letter to school districts, arguing that the family could not be certified or have their curriculum approved, or allow a truant officer or school official to come into their home because of their sincerely held religious beliefs that were protected by the First Amendment.

And it worked!

School district after school district backed off, or simply looked the other way, when faced with the family's right to exercise freely their religious beliefs and the string of court citations that we would include in our "mini-brief" letters that we sent to school officials. We literally sent thousands of these letters out, and God used them to protect most of the families.

Additionally, the Free Exercise Clause has been effective in influencing legislatures over and over again. I presented First Amendment arguments in my testimony before legislative committees who many times have either killed bad bills that would have limited homeschooling freedoms or passed good bills that would protect homeschool freedoms.

So I learned quickly that the victory was not always in the courtroom. In fact, it usually wasn't in the courtroom. I learned, if at all possible, to avoid the courtroom because it is completely unpredictable. You can be as right as right can be on the constitutional protections of the family, but a court can and will still rule against you.

The better way has always been to go school district by school district, educating the educators and not taking no for an answer. And, of course, going to the legislature, where the people's voice can be heard loud and clear to change the law and protect homeschooling.

State Statutes Protecting Religious Freedom

Currently eight states have some type of religious exemption from various aspects of compulsory attendance laws. Alabama, Alaska, Pennsylvania, Tennessee, and Maryland allow for situations where homeschoolers can enroll under the auspices of a church or Christian school.

In Nebraska, homeschools are considered private, nondenominational, or parochial schools and can be exempt from all approval and accreditation requirements. This statutory right recognizing religious freedom for private and homeschools did not come easily. In fact, it was one of the toughest battlegrounds in the country.

Pastor Sileven of Faith Baptist Church operated a Christian school that was neither accredited nor using certified teachers as required by law. The local superintendent did all that he could to shut it down and took the school to court. Mike Farris was involved in parts of that case to defend seven fathers who sent their children to the Christian school and were subsequently jailed for seven months.

He also filed a suit against the state for dragging out sixty-six pastors who were inside the church to pray for the situation when the sheriff came to padlock the church and school's doors. Many cases had already come down from the Nebraska Supreme Court condemning homeschooling and Christian schools. The legal atmosphere was near impossible for any homeschools to function.

The major turning point was when Pastor Sileven had the removal of the pastors and the padlocking of the church video-taped, and that videotape went around the country, appearing on various programs and TV shows. In response, Governor Kerry instituted a commission to look into the Christian school problem. The commission came back with a recommendation that these Christian educators should just be exempted. It was not long until the legislature passed the bill that is still in effect. It allows homeschools and Christian schools to be exempt from the "requirements for approval and accreditation if they violate sincerely held religious beliefs of the parents or guardians."

Nebraska was truly another "Soviet Union" for several years, but now it is the land of the free.

Vermont has a limited religious exemption from certain aspects of the homeschool law. Virginia has one of the best statutory religious exemptions in the country, but it was an intense battle with dozens of court cases and hundreds of school board hearings to finally convince the school boards to apply the law properly.

Virginia: The Best Religious Exemption in the Country

You have heard the expression "No pain; no gain." That succinctly describes the battle for religious freedom in Virginia!

When I began working at HSLDA in 1985, few home-schoolers were able to obtain religious exemptions from the compulsory attendance law from their local school board. The law states, "A school board shall excuse from attendance at school ... any pupil who, together with his parents, by reason of bona fide religious training or belief is conscientiously opposed to attendance at school." No other requirements apply.

I was able to show school boards that the statute exempted children from school, and the only thing parents had to prove was that they had sincere religious beliefs that made them opposed to sending their children to public school. I figured it was fairly easy to prove this in light of the solid convictions that families had and the clear call of the Holy Spirit that they needed to homeschool without government oversight. In those days many families were called to a school board hearing after they had sent in information describing their religious beliefs.

Nonetheless, time and time again I found out that it was not so easy. I would go against local school boards who would insist that the religious exemption was only for the Amish—not for any other Christians.

The school boards attempted to interrogate those families and their children. Sometimes it was awful.

Interrogation of a Seven-Year-Old

One of my first school board hearings in 1987 was with the Wilkerson family in Spotsylvania County. We came early to the meeting, but the school board made us wait until 10:00 p.m. before they heard our case. Then from 10:00 to midnight, the hostile board quizzed and interrogated the parents.

Fred Wilkerson, a blue-collar man, explained his religious beliefs simply, "We just believe God called us personally to teach our children."

When the board baited him with a question, "What is wrong with the public schools?" Fred told them in a straightforward manner.

This only got the board members upset as they disagreed with his opinion. They argued with him for a half hour or so about the conditions of the schools. I learned the hard way that you cannot win if you criticize the public schools with a school board. I counseled families from then on to stick to the call of God and His command to teach the Bible, which the schools can't do.

Then one of the board members said, "The statute mentions the 'pupil.' Let us see if your son has a religious exemption."

I shook my head "no" to the father but then told the board it was up to the father.

Fred decided to let his seven-year-old child answer a few questions. This was a big mistake. When I saw what enfolded, I decided then and there I would never allow another child to be questioned by the school authorities again.

The seven-year-old child was not prepared for the kind of questions that were asked. A school board member asked him why he did not want to go to public school, and he said, "Because I get beat up a lot at school by black children." The black members of the board immediately took issue with that and tried to contradict what was really happening to this child.

It was too late; the grilling became more intense as the father stammered to stop it.

Tensions grew—I knew all was lost. At the end of the hearing at midnight, the board denied the family's right to have a religious exemption.

Yet after a few weeks of fear, God delivered this faithful family. By God's grace I was able to get the family enrolled in a satellite program with a private school to be a legal covering for their homeschool and thus avoid a criminal truancy action.

More Families Face the Wrath of the State

Although homeschool religious exemptions were still not commonly recognized in Virginia, more and more families in Virginia were convicted by God not to comply with the Virginia homeschool law that required an annual test or evaluation.

In 1988 religious exemptions started moving at lightning speed. Families were applying for religious exemptions all over the state. Religious exemptions in Virginia were new to us as far as knowing all the arguments and procedures that would work best. Needless to say, I discovered that there was a certain amount of trial and error that we needed to do.

In Bedford County, the Shifletts applied for a religious exemption. Ron, the dad, also served on the board of the Home Education Association of Virginia.

The main reason they were denied a religious exemption by the school board was because "it would set a very dangerous precedent." This was ridiculous, yet the school board had the power of the state behind them.

The family was quickly charged with criminal truancy, and a court date was set. I prepared a brief, and Mike Farris and I traveled down to southern Virginia. I had subpoenaed all the members of the school board, which did not make them too happy.

Needless to say, God gave us a quick resolution. When the prosecutor found out that Mrs. Shiflett had a teaching certificate, all charges were dropped. Not exactly the victory we wanted, but the family was free to educate their children without government oversight.

Meanwhile, families in Fairfax County, who were applying for religious exemption, received a letter stating that they had to go under the homeschool law. We ignored the letter and still had the families operate under the religious exemption—with or without recognition.

More of His Mysterious Ways

All these years God was enabling family after family to get religious exemptions in spite of a hostile climate.

One particularly unusual move by the Holy Spirit was seen in my being invited in 1989 to a meeting of school board attorneys across the state. The attorney, Patrick Lacy, who was the president of the Virginia School Board Attorneys Association, laughed as he called me on the phone to invite me to be the "token Christian." He wanted me to give my interpretation of the religious exemption law. Then he would have the opportunity to annihilate my position with his cohorts who believed the statute was only for the Amish—everyone else should be denied. Mr. Lacy represented several school boards and was the opposing counsel in some of my cases.

When I arrived, there were approximately sixty school board lawyers from around the state—all suspicious of me.

I made a presentation and passed out a legal memorandum, describing the proper way to handle religious exemption claimants. After speaking for half an hour, I concluded that school boards had to grant religious exemptions unless they had evidence to prove that the families were not sincere or were fraudulent.

When it was Mr. Lacy's turn to get up to rebut my position like he was planning on doing, I noticed that *he was missing*. Upon inquiring of the secretary, I learned that during my speech, Mr. Lacy had a kidney stone attack! He subsequently was rushed to the hospital. No opportunity for an opposing presentation that day!

The school board lawyers afterwards came up to me, shook my hand, and said, "Now we know how to apply religious exemptions. Thank you for your memo."

God sure works in mysterious ways!

In fact, I was able to use the legal memorandum I passed out that day to send to hundreds of school board members.

It carried an official title that made it look more persuasive: "Presented before the Virginia Association of School Board Lawyers, May 1989."

I used it as I argued in front of scores of school boards at hearings throughout Virginia over several years, educating the school boards.

God superintended over it all—even the smallest details.

Snatching Victory from Defeat

The worst county in which to homeschool was Prince William County. In 1989 Tracy and Kathy Johnson were homeschooling their two oldest children and were convicted by the Lord that they had to operate under the religious exemption. They were convinced that they couldn't send their children to public schools because it would be a sin to do so. They submitted a letter to the Prince William County School Board and were subsequently summoned to a hearing. I talked with the school district attorney and explained that the only issue to be discussed was whether the family's religious beliefs were bona fide. He guaranteed to me that he would recommend that the school board grant them a religious exemption and that I did not need to attend.

Much to my shock the school board grilled the Johnsons for an hour, attacking their religious beliefs and arguing with their beliefs concerning the public schools being wrong for their family. They also wanted to approve their curriculum. The school board ended up denying their religious exemption, based on the counsel of Joe Dyer, the attorney for the school board who countered the school attorney Bob Bendal.

Within thirty days I appealed the school board decision to the Prince William Circuit Court. In the meantime, the school board attorney Joe Dyer filed a demur to try to dismiss the case since I did not name the children in the appeal—only the parents. He stated that the children were indispensable parties.

This was a smokescreen. We went to the Prince William County Court, and I was able to get the demur dismissed, thus saving the appeal.

When we went before the judge at the Prince William County Courthouse, he gave us approximately three hours to argue the case. No further evidence was allowed to be produced at the hearing. We had only the barely discernable record that was recorded by a tape recorder at the school board hearing.

Attorney Dyer cast many aspersions upon the family's beliefs. I had also brought another case, the Morgans, to the Prince William County Court since the Prince William County School Board also denied them the religious exemption. Both of the cases were combined together. Neither the Johnsons nor the Morgans were allowed to testify before the judge although they sat in the courtroom.

Since there were no witnesses, Joe Dyer could say anything he wanted to—and he did—in order to convince the judge to uphold the school board's decision. After a long day the judge finally ruled in favor of the school board, upholding the denial of religious exemptions. Over the next year we appealed to the court of appeals, and they kicked it up to the Virginia Supreme Court. I went to Richmond to argue before a panel of supreme court justices to convince them to take the case—and they did. This was a miracle because the court only decides to take a fraction of the cases that come to them.

Finally, I argued the case before the Virginia Supreme Court. I explained that Prince William County was wrong to state that the religious exemption was only for the Amish, and that the family had to prove opposition not only to the public schools but also to the homeschool statute. The justices were completely fascinated with the case and asked many questions of both sides.

On April 19, 1991, the Virginia Supreme Court ended up voting *unanimously* on the legal issues, striking a blow to all of the misapplications of the law by Prince William County. The *Johnson* case has paved the way for every other religious exemption in the state ever since. God used this case to drastically change the legal climate opening wide the religious exemption option to all people of faith.

The *Johnson* case helped everyone but the Johnsons! The court separately voted four to three against the Johnson's personal religious beliefs as expressed at the school board hearing, questioning their sincerity.

I was elated and devastated at the same time. I have learned this is often how God works. He wants all the glory to go to Him.

I did not win the case for my client. My good friends, Tracy and Kathy, with whom I went to church, were in jeopardy.

Yet God in His great wisdom and mercy used this defeat to win the right of religious freedom for everyone else in Virginia.

The *Johnson* case, ever since, has greased the way for hundreds of families to get religious exemptions because the school boards no longer deal with issues such as curriculum, teacher qualifications, and whether or not the family is a member of a religious sect that forbids attendance at the public schools. Instead, families can apply for religious exemption in Virginia and simply prove that it would be a sin for them to send their children to public school. The school boards have no choice in the matter. They have to completely exempt these religious families from all compulsory attendance and testing.

Also from the Johnson experience, I learned always to make sure we hired a stenographer at the board hearings so that no one can misunderstand what transpires. Just having the stenographer there at the hearing helps to keep the questions much more limited. We also have families seeking a religious exemption submit letters from friends who vouch for their sincerity and a pastor who confirms their beliefs concerning education are religious.

Police Come to Arrest but Leave Wanting to Homeschool

By the way, we were not going to take no for an answer for the Johnsons; we simply reapplied for a religious exemption the very next year.

Meanwhile, the current school year still had another month to go. I tried to get Prince William County School District to hold off until summer, but they did not want to make a deal.

The school district wanted the Johnson children in school now—or else. They may have lost for the rest of the state, but they had won the battle to deny the Johnsons.

In a short time two women police officers came to the door at night to arrest the Johnsons and serve criminal truancy charges against them. They knocked, and when Kathy opened the door, she almost went into shock.

Thoughts ran through her mind, "What are we going to do? What will happen to our children? Help us, Lord!"

Tracy and Kathy were scared, but God gave them a peace that passes all understanding—just like He promises.

They calmly talked to the officers explaining their children were asleep. Then Kathy began telling how wonderful their education was doing. Tracy and Kathy shared their love and sacrifice for their children, told about their curriculum provided through a Christian correspondence course, CLASS, and shared the gospel.

The two police officers were transformed. They left without arresting the Johnsons, and the crisis was averted. One of the police women even asked Kathy, "What do I have to do to homeschool? Could you homeschool my child?"

God turned it around for the Johnsons. They finished homeschooling that year. Then we resubmitted their religious exemption to the school board—this time with three affidavits from pastors stating their beliefs were religious and seventeen letters of individuals vouching for their sincerity.

There was no further objection. The school board granted them their long sought religious exemption. We immediately had their criminal charges dropped. The Johnsons finally won the war. God delivered them.

The Last Battles Begin to Wane

Over a hundred families applied for religious exemption across the state in a two-year span. I was crisscrossing the state at school board after school board hearings, bringing a stenographer.

In Roanoke County, the Jones family and the Eales had two-hour "trials" where the school board attorney put on witnesses for the school board and tried to destroy the credibility of the families. In the case of the Joneses, the family was denied, and I filed in the circuit court and simultaneously asked for a rehearing. The school board granted the rehearing and decided a court fight was not worth it. They reversed themselves and granted a religious exemption at the rehearing.

With the Eales, the school board voted with us the first time—and against their own attorney.

Meanwhile, the Wades in Mecklenburg County were denied a religious exemption after a long hearing without my attendance. I appealed to the circuit court but made a motion again to have a rehearing, which the school board granted. Upon arguing the case, the school board finally reversed themselves.

Culpeper County had denied two families. Upon asking for a rehearing and bringing a stenographer and presenting all legal arguments, the religious exemptions were granted. In county after county, we submitted legal memorandums, affidavits from the family's pastor describing their religious beliefs as truly religious and providing many letters from individuals who know them, who would vouch for the sincerity of their religious beliefs. If those things were proven, school boards had to grant religious exemptions.

Meanwhile, in Arlington County, the Rolands were first turned into the Child Department, which sought to investigate an educational neglect allegation and question the children because they were not in school. I intervened in their behalf and was able to get the allegation dismissed in spite of the objections from the social worker. Within a few weeks, we met with a school official who made a favorable recommendation to the Board, and they were granted a religious exemption.

After that we began to see more and more families granted religious exemptions. That combined with making life miserable for school boards and going through our hearings with stenographers and making appeals to the circuit court and subpoenaing board members, the school boards began to start interpreting the law our way and granting religious exemptions across the state. Then armed with the 1991 decision from the *Johnson* case, we could now limit the inquiry to only the religious beliefs and not issues of qualifications and curriculum.

God be praised! He granted a victory through defeat, and now religious exemptions are commonplace throughout the state of Virginia. I enjoy a religious exemption with my seven kids, and every lawyer in our office who lives in Virginia has a religious exemption as well.

Religious Freedom Acts

The U.S. Supreme Court did violence to the Free Exercise Clause of the U.S. Constitution in the *Smith* decision out of Oregon in 1990. In that case the U.S. Supreme Court gave the lowest level of protection to religious liberty—one of the foundational freedoms for homeschooling. Using this ruling, a state could override an individual's right to freely exercise his religious beliefs merely by proving that the state's regulation was "reasonable." It's easy to show that teacher certification is "reasonable" since it is required by public school teachers. We would lose with this standard.

HSLDA helped form a coalition that drafted and promoted the Religious Freedom Restoration Act. Three years later Congress passed the RFRA into law, reversing the disastrous effects of the *Smith* decision and restoring religious freedom as a fundamental right.

Unfortunately, another case went up to the Supreme Court, and in the *City of Boerne v. Flores* case, the U.S. Supreme Court struck down the Religious Freedom Restoration Act as applied to the states. This left the states completely defenseless. As a result, we have worked hard to get individual states to pass religious freedom acts, restoring the proper compelling interest test.

After much involvement in a national coalition of religious groups, drafting religious freedom acts, lobbying legislators in various states, and flooding the legislatures with calls from homeschoolers, we contributed to the passage of religious freedom acts in thirteen states: Alabama, Arizona, Connecticut, Florida, Idaho, Illinois, Missouri, New Mexico, Oklahoma, Pennsylvania, Rhode Island, South Carolina, and Texas.

We are continuing to this day working to pass religious freedom acts so that the most important of all freedoms is protected in all fifty states. Needless to say, God is good.

$$\text{❋} 12$$

Treated Like Criminals: Homeschoolers Arrested

But we also exult in our tribulations, knowing that tribulation brings about perseverance; and perseverance, proven character; and proven character, hope; and hope does not disappoint, because the love of God has been poured out within our hearts through the Holy Spirit who was given to us.

ROMANS 5:3–5

In September 1991, Randy Maas was visited by two local school officials at his front door. He was planning on moving to the state of Georgia with his wife and two children within the next week.

Randy patiently explained that he and his wife were properly and legally homeschooling and informed the truant officers of his upcoming move. One truant officer hastily threatened, "You have to put your children in public school immediately or else!"

Randy, remembering his precious children, began to think frantically. "Who do these people think they are! They are my wife and my children—not theirs!" Randy, who was a big man, said something he probably should not have. He flatly declared, "Over my dead body."

The truant officer suddenly pulled out his gun and shot him. No, I am just kidding! We all know that truant officers do not carry guns.

Seriously, the truant officers did abruptly leave their house. Within a few hours they arrived back at the Maas property accompanied by a police officer. He promptly arrested Randy and took him to jail in handcuffs.

We received a call and were able to help Mr. Maas be released the following day, after posting $300 bond.

"We Don't Do That Down Here!"

I scoured the compulsory attendance law and found a statute in the Alabama Code that requires that anyone suspected of truancy must receive "three days written notice" before they can be prosecuted criminally for truancy. When I contacted the prosecutor and explained the law to him, he just laughed and said, "We don't do that down here."

We secured Jim Hess of Huntsville, Alabama, to represent the Maas family. At court, we argued the statute had been violated that required three days written notice. This due process requirement was state law.

Nonetheless, the judge arbitrarily ruled in favor of the school district ignoring the due process statute acting like he did not need to follow this particular statute in his county.

This was similar to the many situations that I ran into before with "small town justice." Sometimes judges had their own version of the law. It did not matter how right we were—they would enforce the law their own way.

Guilty!

The judge found Randy Maas guilty and fined him $400. He also was sentenced to sixty days in jail. Since the family had moved to Georgia, however, the judge suspended the sentence on the condition that the Maas place their children in public school, should they ever resume residence in Alabama.

I appealed the decision to the Alabama Court of Criminal Appeals. I argued that Mr. Maas had a due process right guaranteed by the Alabama code, but it had been violated. On May 15, 1992, the court of appeals slapped the hand of the local judge and reversed the conviction of Randy Maas. The court held that the three-day written notice was an "essential element" of the state's case, and the court had erred by refusing to grant a dismissal.

Mr. Maas was vindicated by the decision, and his record was cleared. His family was free to relocate in Alabama. We all praised God for intervening, restoring this family, and bringing justice.

Unintended Consequences?

We were just trying to clear Randy Maas. God intended a much bigger result. After this ruling, we never had another family charged with criminal truancy in Alabama. Up until this time, we had homeschool families regularly taken to court.

We now had three-days written notice before any family could be charged. This gave us three days either to persuade the school district that the family was legal under the church school exemption or at least to threaten a civil rights suit against the school district if they proceeded with a criminal charge. After that, we were able to stop the "lightning speed" tactics that school districts had previously used in order to intimidate families by bringing charges against them immediately before we could even talk to the school district.

Handcuffed for Homeschooling

A homeschool family, the Peblers, were happily homeschooling when they started receiving letters from the intermediate school district superintendent, and the local principal, telling them that their homeschool was illegal, and they would "face fines and/or imprisonment."

What would you do? Imagine the fears that ran through the mind of Laurel Pebler. I immediately wrote a letter explaining to the school district that they were legal; and if they had any trouble with the family, they needed to follow the state code which required an administrative hearing to be held by the department of education for any "private school" they believed was not in compliance. We had argued consistently to hundreds of school officials and prosecutors that homeschools are private schools in Michigan.

Of course, the other section of the law required that private schools use certified teachers. That was a huge obstacle, but as you will see below and in chapter 6, God provided a way of escape for His people—just as He promised.

Our "Don't Ask, Don't Tell" Certified Teacher Policy

The Peblers' private school in the home did not use a certified teacher. But we were not going to divulge that information until we had a proper administrative hearing by the Department of Education; then we could argue the constitutional issues against teacher certification.

Up until this point, the Michigan Department of Education never held a hearing for any private school (which homeschools were recognized as by case precedent). Local school districts would just bring criminal charges and skip that process.

After weeks of arguing with the school district, the school district added insult to injury by simply turning the family over to the Department of Social Services to investigate for educational neglect. They figured there were two ways to skin this cat.

Furthermore, the mother, who was a single parent, received at least a half a dozen visits from various combinations of police officers, school officials, and social workers. I spent more time talking to the social workers and explaining that they had no jurisdiction to even investigate, it was solely the school district's responsibility.

By God's grace, the mother, Laurel Pebler, was strengthened to withstand this continual harassment that any normal person would have collapsed under.

Mug Shots and Fingerprints

Saint Joseph County stubbornly insisted on following their anti-homeschooling crusade no matter what. They filed three counts of criminal truancy charges against Laurel Pebler.

But that is not the worst of it. Laurel Pebler, innocent homeschool mom, was not just summoned to appear in court but was arrested, fingerprinted, and mug shots were taken! Her crime? Loving her children so much she was sacrificing her own time to diligently teach them at home.

My negotiations with the prosecutor failed, and the case was set for a hearing. HSLDA secured attorney Dave Kallman, and he and I filed a brief with the court. On June 17, 1991, I met with the judge, prosecutor, and Dave in the judge's chambers before arguing the case before the district court. After returning to the court room, the defense presented their evidence. Then I stood up and made a motion to dismiss based on several issues. Miraculosly, the court granted the motion to dismiss that I had presented.

Vindicated!

Amazingly, the court listened to us and found that the Department of Education had not held an administrative hearing prior to the initiation of criminal charges against Laurel Pebler. Even more amazing, the court found that the compulsory attendance law, as applied, was vague and unclear as to what specifically constituted a violation of the law. And therefore, Laurel Pebler was not given fair notice of what is legal and what is not legal.

This was so incredible because in reality the state statute couldn't be clearer: all teachers in the state of Michigan needed to be certified—no ifs, ands, or buts about it. Nothing vague about that.

Laurel Pebler was not certified. The *DeJonge* case that I had presented three times to the Michigan Court of Appeals and lost every time held that homeschoolers needed to be certified teachers. God had enabled us to use a certain technical legal argument that no administrative hearing had been held before charges were brought. Furthermore, we had argued that there was no mandated, statutory procedure where Laurel had to divulge to the state that she was not a certified teacher in the first place.

This is nothing more than a miracle that God had allowed to unfold. I used this nonprecedent case a hundred times over to prevent charges from being brought against other families.

Lock Up that Six-Year-Old!

On March 10, 1992, we came close to losing a homeschooled child to the authorities. Until this point we had never lost a child.

In fact, in all the history of HSLDA, we have never had a child taken from a homeschool parent, nor have we ever had a homeschool close down because the family was homeschooling. All glory goes to God. The legal atmosphere was downright nasty; yet God's hand was on the homeschool movement, and He continues to protect it today as He did on that day of March 10, 1992.

A year earlier five of the Loudouns' homeschool children were separately charged with criminal truancy in Michigan. Even the five-year-old, who was below compulsory attendance age, was charged. This was somewhat unusual since the authorities generally charged the parents for contributing to the delinquency of a truant, not charge the little homeschool children.

At the hearing the prosecutor approached Dave Kallman, our local HSLDA attorney who was representing the family, and indicated that he had reviewed the case file and my earlier letters to the school district and agreed to dismiss the charges against all of the children. The judge did dismiss the case, and it seemed that the ordeal was over.

In February 1992, however, the Loudouns were notified that their now six-year-old daughter was truant. They were summoned to appear before the court. We immediately contacted the court referee and reminded her that the case had been dismissed. The court referee simply told us to ignore the summons.

Warrant to Arrest a Child

Yet two weeks later police officers arrived on the Loudouns' doorstep with a warrant signed by the judge for the arrest of the family's six-year-old daughter. The family immediately placed a call to me.

As I answered the phone, the mother, crying, said, "The police are here to take away my six-year-old daughter. Can you stop them?"

My heart began pumping faster as I swallowed hard and quickly prayed. I found these emergency prayers were becoming more and more frequent and needful!

I mustered up courage and asked if I could talk with one of the police officers. I explained, "This warrant is a mistake, this case was dismissed last year, and the court referee told us to ignore the summons."

But the officer dutifully declared, "Without the court telling us that the warrant was improperly issued, we must remove the child from the home." After ten more minutes of wrangling, I asked the police officers, "Will you just sit down for five minutes and have a cup of coffee and don't take the child while I call the prosecutor?" I could sense the officer was not crazy about arresting the little girl so he agreed to wait five minutes.

I immediately called the court referee who had told us to ignore the summons. Surprised that the warrant for the arrest of the six-year-old had been issued, the referee nonetheless refused to rescind the warrant. In a half second I was calling the prosecutor while I was praying once again.

Surprisingly, the prosecutor had no difficulty remembering the case, recalling with amusement that they had mistakenly charged a child under compulsory school age.

The Five-Minute Miracle

I was trying to trust the Lord through this whole process—that I would be able to contact the right people in time. Already, finding the court referee (judge) in her office was a surprise. But an even greater surprise was that I was able to talk to the prosecutor instantly. Usually they don't return phone calls for days, or they are in court most of the time.

Upon learning that this same child was about to be arrested on truancy charges, the prosecutor "hit the ceiling." With loud exclamations and the passing of only a few minutes, the prosecutor was in the office of the court referee while I was hanging on the line. He told her to immediately cancel the arrest warrant. He then called the police officers in the Loudoun's home and informed them that they were free to go and that the warrant was rescinded.

In the space of about ten total minutes, the situation was resolved!

Later I learned the source of the wrongly issued warrant. After the earlier hearing, the court clerk had neglected to record the dismissal of the charges against the youngest child, who was only five years old at the time. The charges resurfaced when the child reached compulsory school age, and the warrant was issued.

God's hand of protection was on the Loudoun family—their child was not traumatized by the social workers or police and taken away. He granted a miracle and answered a prayer by enabling me to contact two crucial officials in such a short amount of time. Praise God—He proved to many homeschool families in trouble that He cares about the details.

Underprivileged = Guilty of Truancy

Maxine Allen was a single black mother who was faithfully teaching her children at home. Without warning the police swooped down on her home, arrested her, fingerprinted her, and took her in. I received a call from the jail and was able to help her be released on bond the next day.

Many times we find that there is discrimination with some government officials' attitude to families who do not have as much. There is an unspoken assumption that poorer people are not "smart enough" to teach their children at home. Maxine was a pastor and loved the Lord. She ministered in Jesus' name everywhere she went.

Thankfully it was not long before we were able to get her case dismissed because the *Leeper* decision had already been handed down from the court of appeals, and homeschooling was legal. The fact that her children were not in the school was not a proof of violating the compulsory attendance law.

Furthermore, the law enforcement authorities far exceeded what was necessary to deal with the situation. To arrest her and fingerprint her for simply supposed criminal truancy was over-kill. Nonetheless, Maxine kept the faith the whole way, her case was quickly dropped, and she was able to continue to home-school without even the necessity for a trial. She was extremely forgiving and did not want to pursue a civil rights action. Once again God delivered.

Frequent Scare Tactics

Time and time again families were threatened with unbelievable scare tactics by the authorities. One family in Maryland had a police officer pounding on their door one night. It was about ten o'clock, and this family called our emergency hotline that we have available twenty-four hours a day, seven days a week.

The mother was frantic, saying, "Help me! This police offi-cer wants to take away my children!" As I talked to the family on the phone, I could hear in the background the policeman yelling, "I'm going to break down the door if you don't open it! I will take those children away!"

I had the family open the door and pass the phone to the police officer, and I calmed him down. Apparently, the older teenage child in the home was rebellious and had called the police with a tip because she was not allowed to use the com-puter as part of her discipline for disobedience.

By God's grace, and after fervent prayer during the whole process, the police officer left without arresting or taking anyone, and we were able to resolve the situation within a few weeks.

Many such near misses could be testified to by all of the attorneys at HSLDA. But we saw God always deliver His people!

✳13

Invasion of the Social Workers

Be sober, be vigilant; because your adversary the devil walks about like a roaring lion, seeking whom he may devour. Resist him, steadfast in the faith, knowing that the same sufferings are experienced by your brotherhood in the world.

1 PETER 5:8–9 NKJV

Mother was at home diligently teaching her child when she heard an unwanted knock at the door. She hoped that it was just a salesman, but deep inside she knew that it was probably a public school official snooping around about their homeschool. She offered a short prayer and answered the door.

To her horror, instead of a truant officer, she found herself face-to-face with a child welfare agent. The agent immediately accused her of child neglect and demanded entry into her home. He insisted on being allowed to interrogate all of her children alone. When she refused, the agent threatened to get a court order and a police officer. But she was innocent. Where could she go? What could she do? Inside she screamed, "Help!"

This is a true yet typical story of what many homeschool families during the last twenty years have faced when a social worker comes to their door—and they are completely innocent. It is often the result of anonymous tipsters who call a child abuse hotline and fabricate allegations against the family. They use the system to hurt their neighbor or relative because perhaps they are Christian or they simply don't like homeschooling.

When I received this first call as a young attorney at Home School Legal Defense Association, I was shaking in my boots. What should I do? They are threatening to get a court order. I thought, *Maybe they will even lose their children!* This was an overwhelming fear I felt as I contemplated talking to the social worker at the door and being responsible for the consequences of harm to the family.

I built up my courage and prayed to God for strength. Then God made something clear to me: call their bluff!

I had previously talked with other veteran attorneys, who were friends of mine, and asked them what I should do when faced with a homeschool family being investigated by a social worker. They all answered me with the same response, "Social workers can take the children. They have a lot of power so it is best just to cooperate and try to minimize the damage. It is unavoidable to keep them from talking with the children."

This Is America, Not Communist China

God was making it clear to me that this counsel was wrong. This was not communist China; this was America. I learned in law school that parents have certain rights that are protected by the U.S. Constitution under the Fourth Amendment. The state or the social worker has to have probable cause before they can even obtain a warrant that must be signed by a judge. They are not allowed to enter a home by a mere anonymous tip. All these thoughts were running madly through my head as I faced my first social worker on behalf of an HSLDA member family.

As I talked with the social worker, I stood my ground. I explained that the family had done nothing wrong and that they needed a warrant or a court order if they wanted to enter the home or talk with the kids separately. However, I did offer to have the pastor speak with the children and write a letter describing his conversation to assure the social worker that nothing was wrong. The social worker "huffed and puffed" and said, "Everyone else cooperates with me!" Then he stormed away threatening under his breath that he was going to come back with the police.

He never returned with the police. In fact, within a few weeks, we were able to close the case. Thus began my long journey dealing with nearly one thousand social workers and realizing that their most effective weapon is bluffing.

No State Is Safe from Social Workers

As I continued to represent families with social worker contacts, I realized that no state was safe. For example, in Georgia, one of the most favorable homeschool states at that time, one family following its religious convictions concerning home education was harassed by the local truant officer. After a while, since he was not making any progress, the truant officer decided to turn them over to a social worker for educational neglect, just to increase the power of intimidation. Another HSLDA member in Georgia was a single parent who lived in subsidized housing. Since she was poor, the social worker assumed that she could not possibly be smart enough to homeschool and even threatened to take her children. In each instance I stood on the Fourth Amendment, called their bluff, and the cases where resolved without the children being interviewed or removed and without the social worker even entering the home.

In Colorado a family was investigated by a social worker under somewhat bizarre circumstances. In the middle of the night, the family heard someone trying to break into their house. They called the police who came into the house to inspect the door to which forced entry was attempted. Instead of writing a report on the attempted burglary, the police officer started "snooping around" while asking questions concerning their children. After he left, he contacted the social worker to investigate the family for child abuse. The allegations were "clothes lying around the house, dishes from the night before were still in the sink, and there was a strange odor in the house." With four children who were very young ages, it was true that there were some clothes lying around. The family had figured that they were too tired that night and would do dishes in the morning. As for the odor, it was the middle of the winter, and the family had just had an Italian dinner that night. Not much opportunity for them to open windows and air it out. It sure didn't sound like major child abuse. We are all child abusers if this constitutes child abuse.

When the social worker came to the door, the family mistakenly let the social worker in. Then they quickly called me on the phone. They had explained to the social worker that she could come in no further, but the social worker craned her neck to look to the left and right and all around as she took "baby steps" further inside. The family explained once again that no, she could not come in, and the phone was handed to her.

I immediately explained to the social worker that she had no right to be in the house, and the family wanted her to leave. I further promised that we would give them a letter from a third party who would walk through the house and give them a report. The social worker left to the great relief of the family.

In Oklahoma a child welfare agent came to the door as the result of a neighbor turning the homeschool family over for child abuse simply because they were homeschooling. Oklahoma recognizes the right to homeschool pursuant to their state constitution. It is the only state in the entire country where homeschooling is a constitutional right. But social workers do not care. Most really believe they are above the law. Within days the case was closed. Certainly no state is safe.

One family, in Barabou, Wisconsin, was contacted by the Sauk County Department of Human Services, based on an anonymous tip. Apparently, one of the children's grandmothers had been harassing the family and reported to the social worker that the children were having "trouble with their mom." The children were all homeschooled and the relative was not pleased. I intervened and was able to convince the social worker to close the case after she had just one conversation with the mother. The children were never interviewed.

Now, the reader must remember that Wisconsin was one of the earliest states to pass a homeschool law. In fact, to this day, it has one of the best laws in the country. A homeschool family needs merely to notify by October 15 of each year that they are teaching their children at home and check four boxes on a form indicating that they are teaching certain core subjects for a certain number of days, and that they are not using the law to circumvent compulsory attendance. Nevertheless, as I have found over and over again, it doesn't matter when it comes to social workers.

I began to keep a log of the type of contacts I was receiving because the fabrications that social workers would seriously investigate were so outlandish. Usually it was a combination of factors. For example, a common allegation was neglect of education and an untidy house. Sometimes there were accusations that children were observed regularly playing outside during school hours or were seen playing outside at dusk. Many times families received accusations of having children with "worn out" clothes. In some instances, simply spanking was the allegation.

Let's take a moment and look through the real-life stories that homeschoolers had to face in the 1980s and 1990s.

Truly Ridiculous Allegations

A single mother in a low-income apartment in California was reported to the social service agency for "a child not in attendance in school" and "a messy house." The social worker came to her door and demanded entry. When she refused and asked for him to put his questions in writing, he left. Within the hour, however, he was back with a police officer who also demanded entry. He wanted to "see if the house was sanitary, whether the child was fed, whether there was food in the house, and to ask the child a few questions." He also wanted to see proof of an education taking place.

The mother handed the phone out the door to the policeman, and I told him that he had no right to go into the home without a warrant. He agreed. Over a forty-five-minute period, I kept talking to him and then to the mother to see if the situation could be settled. Meanwhile, the mother and daughter, who were packing for a move to another apartment, picked up around the house while I talked with the officer. I finally convinced the officer to agree not to question their homeschooling, talk with the daughter, or let the social worker come into the house. Based on my assurances, the police officer promised to go alone into the house for one or two minutes and not to scrutinize it too closely. Under those limited conditions, the family let the police officer in. He was in and out in a few moments. When he found everything to be fine, the case was closed.

One of the most ridiculous allegations against a homeschooling family that I ever heard was from a child welfare agent in Michigan who received an anonymous tip that the mother was seen selling all of her children's shoes and coats at a rummage sale. I chuckled, "Are you serious?"

He responded, "It is my job to investigate all allegations—no matter what they are. Besides this could be a problem." The mother had obviously only sold clothing that would no longer fit the children. The case was resolved after I let the agent stop by and see the kids from a distance standing at the door wearing their shoes and coats!

A family in Texas was investigated by a social worker based on the following allegations: (1) the children were not in attendance at school; (2) the children were unsupervised and running around the neighborhood; (3) the children were dirty and abused; and (4) the house may be used for drug trafficking since people were frequently coming in and out of the house. The social worker demanded to interview the children, a six- and seven-year-old, or she would be forced to seek a court order.

The social worker knew nothing about homeschooling, and I was able to convince her not to pursue the matter further. Concerning the other allegations, the mother simply explained to the social worker that they were false. The children had recess during the day but were always supervised and mainly played in their fenced yard. Occasionally the boys would catch frogs in a nearby ditch and get a little muddy, hardly abnormal for little boys. The mother was a curriculum supplier and had people occasionally come by to pick up their curriculums. So much for being a drug pusher! The mother stood firm and would not let her children be interviewed separately in spite of threats by the social worker to obtain a court order. Finally the social worker, having no evidence, closed the case.

Another family in Texas had a visit from a social worker who had received allegations that the family was (1) homeschooling, (2) they had home births, and (3) they used homeopathy. Social services had received the tip anonymously. The family knew that it was particular relatives they had just spent a holiday with who had commented about those things and was very concerned. So being good relatives, they called the social service agency and turned them in.

The family refused to allow the social worker in and called me on the phone. The family passed the phone out to the social worker, and I explained that these accusations were not neglect. Families had the right in Texas to homeschool, and they had the right to practice homeopathy and do home births. The social worker, realizing how ludicrous the allegations were, began to stutter and stammer but stuck to her only point left, "I just have to interview them anyway." Needless to say after a tug-of-war, we were able to keep the social worker out of the house and away from the kids.

One outlandish investigation of a family legally home-schooling occurred in New Jersey. On the first visit the agent from the Division of Youth and Families Services accused the mother of kidnapping some of her children because she had so many children. The mother produced birth certificates to prove that all of the children were hers. The following year another agent came by and said someone called and reported that "the children were seen outside during school hours." The social worker demanded to enter the house, but the mother, under my instruction, refused. The agent then said that she would be back with the police. She never carried out her bluff. I called her and proved that the family was legally homeschooling.

Investigated for Running a "Day Care"

Some homeschool families were turned over to the social ser-vices department for running "day care centers." For instance, in Florida a social worker investigated a homeschool family's home based on an anonymous tip that the family was running an illegal and unlicensed day care center. It turned out that all six children going in and out of the home were members of the same family. I guess this social worker did not know that home-school families tend to have more than the national average of 1.8 children.

In Alabama a homeschool mom was reported to the social worker for operating an unlicensed day care center because she started taking care of one infant five days a week. She was threatened with a felony, and the social worker demanded entry into the home. I discovered as usual the social worker was stretching the truth since running an unlicensed day care center was not a felony. However in Alabama, anyone taking care of a child more than four hours a day who was not a relative must get a license. In order to avoid further investigation, the family chose to no longer watch the infant.

Families in Trouble for Child Discipline

A homeschool father in Michigan picked up his two-year-old child by her arms, taking her into the house while she was crying and was reported for child abuse by a nosy neighbor. I set up a meeting with the social worker and counseled the family on what they should say. I told them to explain their religious convictions concerning raising their children from "a positive standpoint" avoiding Bible verses like if "you beat him with the rod, he will not die." Or, if you "beat him with the rod," you will "deliver his soul" from hell. Not a good idea. Social workers just don't understand those verses.

Instead I told them to explain their beliefs by emphasizing verses such as Matthew 18:6 that states that if you harm or offend a child, it is better that a millstone be tied about your neck and you be thrown in the deepest part of the ocean. In other words, their religious convictions demand that they do not do anything that will harm their children. When the family began presenting these religious beliefs to the agent, he became visibly uncomfortable and suddenly announced that he would close the case. He then abruptly left. This by the way is a valuable lesson to remember for all of us concerning what type of information about your religious beliefs you should share with a social worker.

In Colorado a homeschooler was reported after spanking a child in public. Someone had followed them to their car and written down the license plate number. The father, in order to avoid embarrassment for the child, had marched the child to the car and spanked the child there for acting up in the store.

Even though spanking is legal, families routinely get turned in by anonymous tipsters. I learned over the years to spank in private not in public, no matter what the circumstance. It is better to discipline them at home, or you may find yourself the object of a full-scale investigation.

In Fairfax County, Virginia, a pastor gave a seminar on child discipline that included the requirement in the Bible to spank. A parishioner had to discipline her child while a neighbor was visiting a few days later. She spanked the child in the other room and then explained to the neighbor a little of what she had learned from the pastor.

The neighbor, who happened to be against spanking, reported the pastor to the child welfare agency for "bruising their children and for twenty-minute spanking sessions." The social worker who then initiated the investigation told me she thought she might have a religious cult on her hands that abuses children. I expressed my disbelief to the social worker that she was seriously investigating what an anonymous source claimed she heard from a person who heard it from another person. That is thrice removed hearsay. I told her that her evidence was flimsy and set the parameters for a meeting.

In preparation for the meeting, I told the homeschooling pastor and his wife not to recount any specific incidents of spanking since the social worker had nothing on the family that would stand up in court. I told them that they should emphasize again the positive verses such as Matthew 18:6. Since the social worker had no evidence, the only evidence she could acquire would be from what information she could gather from the pastor and his wife. Since the parents carefully avoided all specific examples and spoke in general terms, the social worker had nothing and had to close the case.

One HSLDA family had just moved to Alabama two weeks earlier and had not yet met anyone in their neighborhood. However, the Department of Human Resources agent received an anonymous tip that the children had bruises and demanded a strip search. The family handed the phone out the door, and I said, "A strip search is not going to happen." The social worker exclaimed, "No one else ever refused a strip search before." She also implied that the family had something to hide, which I have found over the last twenty years is the usual tactic to embarrass and scare the family to let them in. I had the family get a statement from their personal physician who verified that the children were all fine, and the situation was soon resolved.

A family was homeschooling their children in Palm Bay, Florida. Little did they know that their life would be turned upside down when the dad was seen lightly spanking their two-year old on the diaper in a parking lot.

The anonymous tipster called the police, who met the homeschool father when he returned to the house. The father showed the two-year-old to the police, and they were satisfied that there was no injury.

However, the incident was still referred to the Florida Department of Children and Families. A social worker came to the home and talked at length with the parents and children. Although the social worker found no evidence of abuse, she demanded that the parents (1) take twenty-two weeks of parenting classes through the county, (2) have a social visit once a month for an indefinite period of time to see how they were doing, and (3) sign a statement of release to allow the social worker to get documents and medical records from any source they chose. Then she indicated that they would seek a court order if the family did not cooperate. At this point the family contacted me, and I called the social worker and investigator. They did not back down from any of their demands.

The social worker indicated that the family was "at risk." When I asked why, the social worker said that the family was "at risk" because they had (1) a large family (four children), (2) they homeschool and have a low profile in the community, (3) they do not have daily contact with trained people who can detect child abuse, such as those who run the local public school or day care centers.

After much discussion on the phone, the social worker insisted that they would need to get a court order if their earlier demands were not satisfied. We immediately responded with a four-page letter that summarized Florida law that allows for corporal punishment as long as there are not significant sprains, dislocations, or bruises. Finally we were able to convince the social worker to back down, and the family did not have to go through with any of the demands.

The Bogus Lack-of-Supervision Claim

I often ran into situations where families were accused of lack of supervision. For instance, in Michigan some particularly nasty neighbors looking for an excuse to get a homeschool family in trouble saw one of the children outside one night. The neighbors called the child welfare agency to report the incident as "lack of supervision." The social worker wanted to enter the home and interrogate the children. We refused and explained that the child only ran outside for a moment to catch a cat that had escaped. That is a common experience in our home with our cat named Crockett who escapes and runs out the door whenever he gets a chance.

Another Michigan homeschool family was reported by an anonymous tipster who claimed that the children were not supervised, the children did not attend school, the boys ran around barefoot, an old rusty car was in their yard, the boys slept in the attic, and one boy liked to kill mice. (Can you believe that anyone would want to kill mice?) I talked with the child welfare agent who said that she would prosecute the family for neglect and get a search warrant. She also wanted a special study done on the child who killed mice because she thought he might have psychological problems.

We were able to prove to the social worker the children were being legally homeschooled; there was no rusty car in the yard (except their own functional, slightly rusty car parked in their driveway); and the children did not sleep in the attic. As far as lack of supervision, I told the agent the charges were false, and the children have the right to play in their yard. In regard to killing mice from a nearby swamp, we have no apologies but wondered about the competence of the agent. The case was closed.

One homeschool family had recently moved to Florida. Within weeks they were visited by a truant officer who questioned the legality of their homeschooling. The truant officer left and reported them to the Health and Human Services Department (HHS). A few days later an HHS agent appeared at the door and demanded to interview the children within twenty-four hours or he would send for the police. The allegations were that "the children were home during school hours and the children were sometimes left alone." I explained the legality of homeschooling and denied the "lack of supervision" charge (the family had only one car and the father took it to work leaving the mother at home). I then called his bluff and refused to have the children interviewed. After talking with the parents, we allowed him to come by the door and only see the children from a distance. He ended up closing the case since he had no evidence other than an anonymous tip.

Know Your Family Doctor

We have had numerous situations where doctors turned homeschoolers in to social services because they found a bruise or a mark on the child, even though the parents would explain how it happened, and it was an accident. For instance, one seven-year-old son had been using a teeter-totter, and another, larger kid, bounced him on the teeter-totter, where he ended up bruising himself in the pelvis area.

When he went in for a checkup on other things, they noticed the bruise, and in spite of the mother's objections, the doctor insisted on turning the family over to the social services agency. In Colorado, where this family was living, the social workers are particularly aggressive. To avoid their going to get a court order, I quickly had the family get a second opinion from another doctor who was easily able to explain the bruise and that it had nothing to do with abuse or neglect.

I learned early on that each family needs to know their doctor well. If the doctor is familiar with the patients and trusts them, they do not have to turn them over to a child welfare agency, even if they have a mark or bruise. It is completely the doctor's discretion.

Being "Born Again" Makes You Suspect

One particularly ridiculous example occurred in Wisconsin. A homeschool family was reported by an anonymous tipster. I was able to secure a copy of the report by the social worker, who said:

> The caller was concerned because the children were all thin, and thought that removal of food was possibly a form of discipline. The caller thought this discipline may have been a practice of the parents' religion, which was thought to have been "born again." The caller thought that these parents give a lot of money to the charge and spend little money on groceries. The caller's last, somewhat passing concern, was that the mother homeschools her children.

As usual, the anonymous tip was a complete exaggeration. It is apparent from the report that the caller was biased against both the fact that the family was homeschooling and that they were Christians. This has always been a common thread that

I have seen as I have represented homeschoolers facing social worker allegations.

Watching the History Channel Is Abuse?

Another family owned and operated a farm in Buffalo County, Wisconsin. For the last two years they homeschooled their two children in addition to teaching them all of the tasks necessary to run a farm. Unfortunately, a relative did not like their home-schooling and turned them in to Health and Human Services, even though the family was in full compliance with the law. The social worker stopped by when they were not home and left a letter requesting to meet with them. The family refused. The social worker followed up with a second letter requesting a meeting, but this time included a copy of the allegations. The family immediately contacted me at HSLDA.

Upon reviewing the allegations, and realizing that there was no identifiable child abuse among the allegations, I advised the family not to cooperate. Some of the absurd allegations, as typed out by the anonymous tipster with various misspellings and typos, included the following: "Neither parent has an education beyond high school. The parents refuse to send one of their children to summer school. Both parents feel that one and a half hours of schooling per day is sufficient." The tipster continued: "They recently purchased satellite television so the boys could learn from the History Channel, and one of the boys cuts his own hair so he can see."

Finally, in addition to the several false allegations, the tipster indicated that "each child gets a new toy every week that the mother shops and the fathers (sic) number one priority is money—they are not financially poor." The tipster revealed his or her prejudice clearly at the end of the letter by stating, "Wisconsin needs stricter laws regarding homeschooling. Compared with Minnesota (sic)." Minnesota has a much more complicated homeschool law than Wisconsin.

Since the family was not required to cooperate by law, they chose not to do so. When I explained to the social worker that there was no crime in watching the History Channel or having a child cut his hair, the social worker realized that they were getting nowhere with this family. She terminated her investigation after realizing she had no real evidence of abuse.

The Battle for the Front Door

An HSLDA member family in Joplin, Missouri, avoided an intrusive social services investigation due to their preparedness and presence of mind. While the mother was going about her daily routine early one morning at the end of January, she heard a knock at her door. When this homeschool mom of seven answered the door, she was surprised to see three police officers (two uniformed police and one detective) and a social worker, standing on her doorstep. Two squad cars and two other government vehicles were parked in front of her house. The mom was terrified.

The group of officials told the mother that she had been accused of abusing her children and demanded that she immediately let them into the house to interview each of the children separately.

The mother had the presence of mind not to let them inside and immediately called HSLDA. I had her obtain the cell phone number of the social worker since the family did not have a cordless phone to hand out the door. After speaking with the social worker, I learned she was not only concerned about the children's homeschooling but that the allegations also stated that the children were often tied up and gagged, food was withheld, and the mother hit the children repeatedly. After talking further with the mother, it was clear that the allegations were completely baseless, and the results of a disgruntled relative. I explained the limits and the powers of the government officials, telling the social worker that if she did not have the parents' permission, she could not enter the home without a warrant.

Yet the social worker insisted that the allegations were severe and that she needed to investigate immediately. I offered a compromise as I had learned to do over the years. The family would provide references of individuals in the community who would vouch for their good parenting, and I promised that they would also take the children to a doctor to obtain an objective report of the children's good health. The family would send the social worker the information as soon as possible. The social worker finally accepted the offer, mumbling under her breath, and left, along with the three police officers. They realized that they had no legal authority to enter the house.

Whew! The worst was over. Our goal of preventing entrance into the house was achieved. Over the years, we have called this "The Battle for the Front Door." We have learned that if we can keep the social workers out, we can limit the damage and the trauma to the family. We can also prevent "fishing expeditions" so that the investigations are steered by the family rather than the social worker.

In preparation for their future meeting to show their references, I explained to the mom and dad that they should make sure they stick to the discussion of the specific allegations and not allow themselves to be dragged or tricked into discussing other issues. In our experience social workers sometimes like to go on "fishing expeditions" into the family's personal information.

The mom and dad met with the social worker in a neutral location a few days later. After reviewing the information submitted by the parents, the social worker admitted that the case was unsubstantiated.

A family in Denton, Texas, was reported to the social services agency by their own neighbor. He was angry because there had been a dispute concerning his dog. As a result, he used the child welfare system, as so many others do, to retaliate against the family.

When the social worker came to the family's door, they were able to explain that the situation was mostly resolved. However, a short time later the child welfare services supervisor assigned another social worker to follow up with the family, as the family had not allowed the first social worker entrance into their home. I contacted the social worker after she went to the house and threatened the family. She said, "When people are uncooperative, they have something to hide."

Of course, she was ignoring the fact that the family had a Fourth Amendment right not to let the social worker into their home, and simply standing on that right does not determine any guilt. A family, even during a child welfare investigation, is innocent until proven guilty. Many social workers do not seem to understand or agree with this principle. HSLDA was finally able to resolve this case and win "The Battle for the Front Door."

In San Antonio, Texas, a member family was visited by the Texas Department of Family Protective Services. The family telephoned me for help when they discovered that the knock at the door was a social worker paying them an unexpected visit. The social worker told me that an anonymous tipster had expressed concern about the family's homeschool program and indicated that the family was "locking their kids in a cage" and had a "mean dog." The allegations were completely bogus. The family had a Saint Bernard that was quite friendly, and they did not lock their children in any cages. They did have a cage, however, that they put their Saint Bernard in when they periodically went away. We were able to resolve the case with a few references and a letter.

A family in Orlando, Florida, was homeschooling, but the parents had decided to separate for a time due to some marriage issues. When the family returned to the home, where the father was still staying, they were surprised to meet a child welfare investigator.

Apparently an anonymous tip came from someone out of state who invented a false story about the father. The family immediately called HSLDA after the social worker came back a second time. The social worker demanded to interview the children and demanded entry into the house. I argued with the social worker over the phone for thirty minutes when she waited on the family's doorstep. Finally in exasperation after getting one police officer, she said, "I will get four more police officers." I responded, "You could get a whole army of police officers, but you still could not come into the home without a warrant." An anonymous tip is not sufficient evidence to get any type of court order.

This homeschool family had restored the relationship that was nearly broken asunder by the harassment of the Child Protective Services. Finally, the Child Protective investigator and the police left the house without gaining entry or interviewing the children. The case was finally resolved; the battle for the front door was successful.

"This Is Why I Spend Twenty-Six Cents a Day"

Another family in Bradington, Florida, was visited by social workers. Allegations were made by one of their seven adopted children, who was the only one not being homeschooled. He had made up a story and told it to his science teacher, who had then passed on the information to a social worker. I was able to talk to the social worker and keep them out of the home and away from the children. The case was finally listed as unfounded. The mom said, "This is why I spend twenty-six cents a day. People are crazy not to join HSLDA. I have an attorney ready to help me at a moment's notice."

At Risk from Social Workers

I could certainly continue with story after story, but I think that you can get the picture. Homeschoolers are at risk. They are not at risk because they have big families or teach their children at home or neglect their children in any way. They are at risk because the child welfare system has lost control. Many social workers are trained in a philosophy that is antiparent, antifamily, and antireligious.

In fact, on March 5, 2002, I attended a Virginia continuing legal education class (CLE) for becoming a "guardian ad litem." Such classes are held so that practicing attorneys can stay up to date on changes to the law. For seven hours, various lawyers, judicial officials, and social workers lectured on many aspects of child abuse and the role of the guardian ad litem. A guardian ad litem is an advocate appointed by the judge in a neglect proceeding to protect the child's rights.

During a lecture entitled "Developmental Needs of Children: Characteristics of Abusive and Neglectful Families and of Children Who Are Victims," Kathleen Nussbaum, a licensed clinical social worker, discussed the three family types that she believed showed the characteristics of these abusive and neglectful families. The first type of family she called "the religious and authoritarian family type." She defined a religious and authoritarian family type as, "A strong focus on male leadership with strong church involvement. Parents are frequently elders or ministers in the church, and they use their religious authority as well as Scripture to maintain control." Such a broad and erroneous definition probably defines 85 percent of the homeschool families in America. The second type of suspect family she called a "rigid and controlling" family type, which she characterized by "rigid, non permeable parental boundaries." She also said that these parents have extremely high expectations for their children.

This shows us one reason social workers tend to target homeschool families. It seems from our perspective that homeschool families per capita are subjected to an inordinate number of social worker visits. There is no doubt that a large percentage of homeschool families are religious and have strong church involvement. Christian homeschool families typically recognize the father as the head of the household, study Scripture on a regular basis, and bring their children up in the nurture and admonition of the Lord. They fit these two "abusive and neglectful" family types to a "T." The social workers amazingly do not understand that Christian families provide the most solid foundation for their children in a loving environment.

It is clear from this guardian ad litem classes given by social workers across the state of Virginia that the philosophy is deeply entrenched. Our president of HSLDA, J. Michael Smith, sent a letter to the Virginia Supreme Court demanding that the class be pulled since the supreme court has jurisdiction over CLE classes. Within a few weeks the chief justice wrote a letter indicating that he essentially agreed with our analysis and ordered that the class materials and lecture be removed from all guardian ad litem training. Praise God for this fast result.

Nonetheless, there is a problem that homeschoolers face through institutional child welfare systems that is truly out of control. We deal with social workers at HSLDA office on a daily basis.

We Are Winning!

Although the road has been hard these many years, all is not dark. The good news is we are winning. In nearly every situation, we are able to convince the social workers to back off. In addition, we are able to challenge the social workers in court and win. Court clerks have told us when we go to court, "No one ever challenges social workers. You are the first ones we have ever seen!"

It is clear to us that the child welfare system, although serving an important purpose, needs to be reigned in somewhat. In Alabama I helped a homeschool family. Helene Richards was a low-income mother who was contacted by a social worker over some false allegation of child abuse and educational neglect. Under my counsel the family refused the social worker to come into the home and interrogate the children. In order to muscle this family, charges of child neglect were brought, based on no evidence whatsoever, and only an anonymous tipster who admitted she did not have personal knowledge of the family situation. Nevertheless, a hearing was held on whether an anonymous tip was enough to force a social worker to enter the home and interrogate the children. Following "hometown justice," the lower court agreed that it was and ordered the family, under contempt of court, to allow the social worker into the home and to interrogate the children.

Michael Farris and Jordan Lorence appealed the decision to the Alabama Court of Appeals on the basis that the Fourth Amendment to the Constitution requires the government officials to have probable cause (some kind of reliable evidence) in order to obtain entry into the individual's home. They asked for an emergency stay in the meantime with Jordan flying down the day after the decision, and it was miraculously granted. Then the Alabama Court of Appeals reversed the lower court's decision and ruled:

> We suggest, however, that the power of the courts
> to permit invasions of the privacy protected by our
> Federal and State Constitutions is not to be exercised
> except upon a showing of reasonable or probable cause
> to believe that a crime is being or is about to be com-
> mitted or a valid regulation is being or is about to be
> violated. The cause shown in this case was unsworn

hearsay and could at best present mere suspicion. A mere suspicion is not sufficient to rise to reasonable or probable cause.

In short, this case clearly concludes that an anonymous tip is not sufficient for a social worker or a court order for parents to submit to a home visit or interrogation of their children.

Another important case that HSLDA won, among others, is the *Calabretta* case. In this situation a policeman and social worker illegally entered the Calabretta home and strip-searched their three-year-old daughter. The policemen and social worker forced their way into the home over the objections of the mother simply based on an anonymous tip. The tipster merely said he heard the child cry one night. After the coerced entry, and interrogation and strip search of the children, no evidence of abuse was found. The police officer and social worker said, "Thank you," and left.

HSLDA believes strongly this is America, not some communist country. Therefore, Mike Farris filed a civil rights suit against the Yolo County Department of Social Services. We had to stop this abuse of innocent families. At the trial level district court judge Lawrence Karlton ruled that unless there is evidence of an emergency, a social worker and police officer investigating a report of child abuse must have a warrant. The court clarified that the Fourth Amendment applies just as much to child abuse investigations and social workers as it does to any other government official in a search and seizure. An anonymous tip or mere suspicion is not enough to reach the standard of probable cause. The government appealed to the Ninth Circuit U.S. Court of Appeals, but they unanimously affirmed the lower court's decision. They stated that "the reasonable expectation of privacy of individuals in their home includes the interest in both parents and children in not having government officials coerce entry in violation of the Fourth Amendment and humiliate parents in front of the children."

The law is clear. Much precedent has come down since we began challenging these suits. Social workers have to obey the Fourth Amendment, too.

Significant Child Welfare Reform

On October 16, 2001, I had the opportunity to testify before Congress, at the Subcommittee on Select Education of the House Committee on Education and the Workforce. The chairman is Representative Pete Hoekstra. Most of the panelists were there in order to convince Congress to give more federal dollars to child welfare agencies in all fifty states. There was a multitude of programs that the panelists were asking for more funds. I was the only witness who spoke to the substantive problem of social workers trampling parents' Fourth Amendment rights. I explained how parents' rights are regularly threatened by application of state child welfare law. I documented scores of examples and even explained what some of the social workers believe.

For instance, after resolving a false allegation with a particular social worker over the phone from Chicago, Illinois, the social worker informed me that well over 50 percent of all referrals to her child welfare agency are unfounded. Unfortunately, she complained that many of the cases are deemed unfounded after the families are broken apart and the children put into foster homes. She explained that many hospitals and health care centers are in the business of always finding child abuse. Expressing her concern about the new training of recently hired social workers, she said that younger social workers are encouraged to go on fishing expeditions. In the old days social workers tried to prove in a report that the family was innocent and considered a family innocent until proven guilty. Now the system operates on the principle that the family is guilty, period. I discussed the other conversations with social workers who indicated that nearly 90 percent of their cases were unfounded; others, 60 to 70 percent. In Alabama and Florida I had met two former social workers who admitted that the routine procedure they were taught and always used to get their way was intimidation.

Some social workers, as I explain the Fourth Amendment, asked me, "What is the Fourth Amendment again?" After describing at length to the very interested congressional committee, I presented five amendments that should be added to the Child Abuse and Prevention Treatment Act to treat the problem.

Two of those amendments were actually adopted by the House, and as I handheld the amendments throughout the House and Senate process, they finally survived; and on June 25, 2003, President George W. Bush signed into law the Keeping Children and Families Safe Act of 2003. Two provisions that I had authored made it into the law that applied to all fifty states. The first provision requires child protective service workers across America to be trained in their duty to protect the statutory and constitutional rights of those they are investigating, and number two, that all child welfare workers will be required to advise individuals subjected to child abuse and neglect investigations of the actual allegations made against them. Praise God, this is the most important child welfare reform that has been enacted in the past two decades! The Health and Human Services Department indicated that the best way to make sure the federal law is implemented is to pass these amendments into the state child welfare codes, so I set out to do that, and in 2004 we were successful in twelve states. In 2005 we were successful in approximately eight more states.

Now, when a social worker comes to the door and won't tell us the allegations unless they are allowed in the house, we remind them of the federal law or, if they are in a state that passed the state law, we point them to that as well. No more

games do we need to play at the door. Instead we can immediately provide evidence of a doctor's report or individual's
references or other third parties to explain the allegations to
be bogus. We are excited about this development because it has
given us the leverage that we have so desperately needed. The
report language that appeared in the Congressional Record
accompanying the federal child welfare act quoted my testimony and stated:

> The Committee looked carefully for ways to ensure
> that the individual rights of parents to be investigated
> on allegations of child abuse and neglect were pro-
> tected, while not compromising the intent of the child
> welfare system. To that end, the Committee wants
> to enhance the training of child protective services
> personnel to ensure that they are knowledgeable in
> practices for promoting collaboration with families and
> they are fully aware of the extent and legal limits of
> their authority and the legal rights of parents in car-
> rying out such investigations. This bill requires that
> states have provisions in place that address the training
> of child protective service personnel and their legal
> duties, which may consist of procedures to inform such
> personnel of their duties, in order to protect the con-
> stitutional and statutory rights of children and families.

Furthermore, in the Senate report they were even more
explicit. "The Committee believes it is important for child
protective services personnel to understand and respect Fourth
Amendment limitations on the right to enter a home when
investigating an allegation without a court order." Thankfully,
we have come a long way in the battle with social workers.

Although the battle is not ended and families still face these
unwanted knocks at the door on a regular basis, we have the
tools to protect the families and win that battle for the front
door in a stronger way than ever before.

We praise God for His protection of His people over the years, and how He has been faithful. In most countries social workers are unstoppable; but in the United States, due to the faithful sacrifice of many homeschool families over the years and God's mighty hand, we have a more even playing field in dealing with the powers and financial support of the government child welfare agencies.

✳ 14

Homeschoolers Impact the Nation

Then Jesus told his disciples a parable to show them that they should always pray and not give up. He said: "In a certain town there was a judge who neither feared God nor cared about men. And there was a widow in that town who kept coming to him with the plea, 'Grant me justice against my adversary.' For some time he refused. But finally he said to himself, 'Even though I don't fear God or care about men, yet because this widow keeps bothering me, I will see that she gets justice, so that she won't eventually wear me out with her coming!' . . . And will not God bring about justice for his chosen ones, who cry out to him day and night? Will he keep putting them off?"

LUKE 18:1–5, 7 NIV

In the early 1980s, homeschoolers were just trying to survive—school district by school district and state by state. Homeschooling was facing great odds from opposition that included the teacher's unions, the National Association of School Boards, the National PTA, the National Elementary and Secondary School Principals Association, and many other of the education elite.

As God would have it, the homeschoolers, though small and insignificant in the nation's eyes, won their local battles in their school districts and their states. The previous chapters in this book record these amazing victories.

By the middle 1990s, the federal government shifted hands, and the Clinton administration was in control. Now many of the child's rights advocates and educational elite were in the driver's seat. Now was the time they could "ramrod" their liberal agenda and impose it on the American people.

The difference between Congress and state legislatures is that in "one fell swoop" Congress can pass a law that applies to all fifty states. Now everything that we had worked so hard for in the last ten years was in danger. Of course, the federal government does not have the authority under the Constitution to regulate education and child welfare issues in the states; they must do it by the "care and the stick approach." They pass omnibus pieces of legislation that provide funding to the states for education and welfare. However, it is always accompanied by massive "strings" that tie up the states and force them to their bidding.

God's Timing Is Always Perfect

Up until the Clinton administration, we had largely been protected from any new harmful developments from the federal government. God in His mercy, wisdom, and perfect timing had allowed us to fight and wage the battles state by state without the added burden of the federal government coming against us. During the years when homeschooling was disorganized, the statewide homeschool associations were small, and HSLDA influence was minimal, God kept the federal government at bay.

Now after ten years of steady and gradual success and expansion of homeschool freedoms state by state, God had made us ready and prepared to face a new foe—the liberal elite in our federal government.

God had just given me a new role too; I had contracted multiple sclerosis. My superiors switched me from the HSLDA legal department where I had worked for ten years to direct our National Center of Home Education that included our federal lobby arm. They wanted to give me a "less stressful" job. But God had other ideas. Over the next five years, I would work harder and longer hours than ever before. In fact, I would work through the night at the office every couple of weeks. My health had been worsening fast, but miraculously God reversed it for that time and made me stronger. This chapter recounts a few of the many fights that the homeschoolers successfully waged in our United States Congress.

Declaration of War on Parents' Rights

On February 14, 1995, the Clinton administration, through Hillary Clinton, "declared war" on parents' rights in America. On that day Hillary Clinton announced that the United States would sign the UN Convention on the Rights of the Child. The next step, she said, was to send it to the U.S. Senate for ratification. Hillary Clinton described the convention as advancing a "noble cause to promote the well being and protect the basic rights of children throughout the world."

On February 23, UN Ambassador Madeleine Albright signed the UN Convention on the Rights of the Child for President Clinton. Commenting on the move by the president, then Senator Bill Bradley of New Jersey stood up that same day in the U.S. Senate and declared:

> This marks a small, but long overdue step towards improving the lot of the world's children. I urge the

President to take a much larger and equally overdue
step and submit the convention at once to the Senate
for advice and consent to ratification. . . . President
Clinton has done the right thing by instructing
Ambassador Albright to sign the Convention. He
should now submit it to the Senate and we should
ratify it without delay.

Other liberal groups were clamoring to urge President
Clinton to hurry and pressure the U.S. Senate to ratify the
convention. In fact, 150 groups including the liberal elite like
the National Education Association, the Children's Defense
Fund, the National Committee for the Rights of the Child,
the National Counsel for Child's Rights, Planned Parenthood,
International School Psychology Association, the National
Counsel of Churches, the International Counsel and Social
Welfare, the American Academy of Pediatrics, and many
more.

The UN Convention on the Rights of the Child was
extremely dangerous. This was the greatest threat homeschooling parents ever faced in this country. Under the treaty
the U.S. would be required to ensure that children are vested
with "freedom of expression." Furthermore, children would
be guaranteed "freedom of thought, conscience, and religion,"
which would give children the right to object to their parents'
religious training and participate in religious services of cults.
Under this treaty children would have the "right to freedom of
association." Parents would be prevented from prohibiting their
children from associating with other children or gangs. A child
under the UN Convention would be given "the right of privacy," which includes the right to access an abortion over their
parents' objection. The child would have the right to "seek,
receive, and impart information of all kinds either orally, in
printing, or in print in the form of art, or through other media

of the child's choice." Children would have the right to listen to rock music, watch television, even have access to pornography.

The scariest part about this treaty is that Article VI of the U.S. Constitution, the Supremacy Clause, in Section II states, "All Treaties made, or which shall be made, under the Authority of the United States, shall be the supreme law of the land; and the Judges in every State shall be bound thereby, any thing in the Constitution or Laws of any State to the Contrary notwithstanding."

In essence, if two-thirds of the U.S. Senate present would ratify the UN Convention on the Rights of the Child, this treaty would become the supreme law of the land. Judges would have to give the UN Convention on the Rights of the Child the same weight as the U.S. Constitution. Our parental rights would be decimated with the passage of the UN Convention of the Rights of the Child.

Bill Clinton stated that, "Hillary wants to be the voice of the children and I want her to be." Hillary Clinton wanted the UN Convention to pass and so did every force against the family. The only thing standing in the way of ratification was the homeschoolers.

Senators Withdraw Support of Treaty

The Senate was already passing around a resolution, gathering names from the senators of those who were asking for it to be brought up and ratified. They already had over fifty signatories. They only needed about six more to have the two-thirds that they were seeking. We immediately, upon hearing of Clinton's signing of the U.S. Convention on the Rights of the Child, began to map our strategy. One of the first things I did was to begin to review the list of senators and see which ones we might be able to convince to withdraw their names from Senate Resolution 70.

God superintended it from there. For example, the year before, I was invited to speak in New York—way before we became aware of the push for UN Convention on the Rights of the Child. I headed to New York to give a keynote address at the LEAH convention, and I brought a handout prepared that exposed the UN Convention on the Rights of the Child. It also included an action item to call Senator D'Amato to convince him to withdraw his name. Just before I left, I had called Senator D'Amato's office and asked his staff if the senator would withdraw his name after I had faxed them information on its danger to parents' rights. The staff member said the senator wasn't changing his position.

At the LEAH convention I described the dangers of this treaty and asked everyone to raise their hands to commit to call. In the crowd of more than two thousand homeschoolers, virtually all of them raised their hand. Needless to say, that next week Senator D'Amato's phones were ringing off the hook from concerned NY citizens.

By the end of the week, I called Senator D'Amato's office, and to my joy I was told that Senator D'Amato was withdrawing his name from the resolution supporting the UN Convention on the Rights of the Child. The pressure from homeschoolers was working.

Senator after senator began to withdraw and the scare was beginning to subside. It only takes thirty-four U.S. senators to block the ratification of the treaty. Even Senator Dole stood before the Senate and condemned the UN Convention on the Rights of the Child. He had received thousands of phone calls from homeschoolers responding to our nationwide alert.

In response to President Clinton's signing of the Convention, we had sent out an alert to our whole membership causing thousands upon thousands to blitz the U.S. Senate.

Meanwhile on the ground, we had called on our Congressional Action Program (CAP) lobbyists from Virginia, DC, and Maryland. These are our "minute men" we can call at a moment's notice. These moms, dads, and teenagers come to an appointed location on Capitol Hill where we brief them for an hour in the morning. We give them succinct handouts in professional folders and a list of targeted senators. Then they disperse throughout the Senate or Congress to meet with various staffers, and if possible, the Senator himself.

One homeschool CAP team, lead by Elizabeth Smith, Michael Smith's wife, met with Senator Dole. Right after the meeting, Senator Dole withdrew his name from support of the UN Convention on the Rights of the Child and later, on the Senate floor, Dole declared:

> Mr. President, in the past several days, I have received thousands of calls from all over the country in opposition to the Convention. My office has not received one call for it. These contacts have raised many serious problems that need to be examined. They have raised questions about Articles XIII, XIV, XV which grant children the freedom of speech, thought, conscience, religion, and association of assembly. Could these articles be interpreted to limit the ability of parents to decide for themselves how best to raise their children? Should U.S. citizens be subject to some sort of international committee that forces compliance with Article XXVIII, which states, "State parties should take all appropriate measures to ensure that school discipline is administrated in a manner consistent with the child's human dignity and in conformity with the present Convention."

Now the tide was beginning to turn.

Homeschoolers can make a difference on Capitol Hill even though most of them live far from Washington, DC. Ever since the battle for HR 6 (which is the next story), God graciously allowed the homeschool movement to come into a position of influence on Capitol Hill.

Homeschoolers Influence Congress

In this day and age when the government seems so big and we seem so far away, especially from the Federal Congress, we often wonder, "Will my phone call or letter really matter?" When the cause is just and the Lord is on our side, our involvement does matter. We must remember that God is in control and that "the king's heart is like channels of water in the hand of the Lord; He turns it wherever He wishes" (Prov. 21:1).

Even in this day of influential PACs, massive teacher unions, and other special interests, a personal letter or phone call to a congressional office is still the most effective way to influence public policy. This is especially the case when homeschoolers are brought into the issue.

I was told by a staffer on Capitol Hill, in regard to an upcoming meeting with powerful members of the educational establishment, that we "came to the table as equals." I said, "How is that since they have over a hundred-million-dollar budget?" The congressional staffer responded, "They can't deliver the grassroots calls, but you homeschoolers can."

Since 1985 I have worked as Senior Counsel for the Home School Legal Defense Association. I have witnessed the homeschool movement grow from ten thousand families to more than seven hundred and fifty thousand families. During this time, I have been engaged in hundreds of legislative battles, representing homeschoolers at both state and federal levels. Without homeschoolers' exceptional activism in political life and ultimate reliance on God's strength, we would have never convinced thirty-seven different states to enact specific homeschool laws, defeated hundreds of harmful legislative proposals, and influenced the most powerful city in the world, Washington, DC.

There is no doubt homeschoolers comprise one of the most politically active groups, per capita, in the country. I am convinced that it is not an overstatement to say that the homeschool movement is grassroots politics at its best. The reason for this is simple: the homeschool movement is future oriented. Homeschoolers want to preserve and gain more freedom for their children and their children's children. The homeschool movement is composed of families—strong, close families—that form the foundation of any nation. Although the movement is decentralized, homeschoolers have a tight network with one another.

To say that homeschoolers are decentralized is not to say that they are not organized. Most homeschoolers are members of local support groups in their community, which range in size from ten to more than two hundred families. These local groups are usually linked to state homeschooling associations. These state associations often establish phone trees, e-mail groups, and other elaborate communication systems for communicating both news and legislative alerts to their members.

One of the purposes of the National Center for Home Education, a division of HSLDA, is to establish and maintain a network with the state homeschool associations in all fifty states in order to facilitate instant communication and rapid response to federal legislation. We alert the state homeschool associations, and they pass the alert down to the local level. Because of the homeschoolers' commitment to the future, they respond.

In addition, we have created the two-pronged Congressional Action Program (CAP), which is comprised of local homeschool lobbyists in each of the 435 congressional districts and local homeschoolers in the Washington, DC, area. These volunteer lobbyists in each congressional district are simply homeschool parents who establish e-alert systems or phone trees in order to deliver constituent calls to their congressman at a moment's notice. Thanks to the wonders of modern technology and the Internet, when a federal legislative issue that may affect homeschooling surfaces, HSLDA can alert our network of homeschool leaders and CAP volunteers at a moment's notice—similar to the minutemen during the War for Independence. These CAP District Coordinators, in response, activate their phones, fax machines, and e-mails enabling us to alert thousands across the nation.

The second lobby prong of CAP consists of volunteer homeschool parents and teenagers in the Washington, DC, area whom we train to conduct lobbying visits on Capitol Hill as needed. This system used properly results in homeschoolers' becoming the most successful "persistent widows" around.

Miller's Amendment

One of the most miraculous examples of God's hand working in a mighty way on behalf of homeschoolers was the battle over the Miller amendment, which was attached to HR 6. This battle over HR 6 also provides us with an example of successful techniques in communicating an emergency "call to action" across the nation in a matter of days. In fact, for two weeks in February 1994, the homeschoolers gave Congress a tremendous lesson on the power of grassroots politics that it is not likely to forget any time soon. This is what happened.

It all started when Congressman George Miller (D-CA) introduced an amendment to HR 6, an omnibus education reappropriations bill. This amendment stated:

> Each state applying for funds under this title shall pro-
> vide the Secretary with the assurance that after July
> 1, 1998, it will require each local educational agency
> within the state to certify that each fulltime teacher in
> schools under the jurisdiction of the agency is certi-
> fied to teach in the subject area in which he or she is
> assigned.

At first glance the provision seems harmless enough, but that is the way bad legislation is usually introduced. The goal of those congressmen who want to limit our freedoms is to make bad legislation look as innocuous as possible.

After looking more closely at this amendment, we discovered that the term school was defined elsewhere in HR 6 as a "nonprofit day or residential school." In other words, Miller's amendment would require every teacher in all schools—homeschools, private schools, and public schools—to be certified to teach in the subject or area in which he or she is teaching. For homeschoolers the Miller Amendment was the political equivalent of declaring nuclear war.

Of course, this mandate is connected to federal funding. If a state wanted to continue to receive billions of dollars in federal funding, it would have to guarantee to the U.S. Department of Education that all its teachers in the state were certified to teach. Based on experience, nearly every state would change its laws in order to receive the money. Thus the danger was apparent and real.

Representative Dick Armey (R-TX), seeing the problem, offered an amendment in the House Education Committee to protect home and private schools from the certification requirement by simply exempting them. This amendment, however, was soundly rejected in committee on a party-line vote. This was further evidence of the seriousness of this attack and the intent behind it.

HSLDA Enters the Fray

At this point, on February 14, 1994, Representative Armey's office contacted Home School Legal Defense Association (HSLDA) for our analysis of the Miller amendment. We immediately contacted Representative Miller's office to express our concern and ask for clarifying language. However, Mr. Miller's staff stated that he would not agree to any amendments. With the vote only nine days away, we were forced to take our next step by preparing and sending out a nationwide alert.

That evening our "Fax Alert" outlining a six-step plan of action for contacting Congress was sent to our network of homeschool state leaders in all fifty states. These state leaders, in turn, lit up their phone trees, which were already in place, and got the word spread out further. We also sent our "Fax Alert" to a coalition of conservative and Christian groups representing national organizations throughout the country and to the Christian media. Earlier that day we were able to send our Congressional Action Program (CAP) lobbyists, including a number of HSLDA personnel, down to the Congress to drop off a prepared packet at each of the 435 congressional offices, which urged the congressmen to vote against Miller's amendment. We asked them to respond within three hours to avoid phone calls. Only a few congressmen took us seriously and responded.

The Second Day: Christian Talk Shows Get Involved

By Wednesday morning thousands of homeschoolers were receiving our information on the dangers of HR 6. Tens of thousands of copies of the "Fax Alert" were being photocopied and distributed. On the morning of February 16, hundreds of calls began to pour in to the congressional offices. The onslaught had begun, which was not to stop for the next six days.

Meanwhile, HSLDA contacted homeschoolers from around the local area to descend upon the HSLDA offices in order to stuff the mailing to forty thousand HSLDA members. The information for the mailing had been dropped off to the printers the night before and just began arriving from various printers from around the local area.

By Wednesday afternoon the Christian radio talk shows were beginning to call HSLDA offices and interview Michael Farris, Doug Phillips, myself, and many of the other HSLDA attorneys. Marlin Maddoux, who hosts the radio talk show, *Point of View* which was one of the first to air the HR 6 Alert to a nationwide audience. All that day, while HSLDA was working frantically, the state homeschool leaders were also frantically spreading the news across the country.

Misinformation Spread by Congress

On the third day, the local CAP lobbyists hit the congressmen for a second time with a new packet of updated information, urging them to vote against the Miller amendment in order to protect homeschools and private schools. Included in that packet was a copy of the DeJonge decision by the Michigan Supreme Court, which was handled by HSLDA, declaring teacher certification unconstitutional (see chapter 17). Little did the DeJonges know that their case in Michigan and the eight-year ordeal they went through would help stop the teacher certification amendment to HR 6. (God's ways are not our ways. We wanted to win that case the first year, but it would have had no precedential value.)

Homeschoolers from all around volunteered to deliver the packets to the congressmen. In fact, my eight-month pregnant wife, Tracy Klicka, was one of the homeschool lobbyists that visited various offices. This time when they visited, many of the congressmen's aides invited the CAP lobbyists to sit down and explain their position. The first time the CAP lobbyists were basically ignored. It is amazing what a few thousand phone calls will do.

Of course, the Christian talk shows were still cranking out the information and spreading the alert far and near. In the meantime homeschoolers were continuing to give copies of the alert on HR 6 to their parents and grandparents, neighbors, church members, and people at work. We heard story after story of people who, for the first time, called their congressman in response to the HR 6 attack.

Misinformation was rampant from the congressmen's offices. This is a common tactic of many aides to confuse the public and deflect opposition. Many aides said, "There is no such thing as HR 6." Other aides stated that "HR 6 already passed. Why are you calling us?" Others would say, "HR 6 and the Miller amendment are not intended to hurt homeschools and private schools." There were also many who did not even know about the Miller amendment.

Remember, what an aide explains concerning the Congress's intention really does not matter, ultimately. We would not be able to defend a homeschooler in court by stating, "Charlotte from Representative Smith's office said that this was not intended to apply to homeschools and private schools." The courts, instead, would weigh heavily on the fact that when Dick Armey tried to amend the Miller amendment to exempt homeschools and private schools, it was soundly rejected, evidencing an intent of the Congress to have this apply to homeschools and private schools.

By Friday the Capitol switchboard was completely shut down. The lines to all the congressmen's offices were completely jammed across the country. In fact, many congressmen were returning home for the weekend and were being besieged in town hall meetings. When the congressmen tried to call back to their aides in Washington, DC, they could not get through because the phones were jammed. Homeschoolers began to tie up local campaign offices and other local offices of the congressman.

Homeschoolers Stir Up State Governments to Fight HR 6

Meanwhile another strategy was being employed by the homeschoolers. They were contacting their state representatives and governors in order to get them to oppose the Miller amendment to HR 6. In Idaho, the state legislature, in response to

an instant rally organized by a homeschool mom of over six
hundred homeschoolers on the state capitol steps, passed a
resolution condemning the Miller amendment of HR 6. The
resolution, in part, stated:

> WHEREAS, the private schools and homeschools
> of our state are an integral part of that educational
> delivery system; and
>
> WHEREAS, the State of Idaho recognizes the
> value of our nontraditional, nonpublic schools and can
> verify their contributions; and
>
> WHEREAS, private schools and homeschools
> educate and graduate students at a level of academic
> achievement comparable to and often exceeding state
> and national averages of academic achievement; and
>
> WHEREAS, the local control of education is vital
> to the maintenance of our republican form of govern-
> ment; and
>
> WHEREAS, any forced imposition of federal stan-
> dards jeopardizes the foundation on which our form of
> government is based; and
>
> WHEREAS, it is the position of the State of Idaho
> that the role of the state in educating her people,
> including the preparation and monitoring of those per-
> sonnel who are responsible for providing that educa-
> tion, is reserved to the state, the local school districts
> and to the parents.
>
> NOW, THEREFORE, BE IT RESOLVED by
> the members of the Second Regular Session of the
> Fifty-second Idaho legislature, the Senate and the
> House of Representatives concurring therein, that we
> emphatically urge resistance to and total rejection of
> any attempt by the federal government to interject
> itself into the educational affairs of the nontraditional,
> nonpublic schools of this state.

In Wisconsin, my father, George Klicka, called the Wisconsin state superintendent and convinced him that the Miller amendment to HR 6 would even mess up the public schools. He ended up having his staff contact the Wisconsin delegation of congressmen to oppose this bill. Many members of the Wisconsin legislature immediately prepared a document condemning the Miller amendment of HR 6. In Virginia, homeschoolers convinced Governor George Allen to write a letter to the Virginia delegation of congressmen to oppose the Miller amendment of HR 6.

The following week Doug Phillips and I flew to Texas to hold rallies throughout the state that had been prearranged. As a result of the HR 6 phone blitz, over one thousand people showed up for the Dallas rally alone. Also on Monday, James Dobson of Focus on the Family had Mike Farris speak to his twenty million listeners on the importance of calling their congressmen regarding the Miller Amendment of HR 6. This caused a second huge wave of phone calls!

February 24: The Miracle and the Victory

Then on February 24, we found out that the Democrats were trying to use a rule called the "Closed Rule" to keep any new amendment from being entertained on the floor. This, of course, would have prohibited Dick Armey's amendment, which we had helped draft in order to specifically exempt homeschools and private schools from HR 6. Armey's amendment stated:

> Nothing in this act shall be construed to permit, allow, encourage, or authorize any federal control over any aspect of any private, religious, or homeschool whether or not a homeschool is treated as a private school or homeschool under state law. This section shall not be construed to bar private, religious, or homeschools

from participation in programs or services under this
act.

In a miraculous series of events, Michael Farris was able to
reach Massachusetts homeschool leaders in order to get hundreds of phone calls directed to Congressmen Moakley, who
was head of the Rules Committee, to change it to Open Rule in
order to allow for an amendment. Within hours, Jayme Farris
happened to pick up one of the thousands of phone calls coming into the HSLDA offices. It was an aide from Congressmen
Moakley's office asking us what we wanted. Michael Farris
took the phone and told him that we wanted him to let the
Armey amendment be voted on the floor. Soon the situation
was resolved, and a vote on the Armey amendment was going
to take place. God worked a miracle.

AT&T estimated that approximately one million to one and
a half million phone calls came into Congress over those eight
days. Congressmen and aides alike said that the homeschoolers
set all the records.

C-SPAN showed congressman after congressman tripping
over each other to get to the microphone to make a statement
to America that they, too, supported homeschooling and would
do nothing to harm homeschoolers. Many of them even stated
that it was a constitutional right. Congress voted 424 to 1 to
completely kill the Miller amendment, with only Miller himself voting for it. Then they voted 374 to 54 to pass the Armey
amendment that would exempt homeschools and private schools
from every aspect of HR 6.

This was a miracle. God was merciful to His people. He
answered millions of prayers and blessed the efforts of homeschoolers across the country. We "lit the match" to start a
"raging forest fire" across the nation. Amazingly, we did an
"end run" around the major press. Many of the major television
stations called our offices after we had already won the battle,
asking what this was about and wanting to do a show or a story.

This proves that we can make a difference if we take the time just to call our congressmen on various issues. Ultimately, God is in control, and He reigns.

Biblical Principle Applied

This also points to some important biblical principles, which the homeschoolers used. Luke 18:1–7 explains why so many congressmen who were against homeschools and funded by the National Education Association voted in favor of homeschools. The Bible tells us in Luke 18:1–7:

> Now He was telling them a parable to show that at all times they ought to pray and not to lose heart, saying, "There was in a certain city a judge who did not fear God, and did not respect man. And there was a widow in that city, and she kept coming to him, saying, 'Give me legal protection from my opponent.' And for a while he was unwilling; but afterward he said to himself, 'Even though I do not fear God nor respect man, yet because this widow bothers me, I will give her legal protection, lest by continually coming she wear me out.'" And the Lord said, "Hear what that righteous judge said; now shall not God bring about justice for His elect, who cry to Him day and night, and will He delay long over them?"

The congressmen, many of whom did not respect God or man, gave in to the flood of phone calls because they had been worn out by the homeschoolers' tireless efforts. The National Education Association Government Relations Manager, Michael Edwards, in the magazine *NEA Today*, stated that the defeat of the Miller amendment "probably killed any possibility of any meaningful legislation in the area of national certification and licensure." The agenda of the NEA, with over

$200 million budget, was defeated by the grassroots response of homeschoolers faithful to their Lord. We praise God for how He preserved us all through the HR 6 battle!

Unforeseen Benefit: Homeschoolers Find Favor with Congress

America's homeschoolers astonished Congress with this political counterstrike that was quick, effective, massive, and decisive. The Miller Amendment was buried 424 to 1 in eight days by over a million concerned homeschoolers and their friends. The whole affair quickly became a permanent fixture in the annals of congressional history.

HR 6 put homeschooling on the political radar screen in a big way. "Remember HR 6" is a phrase repeatedly heard in the corridors of the federal government. As a direct result of the HR 6 battle, HSLDA now has working relationships with many offices on Capitol Hill because lawmakers now realize that homeschooling is a force with which they must reckon. Congressional staffs call us to help draft and redraft major legislation involving education, labor, and parental rights issues. On a number of education and parental rights bills, congressional staff members, upon hearing our opposition to certain aspects of the bill, told me, "If the homeschoolers do not want the language, we do not either. We will remove it." As a result, harmful language has been struck out of many bills—"without firing a shot." Many congressmen and senators go out of their way to include protective homeschool amendments to bills. This could not have happened if each individual homeschooling family did not pick up their phone and call Congress in 1994.

Homeschoolers Fight against Clinton's National Test

During the 105th Congress, I obtained a transcript of a meeting the U.S. Department of Education convened with educators from around the country to discuss the creation and implementation of a national test for all students. A university professor from Kansas, John Poggio, made a startling but obvious statement, warning, "What gets tested must be taught." A member of the Delaware Board of Education echoed a similar sentiment. She explained that Delaware would have to adjust its curriculum to fit the national test. The danger was clear. If Clinton was able to create and implement a national test, it would, by default, create a national curriculum. The federal education bureaucracy in Washington, DC, would control the education of our nation's youth in a more profound degree than ever before. We had to fight this test. But how?

After meeting with the president of HSLDA who agreed battling this national test would be a major priority for us, I contacted Congressman Goodling's counsel and told him we would "pullout all stops" if Goodling introduced a bill to cut off funding to Clinton's national test. The counsel said he would talk to Goodling. A week later he explained Goodling was willing to introduce a resolution expressing the sense of the House opposing national testing. I told him there was no way we could get homeschoolers to flood the Congress with calls over a resolution that had no power to stop testing. I asked him to go back to Goodling and explain we could not help him unless he introduced a bill to permanently ban testing. I emphasized then and only then could we deliver calls. A week later Goodling agreed.

Over the next year and a half, the homeschoolers had the opportunity to prove themselves again and again as we at HSLDA sent out nearly thirty-five nationwide fax alerts. And the homeschoolers responded. Repeatedly the homeschoolers flooded the House with calls, and we organized our congressional action program volunteers to visit every office with packets exposing the dangers of the Clinton's national test. In September 1997, we won the first round in the House—296 to 125 to stop funding of all national testing. The homeschoolers had made the ban on testing viable. A key congressional staff admitted, "Without HSLDA and the homeschoolers, this could not have happened!"

In October 1997 the Senate sold us out by compromising the bill allowing a national test. This was unacceptable. We told the leadership we would unleash another nationwide alert. In high stakes negotiating in conference committee, we achieved a temporary victory. We won a *one-year ban* on national testing. This meant the fight would continue in 1998. We hoped the grassroots would not become worn out.

At the beginning of the next year, our champion, Congressman Goodling, introduced HR 2846, a *permanent ban on national testing*. Riding on a wave of calls from the homeschoolers, the testing ban passed in a vote of 242 to 174. The fight, however, was just beginning. We still had to get the bill through the Senate. Our champion in the Senate was John Ashcroft from Missouri. The only problem is that we did not have a "vehicle" to which we could attach our testing amendment.

Meanwhile I attended a meeting with Senator Coverdell's chief of staff where he was recruiting support for the Senator's "A+ Education Savings Accounts" bill. I told him we could not deliver calls unless something was attached that would really motivate homeschoolers to call . . . something like our prohibition on a national test amendment.

A few days later I received a call from Coverdell's office that they would allow the testing amendment to be attached. The rules, however, required that a separate vote be taken on our amendment. We scheduled a lobby day and set appointments with a majority of senators while simultaneously sending out a nationwide alert to homeschoolers to call their two U.S. senators.

I soon received a call from Senator Lott's office, who was the majority leader, telling me there was not a chance that our testing amendment would be successful. They had done a "whip count" earlier in the day and only found thirty senators who would support our testing ban. They urged us not to push for the amendment because we would lose big. Our lobby effort the day before, however, gave us evidence that we were very close to winning the vote. Lott's office told me it was our call. I said we wanted to go forward with the vote. I thought we could win. Besides, it might be our only chance to get a vote that year. In the meantime the homeschoolers were delivering thousands of calls, and God's people were praying.

On April 22, 1998, the vote was scheduled. It was amazing to watch. Ashcroft's amendment permanently banning national testing passed in a vote of fifty-two to forty-seven—far more votes than the thirty votes predicted by Lott's office. The Senate leadership was amazed. The homeschoolers had pulled it off.

Later in June we were contacted by the leadership in both the House and Senate, asking us if we would agree to have our testing amendment removed so that the "A+ Education Savings Account" bill could go to the president in a "clean" form. (The "A+" bill was subsequently vetoed by the president.) We made Speaker Gingrich and Majority Leader Lott promise, in writing, that our testing amendment would be attached to another bill later in the year. In October 1998 they kept their promise in spite of intense threats from President Clinton. We finally won. A permanent ban on national testing was achieved. The homeschoolers made a difference again. They shaped national policy.

Homeschoolers: "The Most Effective Lobbyists"

The national testing battle and HR 6 made a big impression on Congressman Bill Goodling, the powerful Chairman of the Education and Workforce Committee in the U.S. House of Representatives. He readily testifies to the exceptional involvement that homeschoolers have in the political arena. In an address on March 4, 1998, at the National Christian Home School Leadership Summit in Washington, DC, Congressman Goodling explained to the audience that he often asks other groups who they think are the most effective lobbyists on Capitol Hill. After hearing many responses, Goodling replies, "The homeschoolers are the most effective lobbyists." He described their effectiveness even further, "You have heard the saying, 'When E. F. Hutton speaks, people listen.' I have changed that saying around a little bit. I say, 'When the homeschoolers speak, you better listen!'" This simple testimony speaks volumes.

Homeschoolers Repeal Goals 2000

On November 17, 1999, Chairman of the Education and Workforce Committee, Congressman Bill Goodling along with the House and Senate leadership reached an agreement with President Clinton on the Education/Labor/HHS Appropriations bill. The bill was signed into law by the president on November 30. The biggest victory was the inclusion of specific language in this appropriations bill insisted on by the Home School Legal Defense Association (HSLDA), which officially repeals the worst aspects of Goals 2000 effective September 30, 2000.

Largely because of the efforts of homeschoolers, Goals 2000, as a mandate on the states, is dead. This big government failure, representing all that is wrong with the federal

Department of Education's manipulation of our children, is finally and officially dead. With the federal "seed" money cut off, the troublesome Goals 2000 programs established in the states will likely cease to exist.

Goals 2000 was an attempt by the federal government bureaucracy to set national standards of education that would usher in centralized control of our nation's youth. The emphasis of the Goals 2000 agenda was to create a climate of political correctness focusing on changing the attitudes of children rather than improving academic skills (i.e., reading, writing, and arithmetic). This methodology is called outcome-based education.

Since 1994 we at the National Center of Home Education, the federal lobby arm of HSLDA, lobbied for this repeal. We continued to lobby against Goals 2000 even when the issue dropped off most other organizations' radar screens.

In 1997 and 1998 we lobbied the Congress and orchestrated nationwide alerts in opposition to Goals 2000 by supporting the Gorton Amendment. The Gorton Amendment would have given a block grant of $10 billion of federal education money directly to the states effectively ending all the federal programs such as Goals 2000. In a surprising turn of events, on April 22, 1998, the homeschoolers, almost single-handedly, passed the Gorton Amendment in a vote of fifty to forty-nine. Unfortunately, the congressional session ended before it could proceed any further.

Other lobbying efforts included organizing visits for eighteen hundred homeschoolers from around the country with over 250 congressional offices in conjunction with our Proclaim Liberty Rally, September 23, 1999. This was one of the largest lobbying events ever organized on Capitol Hill.

Earlier in the year, Congressman Goodling did not reauthorize Goals 2000 in response to a request from HSLDA, and the Appropriations Committee would not designate any funds for it. However, a month before the signing of the appropriations bill, the National Center received a tip from a congressional contact that Goals 2000 was to be funded regardless. Mike Farris, president of HSLDA, gave the marching orders to the National Center staff to take action.

After contacting several key offices, the National Center was told "Clinton wants Goals 2000. It is his pet project. There is no way we can repeal Goals 2000."

Immediately I contacted a dozen key members of the Senate on appropriations and education committees and Senator Trent Lott's office explaining homeschoolers' uniform opposition to Goals 2000 and insisting on its repeal. I also met with Congressmen Goodling, securing a promise that he would not settle for anything less than the repeal of Goals 2000. At a key juncture in the negotiations between House and Senate leadership, the Congressional Action Program, led by Caleb Kershner, directed a targeted national alert generating hundreds of calls from homeschoolers to key leadership offices. Doug Domenech, director of governmental affairs, who works out of our office on Capitol Hill, met with members of the House leadership, insisting on killing Goals 2000.

Finally, the word came. Goals 2000, as applied to the states, was specifically repealed in an amendment added during negotiations with the president. This ended all the funding to the states for Goals 2000 programs. The states no longer have to submit reports to the secretary of education seeking his approval for their Goals 2000 plans or coordinate their states' Goals 2000 programs with school-to-work programs. No longer are progress reports to be submitted to the secretary of education and all federal accountability measures are ended. The states do not have to implement national, federal education standards, giving them back local control.

A staffer of the Educational and Workforce Committee, involved in the final negotiations, remarked, "If HSLDA had not brought up the Goals 2000 issue, it would have never seen the light of day."

The fight against Goals 2000 was a long battle for homeschoolers. As one Capitol Hill staffer said, "The homeschoolers kept up a constant drumbeat." This constitutes another example of the effective and tireless work of homeschoolers. Just moms and dads who care and are willing to make a difference. We ultimately thank God for His grace and mercy in all of these situations.

National Homeschool Week Declared

In January 1999 I was contacted by Senator Ashcroft's office for advice on how to fulfill a request he received from the Missouri Families for Home Education who asked him to try to pass a national homeschool resolution. I readily agreed to help. We had one senator down and ninety-nine to go. I worked first on drafting the resolution and chose the week of September 19–25, 1999, to coincide with our planned Proclaim Liberty Rally and Lobby Day on Capitol Hill. I personally lobbied about thirty-five key U.S. senators (many members of the judiciary), and Ashcroft's office lobbied many others. In one of the offices, I was told it was "impossible to pass a resolution anymore."

Undeterred, we moved forward. We called upon four state homeschool leaders to deliver a few calls to four key Democrats on the judiciary at a key juncture. Senator Lott agreed with us, along with Senator Hatch, to push this through.

God once again had the homeschoolers find favor with our government. Our U.S. Senate Home School Resolution (Sen. Res. 183) was passed on September 14 by unanimous consent. This means the week of September 19–25 was officially National Home Education Week. This was truly a historic development.

It is particularly amazing in light of the fact the Senate rarely passes resolutions and liberal senators like Ted Kennedy and Charles Schumer did not object. It only took one senator to object to kill the resolution. In addition, it had to pass the Senate Judiciary Committee first where we were told they apparently debated a half hour before passing it unanimously on to the Senate.

Here is the text of the resolution, which can be used to demonstrate to governors, school districts, congressmen, and media the legitimacy of homeschooling.

Senate Resolution 183

IN THE SENATE OF THE UNITED STATES

Mr. ASHCROFT (for himself, Mr. ABRAHAM, Mr. COCHRAN, Mr. COVERDELL, Mr. DeWINE, Mr. GORTON, Mr. GRAMS, Mr. HAGEL, Mr. HELMS, Mr. INHOFE, Mr. GREGG, Mr. SMITH of New Hampshire, Mr. SMITH of Oregon, Mr. THURMOND) submitted the following resolution; which was referred to the Committee on the Judiciary:

September 14, 1999

Designating the week beginning on September 19, 1999, and ending on September 25, 1999, as National Home Education Week.

Whereas the United States is committed to excellence in education;

Whereas the United States recognizes the importance of family participation and parental choices in pursuit of that excellence;

Whereas the United States recognizes the fundamental right of parents to

direct the education and upbringing of
their children;

Whereas parents want their children to
receive a first-class education;

Whereas training in the home
strengthens the family and guides
children in setting the highest standards
for their lives which are essential
elements to the continuity of morality
in our culture;

Whereas homeschooling families
contribute significantly to the cultural
diversity important to a healthy society;

Whereas the United States has a
significant number of parents who teach
their own children at home;

Whereas home education was proven
successful in the lives of George
Washington, Patrick Henry, John
Quincy Adams, John Marshall, Robert
E. Lee, Booker T. Washington,
Thomas Edison, Abraham Lincoln,
Franklin Roosevelt, Woodrow Wilson,
Mark Twain, John Singleton Copley,
William Carey, Phyllis Wheatley, and
Andrew Carnegie;

Whereas homeschool students exhibit
self-confidence and good citizenship
and are fully prepared academically to
meet the challenges of today's society;

Whereas dozens of contemporary studies continue to confirm that children who are educated at home score exceptionally well on nationally normed achievement tests;

Whereas a March 1999 study by the Educational Resources Information Center Clearinghouse on Assessment and Evaluation at the University of Maryland found that homeschool students taking the Iowa Test of Basic Skills or the Tests of Achievement and Proficiency scored in the 70th to 80th percentiles among all the students nationwide who took those exams, and 25 percent of homeschooled students were studying at a level one or more grades above normal for their age;

Whereas studies demonstrate that homeschoolers excel in college with the average grade point average of homeschoolers exceeding the college average; and

Whereas United States home educators and home instructed students should be recognized and celebrated for their efforts to improve the quality of education: Now, therefore, be it

Resolved,

That the week beginning on September 19, 1999, and ending on

September 25, 1999, is designated as
National Home Education Week. The
President is authorized and requested
to issue a proclamation recognizing
the contributions that homeschooling
families have made to the Nation.

Passed the Senate September 16, 1999.

I believe one of the main reasons the Home School Resolution
passed against all odds is because homeschoolers stayed involved
by regularly and repeatedly contacting Congress.

Study Confirms Involvement of Homeschoolers in Politics

In the 1996 National Household Education Survey (NHES),
the U.S. Department of Education's National Center for
Education Statistics surveyed 9,393 parents of school-age children. The survey asked numerous questions about the extent of
family involvement in a variety of civic activities. Some of the
questions asked whether the parent had voted recently, telephoned or wrote a public official, signed a petition, attended
public meetings, contributed to political campaigns, participated in community service activities, worked for a political
cause, or participated in a boycott in the past twelve months.
The survey differentiated public schoolers from homeschoolers
and both religious and nonreligious private schoolers. Christian
Smith and David Sikkink of the Department of Sociology at
the University of North Carolina analyzed the data, which was
published in 1999.[1]

By comparing differences in family participation in these
various forms of civic involvement, Smith and Sikkink found
that homeschool families and private school families are consistently *more involved* in all of the civic activities examined

than are families with children in public schools. In fact, by an average margin of 9.3 percent the private and homeschool families are more likely than the public school families to engage in any listed forms of civic participation. Up to 13 percent more private and homeschoolers have given money to political causes, and up to 15 percent more have voted in recent elections and telephoned elected officials. An amazing 26 percent more private and homeschool families are members of community groups and volunteer at local organizations.

The researchers conclude that homeschoolers and private schoolers are "definitely not the isolated recluses that critics suggest they might be. It is rather the public schooling families that are clearly the least civically involved of all the schooling types." Smith and Sikkink closed the article by stating:

> The empirical evidence is clear and decisive: private schoolers and homeschoolers are considerably more involved in the public square than are public schoolers—even when the effects of differences in education, income, and other related factors are removed from the equation. Indeed, we have reason to believe that the organizations and practices involved in private and homeschooling, in themselves, tend to foster public participation in civic affairs . . . the challenges, responsibilities, and practices that private schooling and home education normally entail for their participants may actually help reinvigorate America's civic culture and the participation of our citizens in our public square.

When reviewing both the anecdotal and the empirical evidence, homeschoolers clearly are not separating themselves and sheltering their families from their "sociopolitical" duties. Homeschool families, per capita, are participating at a much higher rate in the life of their communities, states, and nation than their counterparts in the public schools. Homeschoolers are simply following Christ's command to love their neighbors as themselves. That love means they must be involved in our culture and government in order to preserve liberty and our God-given rights for all citizens.

Homeschoolers Do Make a Difference

All of the accomplishments above would not have been possible without the grace of God working through homeschoolers who insisted on protecting their cherished liberties. I encourage each homeschooler to continue to fight the good fight no matter how high the odds are stacked against us. Every call, every letter, every personal visit makes a difference. The persistent widow of Luke 18 was able to obtain justice because she refused to give up even though she was the only one fighting. The millions of "persistent widows" in the homeschool movement of today can accomplish even more. You can make a difference.

✳15

Government Homeschooling: A Trojan Horse

"I have sworn to the Lord God Most High, possessor of heaven and earth, that I will not take a thread or a sandal thong, or anything that is yours, lest you should say, I have made Abram rich."

GENESIS 14:22–23

There is an old adage, "If you can't beat them, join them." The education establishment tried to beat the home-schoolers but failed. So the public school authorities are trying to get the homeschoolers back into public school by creating virtual public schools in people's homes. If they are successful to convince private homeschoolers to enroll in a virtual public school program, they win.

How do they win if a homeschooler enrolls in a virtual charter school? The public school district wins in three ways.

First, the school district receives $5000 to $7000 per child for about $1500 or less of service. Sounds like a good deal.

Second, the public school district gains back *control* over the homeschooler. The homeschooled child becomes a public school student that must do the school district's bidding. Furthermore, the homeschool must be supervised by public school certified teachers. The homeschooler must use the public school curriculum or some secular program approved by the public school. The family loses its privacy since all their children's records are kept by the public school. In addition, the homeschool student has to take the state assessment—designed for the public schools.

Third, the homeschool becomes *secularized.* Christian homeschooling becomes emasculated and compromised. Homeschoolers have to pass the secular state assessment and be tested on all the secular curriculum along the way. What gets tested is what gets taught. Who has time or the money to teach and buy Christian materials in addition to covering all the required secular materials? Certainly, you get a free government computer. But are the freebies worth the significant loss of freedom? Should we think with our pocketbook or stand on principle?

This book is filled with stories of how God's people cried to Him to be free from supervision by state certified teachers, required home visits, and curriculum approval by secular public school authorities and the right to teach their children according to the Word of God. How can we so easily and voluntarily go back to that bondage and control when so many have fought so hard and sacrificed so much to make us free? Is money worth such a high price? I do not know about you, but as for me and my house, we are going to serve the Lord in our homeschool. We will not go back to Egypt.

Yet, private homeschoolers, in the name of saving money, are enrolling their children in these virtual government schools in droves. In fact, it is estimated 80 percent of the virtual public school students are former private homeschoolers.

Even in independent-minded states like Idaho and Alaska and others, homeschoolers are enrolling by the thousands. They are attending the government homeschool conferences (where Christ or God cannot be mentioned) and receiving the secular, government homeschool newsletters. They no longer go to the Christian homeschool conventions. If anything can destroy the Christian homeschool movement, this will.

We need to "just say no" to the government virtual schools or warn our homeschool friends of this "Trojan Horse."

Let us look at some more facts concerning these virtual charter schools to build our resolve not to participate.

The Temptation of Money

It seems that everyone with school-aged children is talking about virtual charter schools. Many are thinking, *This deal is too good to pass up: I can have my children educated outside of the public school system and have the government still pay the bill!* Charter schools along with educational vouchers appear to be harmless since parents are only reclaiming their tax money. Is it really that simple? Let's look at virtual charter schools more closely, examining them from the perspective of freedom rather than asking, "What 'freebies' can we receive from the government?" To accurately understand this issue, we must first define the terms.

What are charter schools? Public schools establish a "charter" listing the school's mission, educational program, and methods of assessment. Charter schools answer to the state or local school board for assessing students and verifying academic progress. Charter schools are completely government funded.

Charter schools now exist in thirty-seven states, the District of Columbia, and Puerto Rico. The Center for Education Reform estimates on its Web site that there are more than two thousand charter schools operating with more that 500,000 enrolled in these schools.

Supporters of charter schools claim that creating competition in the education marketplace will result in more options and a higher quality education. The idea is that if public charter schools draw enough students away from regular public schools, the resulting lack of funds will force public schools to come up with creative alternatives to bring students (and the funding that comes with them) back into the system.

Additionally, proponents claim that charter schools provide an innovative alternative to traditional schooling, allowing creative approaches to teaching, free from the strict rules and regulations of the public school system. They point out that charter and virtual charter schools provide a protective environment, that is, a smaller "private" school or home environment, where students can pursue their own styles of learning.

Charter schools operate on taxpayer dollars, so there is virtually no cost to students. Other often cited advantages are an accredited high school diploma, free computer, Internet access, software, and support by certified teachers. So what's the problem?

I believe the soul of the homeschooling movement is at stake. How we respond to virtual charter schools and vouchers will determine the extent homeschooling remains free from government controls in the future.

Freedom Is the Answer

Since 1983 HSLDA has been working hard to win the right of families to homeschool with minimal regulations. As recounted in this book, many of these battles took place in the courts and legislatures throughout the country. Many families faced fines, jail, and even the threat of the state's removing their children from the home. The families held onto their convictions, and

God honored them in an incredible way. It is now legal to homeschool in every state.

The battle to maintain this freedom continues as some school officials harass homeschooling families with illegal requirements and teachers' unions and other professional education organizations have legislation introduced to restrict homeschool freedoms. A survey by the *American School Board Journal*, published in February 1997, of more than one thousand public school executives found that 71 percent of superintendents whose state or district set standards for homeschoolers did not believe homeschoolers were regulated enough. Ninety-five percent of all the superintendents and principals in the survey believed anything else is better than homeschooling.

The National Education Association passes a resolution each year condemning homeschooling and urging for legislation to be enacted in each state to require that homeschooled children be taught by certified teachers and have their curriculum approved by the state. Prejudice against homeschooling has not disappeared.

Despite these efforts, private homeschooling, with no help from the government, is thriving. Research shows that homeschoolers on average are academically above average from the elementary level all the way through college. All of this success has been achieved without government money. We have had many victories before Congress and the state legislatures because we are not asking for a handout but simply to be left alone.

This liberty is at risk, however, if homeschoolers begin drinking from the public trough. These are the same state governments that once heavily restricted or prohibited homeschooling altogether. If homeschooling families take government money or services through virtual charter schools, they will become dependent on government money and subject to increasing government regulation. Public schools and the state will once again acquire power to dictate homeschoolers' curriculum, teacher qualifications, and methods.

This is not idle conjecture. It is already happening.

Government Homeschooling in Alaska

The old adage "There is no such thing as a free government service," is true. Government money always comes with strings. Governments will demand accountability for funding. States want to be assured that no fraud is involved and that the monies are not used for an improper purpose. The government has the responsibility to spend taxpayers' money frugally. For officials to give money to homeschoolers to participate in charter schools without any conditions would be irresponsible.

Virtual charter schools must be accountable to the state or local school authorities. In addition to dictating the curriculum and teaching styles, virtual charter schools can impose requirements on the parents beyond that which is required by state homeschool laws in order to assure that the parents are teaching the children "appropriately."

Take, for example, an Alaska program that typifies many virtual charter school programs springing up throughout the country. On June 4, 1997, Alaska enacted the best homeschool law in the nation. Alaska's law has no teaching qualifications for parents, no regulation at any level of government, no notice to anyone of the parents' decision to conduct the home education, no registration with the state, no reporting to anyone of any information about the home education program, no testing of the children, no required subjects, and no evaluation of the program by anyone.

In the same month the Galena School District launched a statewide correspondence study program known as the Interior Distance Education of Alaska (IDEA). According to Galena, school officials want "to provide educational, emotional, intellectual, and financial support to those who would like to work in partnership with a public school district." Despite having more freedom than any other state, a majority of homeschooling families are choosing to enroll their children in IDEA.

Carol Simpson, current Alaska Department of Education homeschool program coordinator, said IDEA was "wildly successful, going from zero students in mid-June 1997 to 1,157 students ten weeks later."

Families who enroll their children in IDEA are provided curriculum materials, use of a computer with access to the Internet, and assistance from a certified teacher, among other services. However, public funds may not be used to purchase curriculum materials for teaching core subjects if the materials are distinctively religious in content.

The dangers of these types of government homeschool programs are apparent in a September 11, 2001, letter from Carol Simpson:

> When IDEA started in summer of 1997, we began from the premise that homeschooling parents know their kids best and should be free to use any curricular materials that they deemed most appropriate. We bought nearly anything anyone wanted, including Bob Jones, Alpha Omega, A Beka, etc. By November of that year, the Department of Education (DOE) made a new regulation prohibiting school districts from purchasing religious curricular materials. . . .

> The Attorney General of the State of Alaska advised us that we could not purchase anything that is an advocacy of a sectarian or denominational doctrine. . . .

Simpson then proceeded to tell a homeschool speaker, that IDEA had invited to speak at their five government homeschool conferences that the speaker could not sell her books at the conferences. Simpson explained:

I realize that your books are not "Christian books" and that any religious expression in them is incidental, not the focus of the book. However, we must be strict in our obedience to the letter and spirit of the law, honoring our governmental authorities. . . . We must be careful not to give the appearance of promoting sectarian materials. As such, we cannot allow you to sell or promote these books in workshops that we are paying for. . . . Also, we want to avoid the appearance of promoting sectarian materials through your workshops as well. Please do not include references to faith or an emphasis on the inclusion of Biblical teaching in your presentations.

Alaska has now created an approved list of secular homeschool books. Notice also from the letter how gradual the changes have been. At first, the government paid for Christian homeschool textbooks. When 75 percent of the homeschoolers in Alaska became dependent on the government funds, the rules changed.

Simpson's letter plainly explains the danger to homeschoolers' freedom posed by these government homeschool programs. Some parents have told me they circumvent this in various ways and still use the state government's money to buy Christian textbooks. Dependence on government money is encouraging people to be deceptive.

Refusal to reimburse for any religious curriculum is not the only problem. Additionally, students in grades four, five, seven, and nine must take the standardized tests that Alaska uses for public school students at a test site designated by public school officials, and the tests must be administered by a certified teacher approved by the Galena School District. All IDEA students are required to take the Alaska Benchmark Examination in grades three, six, and eight. As further evaluation of the student, each parent must report to Galena School District the progress of all students each semester.

In final analysis the "freebies" are not free after all. The price is too high—a gradual but steady loss of freedom, control, and independence.

Homeschooling in Name Only

Despite all of the attractions for homeschoolers, virtual charter schools are supporting homeschooling in name only. Parents who enroll their children in these virtual charter schools are actually creating small public schools in their home.

Recently a Christian teacher in a large "brick and mortar" charter school program in Colorado told me that many Christian families are using the program and enrolling their children in the school. I asked her if the teachers could teach the Bible. She said, "No, but we can teach virtues."

"Are you allowed to teach the children about salvation?" I inquired.

"We are not supposed to," she replied.

In Milwaukee, Wisconsin, an educational voucher program that has been operating for several years has been touted as one of the best examples of a successful government educational program. What many do not realize is that any Christian school that enrolls students who are using the government vouchers must comply with more than three hundred additional regulations. Two requirements even prohibit the Christian school from mandating that these children with vouchers attend chapel or Bible class.

Homeschool parents originally fought to be separate from the public schools in order to have the right to choose the curriculum that they believe would be best for their children. Many parents removed their children from the public school system because of the non-Christian curriculum. So why would they want to go back to the same humanistic material? But this is happening with homeschoolers who enroll in charter schools or public school programs for homeschooling.

With significant restrictions on curriculum choices, parents in charter schools also face limited ability to incorporate creative teaching methods. The specific curriculum requirements often demand parents to "stick to the schedule" dictated by the public school rather than use creativity in complimenting their child's learning style.

HSLDA members who have participated in virtual charter schools complain of this very thing. As one California homeschooler shared:

> Having been in a car accident and having been limited in my physical capabilities, I found myself not as able to get my kids out as much as I felt they needed. Home educating independently for three years, I was reluctant to try a charter school, but I thought, *How bad could it be? I'd have access to educational materials and my children would have an opportunity to meet other home-educated children.* At first it was exciting, though enrolling was very institutional. Then it came time to meet with a teacher. We sat and talked, and I stated that I had been home educating independently for three years and was not interested in meeting weekly and that I would bring their work in monthly as they are required to turn in work at least monthly. That worked out great the first month. The next month, however, the teacher wanted to plan out what we'd be doing for the following month. After being independent, I was not interested in being told what my kids would be learning, so we agreed we'd do the work we wanted and would write up the plans retrospectively. This was not ideal but doable since the kids enjoyed the Monday co-op (classes) and field trips.
>
> The next time we met, I took the kids' work but left the children behind. I never read or signed anything stating that my children had to be present. To

me, turning in the work was the requirement. It soon became apparent that the teachers were required to talk to the children at these visits and assess them not only on their academics but also on their physical appearance . . . looking for signs of abuse and/or neglect at their discretion. . . .

Make no doubt about it, a charter school is a public school. . . . It's homeschooling in technical terms only. Enrolling in a charter school will give you more freedom than the traditional public schools but still strips you of the independent responsibility of educating our own children. It is still an institution, which believes we need interference from trained government agents, that we are incapable of educating our own children.

When this mother finally tried to remove her children from the charter school program, she was contacted repeatedly by child welfare services, demanding that she place her children in public school.

The Virtual Charter School Experience of One Family

Here is a typical example of an experience of a private homeschooler when they join the virtual school—they feel the strings tighten. This account below is by Vicki Herdt who resides in Boise, Idaho, and is a homeschool mother of three.

I have been a homeschooling mom for over two years now. I have a third-grade student and a kindergartner this year. Homeschooling has offered my family flexibility in schedule, curriculum, and placement unparalleled in any public or private school I've investigated. Last year a new kid appeared on the scene— Idaho Virtual Academy (IDVA). I have heard all the

arguments for and against virtual schools, so
I am writing to offer you my personal experience last
fall with IDVA.

I attended a very interesting and attractive orienta-
tion/information seminar for IDVA last August. I saw
impressive demonstrations of the online curriculum,
lots of attractive books and manipulative, access to
experienced educators, and the ultimate bait: a free
computer. All of these wonderful items are offered free
of charge to families of IDVA students. Who could
resist? I walked away from the meeting full of enthusi-
asm for free everything and an excellent education for
my child.

IDVA experienced the growing pains typical of a
charter school in its first year. There were problems
acquiring the materials necessary to follow the curriculum, but the school worked very hard to accom-
modate families and ship things as quickly as possible.
Our first problem occurred when the promised fourth-
grade math didn't materialize—my child was given
second-grade material across the board. It took a
month to get the level of math he was given; it was
still probably a bit below his level, but we gave up that
battle and let him do fourth-grade math.

I really started having difficulties when the materials started arriving. We received hard copies of the
PDF files required to meet curriculum demands (we
still hadn't received all of the computer by the beginning of November). There were over twelve hundred
pages of language arts (no, that's not a typo), over nine
hundred pages of second-grade math (not including
the actual textbook), almost three hundred pages of
history, one hundred eleven pages for science, and
almost three hundred pages for music. These were
just the worksheets! I had heart failure. My child is a

kinesthetic learner and not very fond of busy work or worksheets—especially not over fifteen a day!

My next difficulty came regarding the number of hours allowed for assorted subjects. We were originally told as long as the hours were for subjects in the school curriculum, we could log the actual hours spent on the different subjects. My child was taking private chess lessons, piano, swimming, and practicing all of these subjects daily. After logging in these subjects under math (logic, analysis, critical thinking skills), music, and PE, we were suddenly told that at public schools children were only allowed two hours a week total for all these subjects, so that's all my child was allowed to log (we spend at least five hours a week on music alone!). Eventually we were allowed two hours a week for each subject but still far less than we really logged in.

Which leads me to the next problem: public schools are drowning in a sea of bureaucracy. IDVA is no different. We were suddenly informed that instead of one official test per school year, we would be taking at least four. We had to log hours every day if possible so the school's funding was validated. We needed to test our child's progress through the online tests every day in every subject taught (teaching alone was not enough—we spent at least an hour a day on the Internet trying to slog through the tests!). We were supposed to submit a calendar at the beginning of the school year for every day we would school and every day of vacation or family time, or we would be placed on a default schedule. I actually spent as much time wrestling with the computer part of IDVA as I spent on one-to-one time with my student. A real time sink!

In December the school's curriculum provider decided to rework all of the online curriculum. We

were suddenly not nearly as far along as the computer
originally told us we were. My child finally blew a
sprocket at trying to double up on all the work to reach
the 80 percent completion the school was asking for.
Then the IDVA teacher started wanting to speak with
my child alone . . . without me. . . . Why, I wonder?

IDVA certainly was not a successful foray into public education for my family. I have heard many people,
especially those who have pulled their child from
brick and mortar schools, have been quite pleased with
their experiences at IDVA. I think it fills a real need
for families looking for public school accountability,
particularly during their first year of having a school
at home. Visual learners would be better served by
the IDVA curriculum than would children with other
learning preferences. And I have to admit, the manipulative and books provided by IDVA are very nice.

In the long run, however, homeschooling provides
my family with so much more scope for customization
in learning that IDVA felt more like a straight jacket
than a blessing for us. My first child began enjoy-
ing school again after we quit "public school" and has
made truly phenomenal progress with just our little
homeschool curriculum. I will never doubt again that
my child is receiving an even better education than any
institution could ever offer him, right here at home.

Is government money worth it? Aren't these the same types
of controls homeschoolers cast off with much sacrifice and risk
in the 1980s? Are we willing to forge new chains to limit our
liberty? Most homeschool parents want to be free to educate
their children without this kind of government oversight.

Federal Court Insists Charter Schools Are "Public Schools"

Homeschooling is the largest successful education reform movement in America, but many people outside the home-school movement hope that charter schools may transform education, too. A recent federal district court case in Ohio provides a cautionary note.

The Riverside Community School in Cincinnati is a charter school, which fired one of its teachers in 2001. The teacher sued for violation of her civil rights, and the school attempted to dismiss the suit by arguing that it was a private school and not a unit of government. The judge ruled that an Ohio charter school is a "state actor," and therefore is bound by the same rules that apply to the government.

The court used four legal tests to determine when private conduct may be considered "state action." The four tests that the court identified were: (1) the public function test, (2) the state compulsion test, (3) the symbiotic relationship/nexus test, and (4) the "entwinement" test.

The court concluded that "free, public education, whether provided by public or private actors, is an historical, exclusive, and traditional state function." This satisfied the "public function test." By "free, public education," the court presumably means education funded by taxpayers, as is currently the practice under Ohio's charter school law. The court also found that Riverside Community School failed the "entwinement" test writing, "Private conduct may become so entwined with governmental policies or so impregnated with a governmental character as to become subject to the constitutional limitations on state actors." The judge concluded that Riverside had been granted the authority to provide free public education to all students in a nondiscriminatory manner. According to the judge, no other entity has been so mandated by the state of Ohio besides local school districts. As such, the judge found that Riverside's conduct was so "entwined with governmental policies" that the court was forced to consider them "public actors subject to the constitutional limitations on state actors."

For homeschooling parents who are committed to providing a distinctively religious education, this case is troubling. The court also notes a Michigan charter school case where the Michigan court assumed, without any need for analysis, that a Michigan charter school is subject to the "separation of church and state" provisions because it was a public school.

Education Officials Warn against Government Vouchers

Although we differ with the philosophy of many of the former federal secretaries of education, their statements are valuable since they evidence the intent behind government funding of private education. Lamar Alexander, Secretary of Education under former President George H. W. Bush, explained the transformation of private education that was publicly funded when he said, "A public school would become any school that receives students who brought with them public monies . . ."

Richard Riley, who served as former Secretary of Education under Bill Clinton, had strong reservations about vouchers and government funding of private education. No doubt, his reason for opposing government funding of private education was mainly to protect the current public school system, but he has some interesting warnings for private schools:

> You have to be accountable with public tax dollars
> . . . when it comes to taking federal tax dollars and giv-
> ing those to parents and then having the absence of
> accountability as far as their children's education. . . .
> If you have accountability, then you lose the private
> and parochial nature of those schools. . . . It's bad,
> we think, for private schools and parochial schools.

It takes away from them the private and parochial strength, which is being totally free from any federal regulations. . . .

[Vouchers] threaten the very nature of private and parochial schools. It makes them less private and less parochial.

Chester Finn Jr., former Assistant Secretary of Education under Ronald Reagan, declared that government controls were inevitable: "There is no doubt in my mind that there will be some new regulations with voucher plans."

If the highest public school bureaucrats in the nation recognize the loss of freedom government funding brings to private education, how can we deny it?

The Experience of Other Nations

Other nations have experienced the effects of government funding. Private education has almost completely disappeared overseas.

For example, in Australia, over a period of ten years, private schools and Christian schools took more and more government funds. The regulations gradually increased until today the differences between public schools and private schools have become nonexistent. Homeschooling is the last bastion of educational freedom in Australia.

In South Africa, the 1996 National Education Act officially transformed all publicly funded private schools into public schools.

In Alberta, Canada, homeschoolers enjoyed more liberty than almost any of the other provinces. Then several years ago legislation was passed giving homeschoolers $500 per child in government funds. The next year one of the most restrictive legislative bills was passed, implementing regulations for homeschoolers. When asked why, the Minister of Education stated that if they were giving money to homeschoolers, they had to know who they are and have certain standards. These regulations apply to all homeschoolers—not only those who receive the government funding.

Many European countries have experienced similar scenarios with government-funded private schools.

Virtual Charter Schools Increase Taxes

Charter school proponents claim that the resulting competition between educational providers will drive education costs down while increasing the quality of education offered.

Charter schools do not charge tuition but are funded according to their enrollment. Charter school students may be eligible for both state and federal funding. There are over eight million children who do not attend public schools in this country. If these children suddenly began using money from the state's treasury for their schooling, taxes would have to be raised to generate the additional revenue. It is highly unlikely that public schools would reduce their budgets in order to provide funds for private schools. Today nonpublic school parents are being double taxed; they pay tuition for both public school children and their own children. With virtual charter schools, these parents would be triple taxed. In addition to footing the bill for their own children's tuition, they would pay for the public school students and the students participating in charter schools.

According to Eddy Jeans, finance director at the Alaska Department of Education, Galena School District received $15,020,053 in state funds for fiscal year 2000. Of this amount $14,093,136, or $4,104 per pupil, was received for the 3,434 students in IDEA. The balance of the funds in the amount of $926,917 was intended for the 226 students who receive classroom instruction as regular on-site students.

Each student enrolled in IDEA receives an allotment averaging $1,600 per year to cover curriculum and related expenses.

Considering the $4,104 per pupil received from the state, Galena School District enjoys a gross profit of over $2,500 per pupil in IDEA for a total of $8,585,000 for fiscal year 2000. What amount of this profit is reduced by IDEA administrative expenses is unknown, but there is no question that this is a moneymaking enterprise for Galena School District.

In Texas, a two-year pilot virtual charter school is being established. Texas Virtual Charter School would receive the tax dollars as a subcontractor to Houston Gateway Academy, a charter school. This homeschool component of Gateway Academy will serve students in kindergarten, first and second grades. By September 26, 2001, the virtual charter school had so far enrolled about three hundred in central and southeast Texas, including Houston and Austin. The virtual charter school could receive $5,000 for each homeschooled student.

Yet research has found the median cost for a homeschool program is only about $400.17. This sounds like a major waste of our tax dollars.

Choosing Freedom

Parents are buying into a free homeschool program and "de-Christianizing" their education in the process. They are trading a mess of pottage for a precious gift of freedom.

In Alaska alone, nearly 80 percent of the homeschoolers have bought into a government homeschool program that now offers government homeschool conferences and a government homeschool newsletter. *Christ* and *Jesus* have been lively excluded and are censored from being mentioned at their conferences and in their newsletter. Homeschoolers are told that they cannot use the money they receive from the school district to put toward Christian books that mention Christ or God. As a result, homeschoolers are resorting to cheating and deceiving by trying to use the money for Christian books but not telling the government. It is sad to see the level that parents are stooping in order to receive a "free" education for their children. Granted, it is better than having their child attend the public school, but why bring the public school into the home?

Furthermore, there comes a problem with potential Fourth Amendment concerns. Right now social workers have the authority to go into public schools to talk to them, interview them, and interrogate them about alleged child abuse. With families enrolling their children in a virtual government school program, their children become public school students. They use public school textbooks and a public school computer. When a social worker comes knocking at their door to talk to their children, will they still have the same authority to say no?

We need to realize that God has risen the homeschool movement out of nothing, and it has a proven track record of education success without help from the government. We need to continue to cry out the warning not to go back to Egypt. The following scenario should serve as a warning to us. This is the way of great civilizations and the way of great movements. Historian and Scottish jurist, Sir Alexander Fraser Tyler, wrote in the early 1800s:

> The average of the world's greatest civilizations has
> been 200 years. These nations have progress through
> the following sequence: from bondage to spiritual faith,
> from spiritual faith to great courage, from courage to
> liberty, from liberty to abundance, from abundance
> to selfishness, from selfishness to complacency, from
> complacency to apathy, from apathy to dependency,
> and from dependency back into bondage.

Homeschoolers need to be careful they are not undermined from within. We need to depend on God rather than government or we will return to bondage.

Let us not give the government an excuse to regulate us and return us under its yoke. Neither let us allow the government to take credit for the homeschoolers success because it gives us money. Abraham in Genesis 14 was offered a government handout by the King of Sodom whom he and his men rescued from an invading army. Abraham simply replied, "I have sworn to the LORD God Most High, possessor of heaven and earth, that I will not take a thread or a sandal thong or anything that is yours, lest you should say, 'I have made Abram rich'" (Gen. 14:22–23).

Government schools are failing in many places. They are not providing students with the moral training necessary in any society, and students continue to fall short of academic standards. Why would homeschool parents wish to support this system by accepting funding to participate in it?

In spite of the enticements offered by virtual charter schools, parents should realize that virtual charter school programs are simply creating little public schools in our homes. The teaching may take place in a private home, but the government is pulling the strings.

The soul of homeschooling has its foundation built on the incredible sacrifices of many parents who risked all in order to win the right to be free from suffocating government control and to be free to teach their children according to God's ways and in obedience to His commands. God honors those who honor Him and who trust in His sovereign love and power.

We do not need the government's "free" money. The price is too high.

※ 16

Homeschoolers Impact the World from Their Home Computers

"Truly I say to you, to the extent that you did it
to one of these brothers of Mine,
even the least of them, you did it to Me."
MATTHEW 25:40

God has blessed homeschooling in America. He has answered the prayers of thousands of faithful homeschool families and their cries for protection and relief. Homeschooling is now legal in all fifty states, but as seen in the testimonies in this book, it was after many trials and tribulations.

Now homeschoolers have an opportunity to impact "the least of these"—our brethren around the world, who are clamoring for the same freedoms that we enjoy.

Unlike our struggle here in the United States, their resources are far more limited in many other countries around the world. They are contacting HSLDA and asking for help for their fledgling homeschool movements. I can hardly keep up.

I have found that the widow at the judge's door principle is just as effective for influencing foreign countries as it has been in America. Instead of writing and calling state legislators or Congressmen, American homeschool families can contact foreign embassies!

These embassies are responsive to American perspective on their country because they want to be America's friend and, in most instances, receive foreign aid. Because they are sensitive to America's perspective of their country, when an embassy receives hundreds if not thousands of phone calls, that message is sent loud and clear back to their foreign governments. When this happens, things change.

Americans Help Free South African Homeschoolers

Our influence to help homeschoolers in foreign nations was fully realized in the summer of 1994 in the country of South Africa. André and Bokkie Mientjies started to homeschool their children in 1991. Their three children were academically excelling—but that did not matter to the authorities. The issue is never education. The issue is always control.

On December 14, 1993, South African authorities, after a short trial, sentenced the Mientjies to prison for homeschooling. Mr. Mientjies received a one-year prison sentence, and Mrs. Mientjies received a two-year prison sentence. I suppose she was the worse criminal since she was doing most of the homeschooling.

Meanwhile the child welfare department removed their three children, who had been staying with their grandparents, and placed them into a children's home. The children's home tried to force the children to go to a state school, but the children stubbornly refused and stood on their religious convictions as taught by their parents. The officials then threatened to send the children to a reformatory.

Ann-Marie Wentzel, president of the Psychological Association of South Africa, said that these children "have been robbed of their chance to develop culturally and socially. To do that, they must be part of society." Another South African psychologist involved with the case said, "In this case it looks as if the children have been indoctrinated by the parents with a distorted view of an unholy humanity. I believe it will take intense therapy to persuade them to try other options in life." A major magazine in South Africa called *You* also commented on the Mientjies situation: "Their religious beliefs say classrooms are no good, riddled with influences that taint young minds. But experts say children deprived of formal schooling fall far behind intellectually and might never catch up."

Homeschooling in South Africa was just beginning to surface, and many still had bias and prejudice in favor of institutional schooling.

Graham and Alison Shortridge sent a fax to me at HSLDA begging for help for this family. I talked with Mike Farris who gave his permission to do what we could to help the family. I then got to work.

I contacted several South African leaders with whom we had contact in the country and called the South African embassy. The South African embassy promised us that they would investigate the matter. Meanwhile, as I began my traveling season at different conferences in various states, I passed out a handout and explained the South African family's plight. We also put information in our *Court Report*.

Locally, the Shortridges and the Front Line Fellowship, a missionary organization, organized a letter-writing campaign to various South African officials on behalf of the Mientjies, per our advice. Meanwhile, hundreds of letters and calls, generated by our "alerts" began flowing, at first with a steady trickle, but later with a flood, into the South African embassy in Washington, DC.

Then a miracle occurred. Without explanation, authorities released the Mientjies from prison after just a short month and allowed them to return to their children.

This provided a significant lesson to all of us: we can have an influence on foreign governments to make changes regarding homeschooling.

We continued to work with the South African government, and we were able to help a constitutional amendment get passed allowing for and legalizing homeschooling throughout all the provinces of South Africa.

German Homeschooler's House Ransacked

In April 2000, when I traveled to Germany to speak to American military homeschoolers located there, I met a father named Johann Harder whose house had just been ransacked by the police simply because he was homeschooling.

Homeschooling was not and still is not legal in Germany.

"They broke in through the window, turned over furniture, emptied drawers, and dumped out contents of the closets searching frantically for the children." Mr. Harder, with tears in his eyes, showed me the photographs that he had taken of this destruction in their house. He explained further through a translator that the police had tried to find the Harder children so that they could force them to attend public school. Most of the children escaped through an attic window, and others remained hidden. (He had eleven children.) Finally the police caught and took one child to the public school that day. Mrs. Harder was crying frantically for her child as she held onto her newborn infant.

Mr. Harder pleaded with me, asking if the American homeschoolers could do something to help him. He was now facing court action that threatened to take away his children and have him jailed for two years. I promised to see what I could do for him.

Upon returning to the States, we launched a nationwide e-lert on June 5, 2000, requesting homeschoolers to contact the German embassy to protest the criminal prosecution of the Harder family for their choice to homeschool. An embassy official told me, "I've received at least one thousand e-mails and between three and four hundred letters from concerned homeschoolers." The official also said the embassy informed the German government about the outpouring of public opinion. In addition to the letter writing in the states, Australian and Mexican homeschoolers and others were contacting their country's German embassy as well at our urging.

Within three weeks the scheduled court hearing for the custody of the Harder children was inexplicably canceled. A few days later their attorney Frau Eckermann received a formal notice that the case had been dismissed and the charges dropped. Some German homeschool leaders wrote:

> We homeschoolers here in Germany cannot offer thanks enough to HSLDA for your involvement and the involvement of thousands of homeschool families in response to your e-lert. Because of all of you, your prayers and actions, the Harders have been relieved of their heavy burden—the threat of their children being taken away from them. You being there for us, your counsel and action throughout this whole ordeal were so helpful, needed, and encouraging. You have given us real hope.

This was an amazing result in answer to prayer. However, the work is still pending in Germany to win the fight for legalization.

Ireland Is Thwarted from Imposing Unannounced Home Visits

The homeschool movement of Ireland is small, but the right of parents to homeschool was about to be severely diminished in late 1999. The Irish Senate passed a dangerous bill that would have required homeschoolers to register and be subject to periodic assessments at the whim of the school authorities. Worst of all, the bill would have required the homeschoolers to submit to home visits where the Education Welfare Officer would observe instruction taking place, inspect the premises, and carry out an on-site assessment of the child's intellectual, emotional, and physical development.

The Irish homeschoolers asked for our help. In response, HSLDA launched a nationwide e-lert, and HSLDA members sent hundreds of letters and calls to the Irish embassy. I worked with a homeschool mother who is also an attorney, Elizabeth Bruton, to help plan a strategy for organizing the homeschoolers and lobby legislature. We used HSLDA's materials and studies to correspond with more than fifteen key members of the Lower House in an attempt to persuade them to derail the bill. The calls that HSLDA members in the U.S. made to the Irish embassy contributed to the willingness of the Irish Parliament members and the Minister of Education to agree to a compromise. Amazingly, after battling for several months, the mandatory home visits provision in the education bill for all homeschoolers was removed.

Homeschool leader Elizabeth Bruton wrote saying, "Thank you for the invaluable help given by HSLDA and your members in lobbying for changes to the proposed homeschool legislation. Homeschooling in Ireland was facing a bleak future. Parents were to be confronted with mandatory home visits and wide-ranging assessments of their children before being allowed to homeschool. As a result of the lobbying by the American home-schoolers, the government has made significant concessions.

Families who diligently educate their children at home can confidently proceed."

Once again we are learning that when homeschoolers lobby they make a difference—even across the ocean.

Homeschoolers Shut Down the Czech Republic

In December 2001, I made another trip, this time to the Czech Republic, where I met with Michael Semin, president of the Czech Home School Association. As we sat over pizza in a downstairs Czech restaurant with my three oldest children and my wife, he described the uphill battle that homeschool parents faced to keep the freedom to teach their own children.

He also told us a wonderful story of his involvement in bringing down the Iron Curtain in the Czech Republic. Michael had been a student at the University of Prague and had been organizing protests against the communist government. Numerous times he was dispersed and hunted down, but he did not flinch. He believed he was called by God to lead students in asking their government for freedom.

With my children riveted around the table listening to Michael, he explained how when all hope seemed to be lost, God delivered His people. Michael had organized another protest at the university, and this time the tanks and military trucks were seen heading down the highway to Prague. Then for no human reason, the whole military turned around and went back home. As a result, the protest continued with the rest of the country watching. Soon the unions and others joined in a nationwide protest, bringing the country to an economic standstill. Within days the communist government stepped down without firing a shot.

Michael still had the same resolve and knew God could turn around the situation for the homeschoolers. I offered our help.

He asked if we would send out an e-lert and ask people to write to the two hundred members of parliament. I also sent him immediately two hundred copies of our homeschool studies to give to parliament members.

The Czech Republic allows for homeschooling for only the first five years of elementary schooling. The Ministry of Education issued a new bill in November 2001 that would only allow homeschooling if the agency decided there were serious enough reasons for the child to be homeschooled. In an interview with agency officials, parents would have to specify the reasons for choosing home education and disclose other private information, such as their facilities and income. Most families would be forbidden from homeschooling.

We organized a massive blitz by members of the Home School Legal Defense Association to lobby by letters and calls on behalf of the homeschoolers in the Czech Republic. In just twenty-four hours, over eight hundred members e-mailed the two hundred members of Czech parliament, resulting in over 150,000 e-mails in support of the Czech homeschooling movement. (We had set up on our Web page the means for families to send one e-mail to us and then we would blast a copy of the e-mail to all two hundred members of the parliament.)

The next day the Czech parliament was shut down. A local Prague newspaper reported that the Parliament e-mail server was shut down by the volume of messages coming in on the homeschool issue.

So many e-mails came in on this issue, the Czech-government server stopped accepting out-of-country or in-country e-mail. The Czech homeschoolers then asked us to do a second wave to make certain their government was aware that homeschool legislation was attracting worldwide attention and encouraging them to recognize homeschooling.

Thousands of e-mails to both the Czech Parliament and embassy added strong effect. We received a report from Michael Semin about the crisis, and he stated, "We are winning. The

U.S. campaign has produced good fruit." He said there was "some angry noise among the parliamentarians because the e-mail letters had pulled down the whole server, so not a single parliamentarian could use his personal e-mail account and Internet during the whole day." He then explained further, "On the other hand they realized their work was being closely watched, not only by Czech homeschoolers but around the world!" Michael believed the U.S. campaign was a complete success.

The Czech homeschoolers were able to see the legislation finally go down in defeat. Michael Semin sent a note, "Please tell all your members how thankful we are for their help and prayers. Wish I could thank each one personally, but then I would have to spend days and nights in front of a computer and probably die from that!"

Homeschoolers Can Impact the World

God is good. He has enabled us to spread the blessing of freedom to other countries. This is just a few examples of what we've been able to do. We've been able to help other homeschoolers in many other countries as well. You can look on the HSLDA Web site at www.hslda.org for updated information on over twenty-five countries and how Americans have been able to help them either by e-mails promoting freedom or by sending in financial contributions to help these fledgling organizations.

Homeschooling has come a long way in America. All the lessons we have learned as briefly summarized in this book are lessons that homeschoolers in other countries are wanting to hear. We are able to counsel them and help them avoid some of the mistakes of our past and give them courage that there is hope in the future that they may see the Christian homeschooling movement grow in their country.

17

Homeschooling Through Suffering and Persecution: The Spiritual Lessons

All things work together for good for those who love Him and are called according to His purpose.

ROMANS 8:28

In the chapters of this book, we have recounted many stories of God's people being persecuted at the hands of the state. Persecution and affliction are not fun. We want to avoid them at all costs.

But we must say with Jesus Christ, "Not my will, but Thine be done." God the Father knows what is best for us. He wants us to trust Him and walk by faith not by sight.

God uses persecution to make us strong. He has made the homeschool movement strong. Yet it can change quickly to a weak, worldly, ineffectual movement if we forget God and the lessons He has taught us.

This chapter recounts some of the spiritual lessons of affliction and wrestles with the question of why God's people suffer. Suffering and hardship are still common to homeschool families. The suffering is not so much in the form of persecution, but the lessons are the same.

Just to keep homeschooling in the face of tremendous difficulty with our health or financial problems is hard. The temptation is to abandon homeschooling and send the children to school. We reason, "We need to get our children away from the situation and make sure their education is not interrupted." As a result, the bond is broken, and the education of our children in the school of life is damaged.

But we need to stay the course, and God will provide during the hard times. This book is filled with examples of moms and dads just like you who stayed the course through difficult times.

If God sustained them, He will sustain you with the grace sufficient to handle your trouble. Just like with the families in this book, He will work all things "together for good to those who love God, to those who are called according to His purpose" (Rom. 8:28). God will not give us more than we can bear, and He will provide a way of escape.

Let us not forget to teach these lessons to our children and recount these stories in this book so our children and new homeschoolers will not forget God's faithfulness.

Afflictions Common to All of Us

We all suffer. Psalm 34:19 says, "Many are the afflictions of the righteous, but the Lord delivers them out of them all." Everyone reading this has suffered in some way. The great man of God, Augustine, being familiar with difficult times, once wrote, "God had one Son on earth without sin, but never one without suffering." As the Suffering Servant, Jesus was no exception. As God's adopted children, we share in that suffering.

Some of you have suffered various types of persecution like those recounted in this book. Since 1985 I have been fighting in the legal trenches alongside homeschool parents fighting for their freedom to train and educate their children. There have been thousands of examples of innocent homeschoolers being persecuted for their beliefs. This book only gives us a glimpse.

Many homeschoolers today still face prejudiced public school officials, hostile social workers, aggressive prosecutors, or statist judges.

Other persecution comes at the hands of relatives, neighbors, friends, or even churches that do not understand homeschooling. It is a different form of persecution, but it is persecution nevertheless.

Remember the disciples, after being beaten and imprisoned, counted it all joy to be considered worthy to share in the suffering of Jesus Christ.

Some of you suffer in the form of diseases or various physical infirmities: cancer, back problems, intestinal diseases, multiple sclerosis, heart problems, and all types of chronic diseases. Sometimes God uses short-term illnesses to shake us up and get our priorities straight.

Many of us have experienced the death of a loved one, and all of us will. The sorrow never completely disappears. On May 29, 1994, my legal assistant, Kimberly Wray, was tragically killed in a car accident along with another legal assistant at HSLDA, Angela Yerovsek. Kimberly and Angela were in their mid-twenties. They were both beautiful Christian girls. They were killed by a man under the influence of drugs. Kimberly had worked with me for three years. She was a close friend to my family and me. Her death was a total shock. It was hard to take. Through the tears I knew she had finally won the race and crossed the finish line. She arrived where she always wanted to be, and she did not want to come back. The joy she is experiencing is beyond our imagination. Both Kimberly and

Angela are with their Savior Jesus Christ. But it still hurt. (See the full story in Appendix A.)

God used this tragedy to build my faith. I saw Him work this tragedy together for good for those who love Him. He lovingly and sovereignly used their deaths to save others. I had the privilege of sharing the gospel with one of Kimberly's close friends, Dana, who worked for our travel agent. I asked her if she knew where Kimberly was. She said without hesitation, "She is in heaven." I asked, "Do you know where you are going when you die," and she said, "No." I asked her if she wanted to know and she said, "Yes." I then told her about Jesus being the only way to heaven. I soon led her to pray to ask the Savior into her heart. I asked some girls in the office to help disciple her by having a Bible study. She has been living for the Lord ever since. In fact, we even hired her to work at my office at HSLDA. Meanwhile, Angela's father, who had been a "line walker," also came to the Lord through this terrible loss.

Financial hardships are another difficult area of suffering. Losing one's job and wondering if you will have enough money to make ends meet is always difficult to bear.

Other types of suffering include having a spouse reject God and sue for divorce or enduring various marriage problems.

We all face routine types of trials of one kind or another: broken-down cars, job hassles, children sick in the night, costly mistakes, accidents, moving, or losing close friends.

As I travel and speak on this topic at state homeschool conferences around the country, many homeschool parents have shared all of the sufferings listed above with me. Many tell stories of God's power in the midst of suffering. Others explain the relief and peace they feel after allowing the Scripture verses and story I shared to penetrate their hearts.

How Will You Handle Suffering?

We will all suffer. So the big question is, how will we handle suffering?

Will we become angry with God? Will we question His love for us? I spoke at a homeschool conference a few years ago, and a mother came up to me fighting back the tears. She said, "I was going to have twins too, but one of them did die. I have been shaking my fist at God ever since demanding why He allowed one to die. After hearing what God has taught you, now I understand how wrong I was and how much God truly loves me."

Will we grow bitter and begin to resent others around us who do not appear to be suffering as much as we are? That is an all too common response. At another homeschool conference, a couple came up to me with tears in their eyes. They said, "We want to confess a sin to you and before God."

I responded, "What do you mean? I don't even know you."

The homeschooling couple continued, "We have been resenting all these homeschool speakers who have perfect families, perfect jobs, and all the money they need. Bitterness crept in. After hearing you tonight, we realize that appearances are not what they always seem to be. God has convicted us of our sinful attitude and how much we need to be filled with thankfulness. We have to trust Him more and accept that He's in control and will see us through."

Does our faith begin to wane and our hope in God die in the midst of suffering? Some homeschoolers at conferences have confided in me that they were beginning to doubt God and their own faith because they were not being healed. Now they began to realize God is not bound by any "name it and claim it" magic words. Rather, He is the awesome, all-powerful God who loves us first and works all things together for good for those who love Him and are called according to His purpose.

When we suffer, do we simply begin to whine and complain and feel sorry for ourselves? Do we take out our suffering on those around us? One homeschool dad came up to me after I spoke and, with an expression of relief and thankfulness, said, "Thanks for what you shared. It was a blessing to hear someone who has had it worse than me not complaining but rejoicing in the Lord. You see, I have had two heart bypass surgeries, and I was depressed that God was not blessing me like others. I was feeling sorry for myself, but now I am beginning to see God's hand in all this working for my good."

Do we give up on homeschooling and stop pursuing what God has called us to do? One of the first things that comes into our mind when we are sick is cutting back and resting more. We begin to reason that maybe we should just send our children to school. It is too hard to continue. We need to focus on ourselves. We forget the call of God on our lives to homeschool. We forget that when we are weak, then we are strong. We abandon God's promises that He will give us the grace sufficient and that we can do all things through Christ who strengthens us. It never was our strength in the first place! We do not realize that He wants us to homeschool by faith and surrender all to Him. God will honor those who honor Him, and He will enable us to fulfill the calling He gives us to homeschool.

Or, in reaction to suffering, do we honor and glorify Him and humble ourselves "in the sight of the Lord" knowing He will lift us up? (see 1 Pet. 5:6). Do we seek the awesome face of God, realize His sovereignty, and say with Job, "The Lord gave and the Lord has taken away. Blessed be the name of the Lord" (Job 1:21)? Do we focus on the Lord and grow closer to Him? Do we look for new opportunities to share the gospel? Do we consider if God is chastening us and repent of our sins? (We always need to do this to some extent.) Do we see our priorities in a clearer light, concentrating once again on training our children's souls in the Lord and daily thanking them for the privilege of homeschooling them? Do we simply thank God and look for the new opportunities He has given us to glorify Him?

One of my favorite hymns that captures the proper attitude God wants us to have in the face of life's trials was written in 1675 by Samuel Rodiguso. A man I always admired greatly, Greg Bahnsen, shared this love for this hymn. He was a pastor, theologian, and author. He suffered through many heart problems and surgeries in his short life. On his last Sunday on this earth, he led the worship with this hymn, knowing his next surgery was that Tuesday and that the surgery was high risk.

What ere my God ordains is right
Holy His will abides
I will be still, what ere He does
And follow where He guides
He is my God though dark my road
He holds me that I shall not fall
Wherefore to Him I leave it all.

What ere my God ordains is right
He never will deceive my soul
He leads me by the proper path
I know He will not leave me
My God is true each morning new
Sweet comfort, yet shall fill my heart,
And pain and sorrow shall depart.

What ere my God ordains is right
Here shall my stand be taken
Though sorrow, need, or death be mine
Yet am I not forsaken
My Father's care is 'round me there
He holds me that I shall not fall
And so to Him I leave it all.

Greg Bahnsen died in surgery at the age of forty-seven a few days later, and he went straight to the arms of his Savior whom he trusted so completely. What God ordained for Greg's life was right.

Suffering Is Our Curriculum for Sanctification

Maryanne Lash, the wife of our pastor at Gainesville Presbyterian Church, Jack Lash, has experienced many times of suffering as a homeschool mother of eleven. She has experienced her house burning down and countless pressures and stresses of maintaining a large family and vibrant ministry at the church. Through it all, she has been suffering for years with a chronic condition called fibromyalgia. During a Bible study Maryanne recounted some of their own hardships and simply said, "Suffering is our curriculum for sanctification."

Maryanne Lash is right. We homeschoolers understand the importance of a good curriculum. The curriculum that God uses for our instruction is the best. Oftentimes the deepest lessons and the most important truths are learned by us and our children when we have a bout with or continually experience hardships and suffering.

Suffering Helps Us to Appreciate Homeschooling

Charles Spurgeon once wrote, "There are no crown-bearers in heaven who were not cross-bearers on earth."

Over these last few years, God has brought my family through major periods of suffering: my car accident, my kidney stones, my wife's incurable ulcerative colitis (which she almost died from in 1989), deaths of close friends, the near death of our twins, and my diagnosis with multiple sclerosis to name the hardest trials. The Lord has helped us understand our suffering in light of His total sovereignty. He taught us that God is in control! His sovereignty is our *only* security because everything else is temporary and fleeting.

Through the fire of our trials, God also helped us understand why we are homeschooling our seven children. We are not homeschooling merely for homeschooling sake; it is not the end in itself. Rather homeschooling is simply the means to the end: bringing our children up in the nurture and admonition of the Lord so they will love and obey God all the days of their lives. Homeschooling is simply the best vehicle we as parents can use to fulfill the commands God has given us to train our children as found in Deuteronomy 6; Ephesians 6:4; and throughout the Word of God. We can't abandon it during the hard times. It would just increase the pain.

But it is true. Suffering is a blessing. God uses suffering to shake us and wake us up. Times of suffering are times God draws closest while intensely molding us, shaping us, and conforming us to the image of His Son. It is an opportunity to see our priorities clearly and to set them straight. We learn to concentrate on what really matters: living holy lives, sharing the gospel, advancing His kingdom, and training our children to love God with *all* their heart, *all* their strength, and *all* their mind. Suffering is a blessing. It is OK to suffer. I can say that with my whole heart.

Suffering Saints

A quick look at the Word of God demonstrates that our Father in heaven, out of great love for His people, has repeatedly used suffering as a means to conform His children more into the image of His Son. He also has used it to increase their faith and prepare them for His work and help them to long for their heavenly home with Him.

Joseph is a prime example. Through no fault of his own, he was hated by his brothers. In fact, he was nearly murdered by them and eventually sold into slavery. Joseph had no rights. He had no hope. He was lonely being raised and trained in a pagan land that worshipped false idols. He couldn't see his family and those he grew up with. He received tremendous injustice being framed by Potipher's wife. He experienced endless postponement of the dreams that the Lord had given him. He spent years in prison forsaken with no hope. Yet Joseph remained firm and was able to say when he was tempted by Potipher's wife, "How can I do this and sin against my God?" Then when he met with his brothers, who had done him such harm and caused him such suffering, he forgave them and said, "You meant it for evil, but God meant it for good." Joseph had unwavering trust in God and His sovereignty that all He ordained is right and that all things would work together for his good because he loved God and was called by Him.

All the disciples and the saints mentioned throughout the Bible, particularly in the New Testament, suffered greatly. Hebrews 11 is filled with examples of the faith that these saints had in spite of their circumstances. It also talks about those who were faithful to the death, even people whose names are now unknown.

Of course, there is the example of Paul. He went hungry, suffered many beatings. He was shipwrecked. He experienced physical weakness. He had a thorn in his side that God never removed even though He was able. God, in fact, told him that he would keep that thorn in order for Paul not to get too prideful. He experienced nakedness and financial want. He was persecuted in town after town and stoned. He experienced years in bondage in prison, waiting for the death sentence. Yet he continued boldly to proclaim the Word of God wherever God took him. If he was shipwrecked and ended up on an island, he shared the gospel there. If he was in prison, he shared the gospel with the Praetorian guard. If he was sick, he shared the gospel where he had to rest.

Suffering Is an Opportunity, Not a Curse

Paul's attitude should be our attitude as well. We should look at each hardship, each suffering as an opportunity to share God's good news with someone new or to let our light shine so people can see how we handle suffering by God's grace. People will see that we have joy in the midst of the suffering and will be amazed and pointed to God for their only hope of salvation.

God has blessed me with realizing how short life is; the multiple sclerosis has steadily taken away much of the strength of my legs and weakened my hands, waist, and other functions of my body. I have stuck to a strict, healthy diet; but it is no longer holding the disease back. But God be praised; He has taught me to make every day count with my relationship with Him, with Tracy, with our seven children, and with my work. I am seeing the hand of God working so visibly in my life. I am learning to walk more and more by faith. I cannot see what is ahead. I am learning to trust Him more completely. All things do "work together for good" for those who love Him—even MS.

As I read the Bible, I am more in love with God and His Word. Most of the time it is the only thing that holds me together. I am so thankful God is with me all the way. My roots, that had sunk deep into this earth during my healthy times, have been cut.

As I Become Weaker, God Shows His Strength

As I get weaker, His power gets stronger. I went to Mexico for a failed attempt to get better, but God used it as a mission trip. I gave Spanish Bibles and tracts to many, shared the gospel with dozens, and prayed with three men to receive Christ. Then I went to the local hospital for four days of failed treatment in another failed attempt to stop the unrelenting MS attack, but God turned it into another mission trip. I shared the gospel with about twenty-five hospital employees, gave out tracts and

Bibles, and prayed with two nurses to receive Christ. This summer in the Atlanta airport, as I struggled to my gate, a man asked to help me. We sat down for an hour and a half, and he prayed to accept Jesus as his Savior. On a trip to Texas, I talked with a restaurant manager; and after two visits with him, he wanted to be a disciple for Jesus Christ.

God is telling us over and over again that He is completely sovereign. He is in control. That is our greatest hope as we go through the suffering. We know there is purpose, and it will be for our good. We are blessed when we suffer. We must choose to say with Job, "You give and take away. Blessed be your name."

We all need an attitude that Jesus Himself had when He asked for the cup to be passed from Him, which was the great suffering He was facing on the cross. But He ended with a humble reliance on God's sovereignty and love. He said, "Not My will, but Thine be done." As Scott Rowley said in his song, "With these seven simple words, the victory is won."

Remember, Jesus Understands

As we face the hardships and sufferings, we wonder why we don't immediately get delivered the moment we pray. If God is sovereign, then His ways are not our ways. But what we do know is that not only does He work all things together for our good, but He understands. Jesus can "sympathize with our weaknesses . . . [as] One who has been tempted in all things as we are, yet without sin" (Heb. 4:15). He is a man of sorrows and acquainted with grief. "During the days of Jesus' life on earth, he offered up prayers and petitions with loud cries and tears to the one who could save him from death, and he was heard because of his reverent submission. Although he was a son, he learned obedience from what he suffered and, once made perfect, he became the source of eternal salvation for all who obey him" (Heb. 5:7–9 NIV). Jesus set the pattern.

God is chipping away at us, molding and shaping us to be more like Him as we go through the hard times. God is working more and more each day to unveil Christ in us. Paul understood when he prayed, "Three times I pleaded with the Lord to take [the suffering] away from me. But he said to me, 'My grace is sufficient for you, for my power is made perfect in weakness.' Therefore, I will boast all the more gladly about my weaknesses so that Christ's power may rest on me" (2 Cor. 12:8–9 NIV). The suffering and hurting process will not end until we become completely holy. That, of course, won't occur until we're in heaven one day. But we have that hope and promise of heaven where there will be no more tears and no more sorrows.

In the meantime, until we get to heaven, God is with us. He is giving Himself. He is constantly holding us, comforting us, never giving us more than we can bear. He becomes a father to the fatherless, the husband to the widow, our counselor, healer, and deliverer. He can do no more than give Himself to us.

And what greater love, what more amazing, incredible love can there be than that God, who created the whole universe, would be pleased to have His own Son die for us while He watched. No greater grief has anyone experienced than God over the death of His Son. Yet He did this because He loves us.

You see, when we go through times of suffering as mothers, fathers, children, homeschoolers, and ultimately, as Christians, we are a billboard for Jesus Christ. The world is looking at us with complete amazement. How we handle our suffering is a testimony to the world of the power that is within us. Humanly, there is no way that we could still have the fruits of the Spirit in the midst of the suffering, but God's supernatural strength can enable us to be gentle and kind and to have self-control, to still be faithful and loyal and patient. The world does not understand but wants to understand and this is our opportunity to share the gospel of Jesus Christ with them.

A few years ago I asked that God would make me more like Jesus—whatever it takes. And He is doing it! We are closer to

God than ever before. He is teaching us to be faithful to the end and to trust Him *completely*. We have also seen the tremendous impact this affliction has had on the spiritual lives of our seven children. The life lessons and spiritual truths are touching their souls. We know this is not in vain when we see the fruit in their lives.

Ultimately, we want to say with Jesus in the garden of Gethsemane, "Not My will, but Thine be done."

The Lessons of Suffering

Through all this, we can learn many important lessons.

First, we have learned that *nothing* can separate us from the love of God (Rom. 8), not even disease or tragedy. God's love abounds. He draws us closer to Him. He uses these hard times to conform us more and more to the image of His Son. He *must* prune us so we can bear fruit (John 15:12); and we are being pruned!

My family has learned to have joy in the midst of suffering:

> Consider it all joy, my brethren, when you encounter various trials, knowing that the testing of your faith produces endurance. And let endurance have its perfect result, that you may be perfect and complete, lacking in nothing. (James 1:2–4)

We must thank the Lord for these hard times, too:

> Exult in our tribulations, knowing that tribulation brings about perseverance; and perseverance, proven character; and proven character, hope; and hope does not disappoint, because the love of God has been poured out within our hearts through the Holy Spirit who was given to us. (Rom. 5:3–5)

Second, we know that "all things [including suffering] to work together for good to those who love God, to those who are called according to His purpose" (Rom. 8:28). Through the eyes of suffering, we are blessed to see God's power and love so much more clearly. In addition, I have seen lost souls saved, believers grow in the Lord, and the struggling conquer problems—all as a result of our suffering.

In Galatians 4:13, the apostle Paul wrote, "But you know that it was because of a bodily illness that I preached the gospel to you the first time." Paul became ill and had to stop in Galatia. It probably was not on his agenda. However, he preached the gospel to the Galatians, many came to the knowledge of Christ, and a church was born. God works all things together for good.

Furthermore, God uses our suffering for good by equipping us to help others in distress.

> Blessed be the God and Father of our Lord Jesus
> Christ, the Father of mercies and God of all comfort;
> who comforts us in all our affliction so that we may
> be able to comfort those who are in any affliction with
> the comfort with which we ourselves are comforted by
> God. For just as the sufferings of Christ are ours in
> abundance, so also our comfort is abundant through
> Christ. (2 Cor. 1:3–5)

Third, we know that God answers our prayers, but it is in His timing and in His way. For some of us, that timing will not be until we get to heaven. That is OK; God's will is better than our will. In the case of Lazarus, Jesus tarried for two days after hearing of Lazarus's sickness (John 11). He waited until Lazarus had died so when He did come, He could raise Lazarus from the dead, giving God, the Creator, all glory. In John 9 a man was suffering from blindness since birth. When the disciples asked why he was born blind, Christ answered, "It was neither from this man's sin nor his parents, but it was in order that the work of God might be displayed in him." That man suffered all his life in order for the special moment when Christ would miraculously heal him. To glorify God is our sole purpose.

In other words, *God is sovereign; He is in control.* Before they were thrown into the fiery furnace, Shadrach, Meshach, and Abednego told the King: "We believe God will deliver us. *But even if He does not,* we still will not bow the knee to your idol" (Dan. 3:17–18, author's paraphrase). Our attitude must be the same. This is the perfect balance: pray for healing but trust God and want His will to be done. As Jesus said Himself, "Not my will but yours be done" (Luke 22:42 NIV). Ultimately, we must bow to God's power and sovereignty.

Fourth, we've learned that God's grace is sufficient. No matter how bad the suffering seems, we can be sure that God will enable us to endure it. Although it may seem as if we can't go on, God will never give us more suffering than we can bear (see 1 Cor. 10:13). Certainly what Paul says is true:

> My grace is sufficient for you, for power is perfected in weakness. Most gladly therefore I will rather boast about my weaknesses, that the power of Christ may dwell in me. Therefore, I am well content with weakness, with insults, with distresses, with persecutions, with difficulties, for Christ's sake, for when I am weak, then I am strong. (2 Cor. 12:9–10)

Fifth, we also know that we will receive the peace of God that passes all understanding.

> Be anxious for nothing, but in everything by prayer and supplication with thanksgiving let your requests be made known to God. And the peace of God, which surpasses all comprehension, shall guard your hearts and your minds in Christ Jesus. (Phil. 4:6–7)

God gave us peace in the midst of terrible suffering. In this book we saw many accounts of God giving peace to people under heavy stress and legal persecution. This peace is supernatural; it is beyond our understanding. God will give it to us. It is a promise.

Sixth, we know we must walk by faith and not by sight (2 Cor. 5:7). We walk so much closer to the Lord when we do not know what is ahead. Faith enables us to trust in the Lord our God and lean not on our own understanding.

Seventh, God teaches us the necessity of rejoicing in Him always and being thankful for all things. In Philippians 4:4, we are commanded to "rejoice in the Lord always; again I will say, rejoice!" (also see Phil. 3:1 and 1 Thess. 5:16).

As my pastor Jack Lash pointed out, "If the joy of the Lord is not in you, how will nonbelievers ever yearn for what you have? How will they ever come to you and ask 'you to give an account for the hope that is in you' (1 Pet. 3:15)?" Joy is a fruit of the Spirit (Gal. 5:22–23), and only the Holy Spirit can give us this joy. In fact, it is called "the joy of the Holy Spirit" in 1 Thessalonians 1:6. If we don't have his joy, we need to repent and ask for His forgiveness.

We know that "the joy of the Lord is our strength." He will give His people a supernatural joy that transcends our suffering and hardships and provides us with strength to go on. It is a joy in Him. If we have nothing else but Jesus, we still have joy. This helps us to develop an attitude of thankfulness even when crossing the roughest waters. We truly have come to the point where we can do what once seemed impossible: "In everything give thanks; for this is God's will for you in Christ Jesus" (1 Thess. 5:18). We can thank God for the hard times because we know it is for our good; we need to complain less and look for the opportunity for our light to shine brighter.

Eighth, God teaches us that this life is short and that we need to see it in light of eternity. What awaits us in heaven far surpasses anything here in this life on Earth. Therefore, believing in Jesus as our Savior and seeking Him first in everything is all that really matters. Without Jesus we have nothing.

Therefore, the *last and most important lesson* is that we must put our complete trust in the Lord Jesus Christ. Since He is the Creator of all things, He also controls all things and is completely sovereign. The Bible states in Matthew 8 that He only needs to "say the word" and we are healed. God, in His sovereignty, may want us to remain handicapped or even die, but it is for His glory. And it is OK.

We can be assured of healing in heaven, where there will be no more tears or sorrow (see Rev. 21:4). But we can only be certain of our healing if we know Jesus as our personal Savior. Without Jesus, we are bound for hell, where the suffering will never cease.

> Therefore we do not lose heart, but though our outer man is decaying, yet our inner man is being renewed day by day. For momentary, light affliction is producing for us an eternal weight of glory far beyond all comparison, while we look not at the things which are seen, but the things which are not seen; for the things which are seen are temporal, but the things which are not seen are eternal. (2 Cor. 4:16–18)

> The mercies of God know no end!

$$\text{※}18$$

The Price of Freedom
Is Eternal Vigilance

And the God of peace will crush Satan under your feet shortly.
The grace of our Lord Jesus Christ be with you. Amen.

ROMANS 16:20 NKJV

We have briefly peddled through only a few of the thousands of stories of brave mothers and fathers who challenged the power of the state. These stories we read are stories of courage and faithfulness. Many families remained unnamed and their stories untold.

How can one do justice to this modern battle for freedom? It is tantamount in intensity and prejudice to the battle for racial civil rights in this country. It is more than that however. It is a supernaturally fought battle as parents who are in an extreme minority continue to lean on their everlasting Father to give them the strength to fight back.

As I said at the beginning of this book, it was no particular organization that began or controlled the homeschool movement. Time and time again I have seen that it was the moving of the Holy Spirit on the hearts and minds of parents to take this leap of faith into homeschooling against great odds.

These odds were in the form of vague legislation that gave school superintendents unbridled discretion in disapproving homeschools. The homeschoolers fought against laws that upheld teacher certification as the one and only way that teachers could be qualified to teach children. They battled against the state's desire to play "big brother" and send in school district "professionals" to monitor and approve homeschoolers by invading their homes with home visits.

You saw how families stood on the First and Fourteenth Amendments of the Constitution that guarantee them both religious liberty and the fundamental right to direct the educational upbringing of their children. In spite of this solid foundation, courts mostly did what they wanted to do; and many of them ignored, misapplied, or merely paid "lip service" to these treasured constitutional amendments.

Leaning on Jesus

This book hardly even touched on the heartache and the emotional stress and fear that each family experienced as they faced threats to have their children taken away while they were dragged into court. These families leaned heavily on Jesus through these times.

Over and over again I heard reports of the prayer meetings and the prayer chains that went forth on behalf of families who were fingered by school districts and social workers. We routinely recommended that people put their legal conflicts on the prayer chains, and we often prayed with members on the phones that God would give them deliverance and courage. And He always did!

Yes, the homeschool movement has been delivered and continues to be protected by God and God alone. He uses HSLDA to defend families' rights, and it continues to be that "bulletproof vest" that the homeschool movement can wear to protect them from the continual attacks by the educational elite.

But HSLDA is not just lawyers and the employees at HSLDA. HSLDA is really homeschoolers across the country who are our members. HSLDA could not have existed throughout the years without members believing in the cause, who were willing to pull their resources together to give us the financial wherewithal to fight back.

Victory Is the Lord's

The successes that are related in this book were not due to the "fancy footwork" of clever lawyers and smart experts. No, the victory has been the Lord's from the beginning, and the victory will continue to be the Lord's to the end.

Homeschooling has been blessed because the homeschool movement has put Jesus Christ as its center. The primary reason families are homeschooling is because they want to be true to the Word of God and follow God's call in their hearts. They are not homeschooling for homeschooling's sake but are homeschooling simply as a means to an end. That end is to glorify God by training their children in God's ways and nurturing their souls.

Remember, these are never-dying souls that have been entrusted to our care. Our children are not some chattel or gift that we can expend in any way we please. Our children are the Lord's, and He requires that they be trained faithfully in His ways. To whom much is given, much is required, the Scripture said. God has given us much freedom in this country, and much is required of us to make certain that we give our children the best Christian education that we possibly can. Homeschooling is an option that not many countries in the world have.

Temptation to Quit or Compromise

If Satan had his choice, where would he want you to send your children to school? I think the answer is obvious. The public schools are easy because in one fell swoop a U.S. Supreme Court decision can turn the whole course of the public schools, remove the Ten Commandments, remove prayer, and bar God from the classroom. With homeschoolers, however, he has to take them one at a time. He has to try to infiltrate the family from within to break them down. He already tried to take us down through the legislatures and the courts. But God saw to it that he failed.

Now, homeschoolers need to be wary about being infiltrated from within. The homeschool movement has started strong, but that doesn't count as much as ending strong. We need to make sure that we don't grow apathetic and simply expect our freedom to homeschool always to be there.

This book provides the evidence of the many hundreds and thousands of people that sacrificed for our freedom to be enjoyed now in training our children at home. Let us not sell our freedom for a bowl of pottage. Let us not return to Egypt and sign our children for government homeschooling, which is so popular today.

Christian home education is where God wants us. It was through private Christian homeschooling that homeschooling has succeeded—without a dime of government help. What makes us think we need government help now?

The Challenge

Therefore, the challenge to all of you is to make certain that you are connected to your statewide homeschool association so that you can be involved in helping with the phone calling and lobby efforts if a bad piece of legislation is introduced that "turns the clock back."

Support your local support groups and attend your state homeschool conference to provide additional support for them and a regular "shot in the arm" for you to help you receive encouragement to keep going.

Make sure that you are members of the Home School Legal Defense Association. (You can join at www.hslda.org.)

Let's not allow the sacrifices of so many families to be in vain for you. Continue to be a member of the Home School Legal Defense Association so you can be a part of the tens of thousands of families, pooling their resources together to have a defense ready for all when and if that unwanted knock comes at the door. Also, so we will be a united force to withstand some other attempt by the state to bring back the regulations and controls of the 1980s and 1990s.

He who doesn't know history is condemned to repeat its mistakes. We need to know the history and tell our children and our children's children so that they can be aware of the heartache and sweat and effort that was made by families who boldly followed the Lord in spite of intense persecution and opposition.

Love Is the Main Ingredient

Homeschoolers have shown the establishment that "mere parents" can teach as well, if not much better, than the government schools. The homeschool parents have proved that parents do act in the best interests of their children. Homeschool parents have proved that love is the main ingredient to successful education, not a teaching certificate. Homeschoolers have proved that children are best socialized using a greenhouse effect, where they are protected from harm, from exposure to illicit drugs, various alternative lifestyles, and crime of every description. Homeschoolers have proved that children can learn about these things from afar and grow up to be honorable, diligent, and productive citizens. They don't need to pool their ignorance together with children of the same age. In fact, parental interaction with children on a regular basis helps them mature faster and helps them perform better as students and college students, employees, and adults.

Most of all, homeschoolers have proved that God is real, and that His desires will be carried out. Time and time again, this book has given you stories of where God turned the situation around in the legislatures or the courts to bring about victory for His people. Sometimes He brought the victory about by defeat, showing it was God and God alone that was going to deliver them. It is much like Joshua and the Israelites circling the city of Jericho, simply playing music and marching, causing the walls to come down. All the Israelites knew and the whole world knew that it wasn't their power that won the day. It was God and God alone. So it has been with the homeschool movement. Fathers and mothers simply being obedient—God is giving us the victory.

God bless you as you continue to teach your children at home.

Never forget the most important goal—to teach our children well in the Lord, so that one day our children will be standing in heaven with us. That is what I long for. That is what I work for. That is why I work to train my children in homeschool. How about you?

Appendix A

Do You Know Where You Are Going When You Die?

Some readers may wonder why I took the time to write this book. The major reason is that I believe homeschooling is the most effective way to plant the Word of God into the consciousness of our children. In other words, homeschooling is a tremendous way to reach our children's souls. Certainly our souls and those of our children are of utmost importance. The time we spend in this world is short compared to the never-ending time in eternity.

This hit home on May 29, 1994, when Kimberly Wray, my legal assistant at HSLDA, was instantly killed in a car crash along with Angela Yerovsek, another legal assistant in our office. The police said the man who hit them was speeding—at least 100 mph—and hit them from behind, knocking them off the road into a tree. Both of these girls were in their twenties, and they were expected back at work on Monday, but suddenly they were gone.

Both of these girls loved the Lord. Kimberly had worked at HSLDA for three years, working as my personal legal and administrative assistant for the last two years. She became a close friend to my family and me. I miss Kimberly very much. She was constantly seeking the Lord's will in everything, and she loved Him with her whole heart, soul, and mind. On her computer were three quotes: "Lord, make me an instrument of thy peace;" "Trust in the Lord with all your heart and lean not on your own understanding" (Prov. 3:5); and "When I am afraid, I will put my trust in thee. In God whose Word I praise, in God I have put my trust: I shall not be afraid. What can mere man do to me?" (Ps. 56:3–4). Kimberly was so talented. Her kindness and cheerfulness was well-known by all of us at HSLDA as well as by the many HSLDA members she helped. She would agonize over the persecution of innocent home-school families by state officials. She gave so much godly and accurate counsel to many families.

God in His wisdom brought Kimberly and Angela home. No doubt, they are where we all want to be and do not want to return. The Scriptures say in 1 Corinthians 2:9, "Eye has not seen, nor ear heard, nor have entered into the heart of man the things which God has prepared for those who love Him" (NKJV). Furthermore, Revelation 21:4 says, "And God will wipe away every tear from their eyes; there shall be no more death, nor sorrow, nor crying; There shall be no more pain, for the former things have passed away" (NKJV).

Kimberly and Angela ran the race and now have received the crown of glory. "Therefore we are always confident in that while we are at home in the body we are absent from the Lord, for we walk by faith and not by sight. We are confident, yes, well pleased rather, to be absent from the body and present with the Lord" (2 Cor. 5:6–8, author's paraphrase). However, we continue to experience great sorrow because we miss Kimberly and Angela, yet we know the Bible says in Psalm 116:15, "Precious in the sight of the Lord is the death of His saints" (NKJV).

Do You Know Where You Are Going When You Die?

The important point in all of this for the reader is that Kimberly and Angela were ready. We know they are experiencing unbelievable joy in the presence of God their Father and the Lord Jesus Christ. But where are you today? Have you thought about your soul and about your children's souls? Have you taken the time consciously to train your children in God's Word? Have you taken the time to get your own life ready with God? Do you have hope when you die?

There is so much more to our lives than this life. This life is fleeting and uncertain. I have been diagnosed with multiple sclerosis. Suddenly my life has changed. I can't run any more, and I have difficulty walking and climbing stairs. My energy has been cut in half. This body is decaying. Some of us are decaying faster than others, but we will all die one day. As I struggle with MS, God has made it clear to me how important it is that we make this life count. The only thing we can do that will last is what we do for Christ. Life is so fleeting and completely hopeless—except for our life in Jesus Christ. God made this clear when we faced the near death of our twin girls. Our relationship with Jesus is the only thing we will be able to bring with us into eternity.

So don't put it off for another day. As we have learned from Kimberly and Angela's lives, we have no idea when we will die. One thing we can all be assured of is that we will all die. There are no exceptions. If you died today, are you sure you would go to heaven? That is a question to meditate upon. If God asked you why He should let you into heaven, what would you say? Would you be explaining to God that you are a good person and deserve heaven? Would you tell God that He owes you something? Would you say that since He is a God of love, everyone must be allowed into heaven? Such answers would be useless. God has made it clear that there is only one way to heaven, and that is explained in the Bible, God's love letter to man.

We Are All Sinners

Romans 3:23 says, "For all have sinned and fall short of the glory of God." Romans 6:23 says, "For the wages of sin is death, but the free gift of God is eternal life in Christ Jesus our Lord." In other words, I am a sinner and you are a sinner. Everyone in this entire world has done wrong. We have sinned against the holy and perfect God who created us. As a result, the Bible tells us that the penalty and wages of sin is death. This death, the Scriptures say, is eternal death in hell where the burning and torment will never ever cease.

You are doomed and I am doomed. In order for us to earn our salvation, Galatians 3:10 makes it clear that we must obey all the law that God has laid forth in the Scriptures. This means we must never lie, never cheat, never steal, never have bad attitudes or use unkind words, never sin in anger, never sin at all. Of course, this is impossible. Just look at your own life. Besides, even if we do an extraordinary amount of good works, God says our "righteous deeds are like a filthy garment" (Isa. 64:6). They cannot save us.

The Only Way to Heaven

However, there is hope because God in His great mercy and love for us has provided one way to heaven. God willingly sent His only begotten Son, Jesus Christ, to this world to suffer and be tempted in all the ways we are, yet He did not sin. God went further by having Jesus Christ, who was perfectly God and perfectly man, to be crucified on the cross for our sins. In other words, as my little four-year-old daughter would explain, you and I should have been crucified on the cross and sent to hell, but Jesus willingly did that in our place. He conquered death by rising again from the dead in three days. Now He sits on the right hand of God the Father Almighty. John 3:16 explains: "For God so loved the world, that He gave His only begotten Son, that whoever believes in Him should not perish, but have eternal life."

God had His only Son suffer untold agony for us! "But God demonstrates His own love toward us, in that while we were yet sinners, Christ died for us" (Rom. 5:8). The Bible declares, "He [Jesus Christ] was delivered over to death for our sins and was raised to life for our justification" (Rom. 4:25 NIV). In other words, Jesus willingly took our place. When we go before God one day, and He looks at us and sees sinners deserving of death, before we are condemned to eternal hell, Jesus Christ will stand in front of us and declare us righteous by His blood that He shed for us on that cross long ago.

There is no other way to heaven. Jesus Himself told Nicodemus in the Gospel of John, chapter 3 that one must be "born again" in order to enter the kingdom of heaven. Jesus explained that this is not where you go back into your mother's womb and be reborn, but this is a new birth of the spirit where we put aside our old man and put on the new. In John 14:6, Jesus said, "I am the way, and the truth, and the life; no one comes to the Father, but through me." As I said, there is no other way. Buddha, who is dead, cannot save us; our own works cannot save us. No other god or religion can save us. We must believe in Jesus Christ as our Lord and Savior. He is our Creator. He is the One who made us as well as the whole universe.

So how can we be saved from our present path straight to hell? God tells us in the Bible in Romans 10:9, "Confess with your lips that Jesus is Lord and believe in your heart that He rose again from the dead. Then you shall be saved!" (author's paraphrase). "Whoever will call upon the name of the Lord will be saved" (Rom. 10:13). No matter what you have done, Christ will forgive you. "If we confess our sins, He is faithful and righteous to forgive us our sins" (1 John 1:9).

Furthermore, the Bible clearly states, "And there is salvation in no one else; for there is no other name under heaven that has been given among men, by which we must be saved" (Acts 4:12). The road is narrow. Jesus is the only way. "Enter by the narrow gate; for the gate is wide, and the way is broad that leads to destruction, and many are those who enter by it. For the gate is small, and the way is narrow that leads to life, and few are those who find it" (Matt. 7:13–14).

We Can't Fool God

It is easy to fool men by confessing that Jesus is Lord of your life, saying that you believe in your heart that He rose again from the dead and paid the penalty for your sins. It is also easy to fool people saying that you have repented, changed, and put on the new man. However, you cannot fool God. God knows the heart. Jesus warns:

> Not everyone who says to me, "Lord, Lord," will enter the kingdom of heaven; but he who does the will of My Father who is in heaven. Many will say to Me on that day, "Lord, Lord, did we not prophesy in Your name, and in Your name cast out demons, and in Your name perform many miracles?" And then I will declare to them, I never knew you; depart from Me, you who practice lawlessness. (Matt. 7:21–23)

Don't try to fool God because it isn't possible. God knows the heart. Repent from your sins. Accept Jesus as your Lord and Savior. As Paul told the Philippian jailer, "Believe in the Lord Jesus, and you shall be saved" (Acts 16:31).

Remember, we will not get a second chance once we die. We know it is easy to die. We could die tomorrow. People die every day. God tells us in Hebrews 9:27, "It is appointed for man to die once and after this comes judgment." There will be no opportunities for us to confess Jesus as our Lord and Savior after we die. We must do it here; we must do it now.

What more important thing in this life do we have to tend to than that of our own souls? Once we understand this, how important the responsibility for us as parents to be sure that we have trained our children in God's Word and presented them with the gospel of Jesus Christ, so they, too, may confess him as Lord and Savior of their lives. What a glory it will be when we are all together in heaven one day.

Caution: Faith without Works Is Dead

One final note involves our lives once we have accepted Jesus as our Lord and Savior. The Bible says, "You will know them by their fruits," and that if we love God, we will keep His commandments. If we truly love God, and if we have truly accepted Jesus into our heart as our Savior and are developing a personal relationship with Him, we will want to obey Him and know His Word as found in the Bible. It is in the Holy Bible that God shows us His will and revelation. I challenge you to read your Bible daily and mediate on God's law day and night as David encouraged in the Psalms. We owe God so much. We owe Him our very salvation, our very life. We need to be "sold out" in our commitment to Him. He deserves no less. We must seek to obey Him in all things and follow His Scriptures. Of course, we must also teach these Scriptures to our children.

Once you are saved, truly saved, you will never lose that salvation. Jesus said:

> I give eternal life to them, and they shall never perish; and no one shall snatch them out of My hand. My Father, who has given them to Me, is greater than all, and no one is able to snatch them out of the Father's hand. (John 10:28–29)

We were all made in the image of God. Only living in His will and knowing Jesus Christ as our personal Savior will we ever have true security in this life and true happiness.

We all know that our bodies are decaying day by day. I know, I am afflicted with an incurable and degenerative disease. Scripture reminds us in 2 Corinthians 4:16–18, "Do not lose heart, but though our outer man is decaying, yet our inner man is being renewed day by day. For momentary, light affliction is producing for us an eternal weight of glory far beyond all comparison." That is what we must look forward to: the great glory God has prepared for us. That is what Kimberly and Angela lived for. They lived for Jesus Christ. As a result, when they died, they immediately went to be in His presence. They had gotten the most important thing in this life in order: the condition of their souls. How brief our lives are.

Please Accept Jesus as Your Savior

How important it is that we take the steps to accept Jesus as our Savior. "He who believes in the Son has eternal life; but he who does not obey the Son shall not see life, but the wrath of God abides on him" (John 3:36). My hope is that every reader of this book comes to the saving knowledge of Jesus Christ. Simply pray to God, confessing your sin and your need for a Savior. Accept in your heart that Jesus died and rose again from the dead, paying the penalty of death for you. Then ask God to forgive you and fill you with His Holy Spirit so you will be saved for all eternity. Repent and turn away from your sins and make Jesus Christ the Lord of your life. Read and obey the Bible, His words and commands to us. God will forgive your sins, but the road will not always be easy, and the race will be hard. But when you reach the finish line, you will be with God in the perfect place He has prepared for you forever.

Jesus is the only thing that matters. Remember, "Now is the day of salvation" (2 Cor. 6:2). You do not know what tomorrow may bring. Kimberly and Angela did not expect sudden death that day, but they were prepared. Are you? Eternity is a long time. Can you afford to wait any longer?

The Advancement of Homeschool Freedoms Time Line

NOTE: Non-HSLDA cases are marked with an "."*

1983

This year homeschool statutes or regulations were adopted in Wisconsin and Montana.

March 26, Washington

Michael Farris and J. Michael Smith founded the Home School Legal Defense Association.

April 26, Wisconsin

Monumental changes were made in the Wisconsin law relating to home education. The state court of appeals declared the state's compulsory attendance law unconstitutional in *Wisconsin v. Popanz.**

May 18, Washington

Because they were being denied the right to educate their children, home-schoolers led by HSLDA challenged the constitutionality of the Washington statute when they filed the *Caproni* case. This contributed to the passage of a new homeschool law in 1985.

1984

This year homeschool statutes or regulations were adopted in Georgia, Louisiana, Rhode Island, and Virginia.

August 16, Nebraska

The State Department of Education announced that parents with a sincerely held religious conviction against state educational standards can privately educate their children as long as the children are taught equivalent branches of learning and are submitted to periodic state testing.

November 15, Louisiana

The State Board of Education adopted Home Study Guidelines. The legislation stipulated that for the 1984–85 school year, all applications for homeschooling would be automatically accepted. In 1985–86, however, homeschooling parents must meet one of three requirements.

December 19, Indiana

The United States Court of Appeals for the Seventh Circuit ruled in favor of the Mazanec family and upheld the right of homeschools to operate as private schools, saying, "It is now doubtful that the requirements of a formally licensed or certified teacher . . . would pass constitutional muster."*

1985

This year homeschool statutes or regulations were adopted in Arkansas, Florida, New Mexico, Oregon, Tennessee, Washington, and Wyoming.

January, Kansas

A Kansas state court dismissed all charges against Kim and Constance Jost, who had been criminally charged with truancy for operating their homeschool as a private school. The court ruled that the law was somewhat vague but that the Josts had a legitimate school.

February 18, Texas

Three of five families from Katy, Texas, were found guilty of violating the state's compulsory attendance law. Several days later the fourth family was found guilty. However, all these cases were put on hold due to the pending *Leeper* case, and the fifth family was victorious in May.

March 12, Texas

Leeper, et al v. Texas Education Agency, et al was filed, suing the Texas Education Agency (TEA) and the state's 1,060 school districts in response to the continued violation of homeschoolers' civil rights. Fort Worth attorney Shelby Sharpe handled the case. HSLDA joined as a plaintiff.*

April 23, Michigan

Warrants for the arrests of Mark and Chris DeJonge, charged with criminal truancy for homeschooling without a certified teacher, were issued. Attorney David Kallman was retained to assist with their case.

May 7, North Carolina

In *Delconte v. North Carolina*, the North Carolina Supreme Court unanimously ended prosecution of homeschoolers by holding that homeschools qualify as private schools under the law and thus fulfill the compulsory attendance law.*

1986

This year homeschool statutes or regulations were adopted in Missouri.

February 20, North Dakota

In the Larsen case, the state supreme court ruled against the Patzer, Larsen, Reimche, and Lund families, who had been charged with violating the state's compulsory attendance law.*

March 10, California

In *People v. Darrah and Black, et al*, the municipal court ruled that because *§48222* fails to provide fair notice or establish guidelines as to what constitutes a "person capable of teaching" and what constitutes a "private full-time day school," it is unconstitutionally vague and unenforceable.

June 17, Michigan

The court ruled in *Haines, Smolls, Gibson v. Runkle* that homeschoolers do not need to seek approval and that the state must exhaust their administrative remedies before bringing criminal charges against families for homeschooling. David Kallman represented the HSLDA families involved.

October 22, Iowa

The Iowa Supreme Court agreed to hear HSLDA's appeal in *Iowa v. Trucke*. The Trucke family was charged with violating the state's compulsory attendance law because they were not using a certified teacher for at least 120 days of the school year.

December 4, Ohio

Judge Joseph J. Nahra of the court of appeals of Ohio Eighth District ruled in favor of HSLDA homeschoolers Don and Karen Svoboda, saying that the Svobodas had been denied their due process rights. The case was remanded for further proceedings, and the family's right to homeschool was finally recognized by the lower magistrate.

1987

This year homeschool statutes or regulations were adopted in Maryland, Minnesota, Vermont, and West Virginia.

February 4, South Carolina

South Carolina homeschoolers and HSLDA were able to convince the legislature to kill the South Carolina Department of Education regulations, which would have required all homeschool teachers to have a bachelor's degree.

February 16, Maryland

Maryland home educators and HSLDA convinced the Maryland Legislature to remove the home-visit requirement from the Department of Education's regulations.

March 5, Maine

The Maine Commissioner of Education reversed a local school board's denial for the Dionne family, thereby allowing them to homeschool. The family earlier had a truant officer enter the home insisting on taking the children to public school until HSLDA warned him they would bring kidnapping charges.

March 17, Nebraska

Nebraska homeschoolers and HSLDA defeated LB 682, which would have repealed the religious exemption provision and restored the teacher certification requirement.

March 25, Ohio

The Ohio Supreme Court upheld the conviction of an HSLDA family, the Schmidts, in *Ohio v. Schmidt*. The Court relied on the prosecutor's version of the facts, which asserted that the family did not exhaust their administrative remedies. The facts presented at trial, however, showed that the Schmidts had met with the superintendent several times. Since the record of the trial was destroyed by the Court of Common Pleas' defective recording equipment, the court could not compare the prosecutor's version with the actual record.

March 26, North Dakota

Gerald and Sheryl Lund and Richard and Kathy Reimche were put on trial—again—for the crime of homeschooling their children. Both were again declared guilty. HSLDA appealed their case to the North Dakota Supreme Court.

April 13, Texas

Leeper, et al v. Arlington Independent School District, et al, round one: Judge Charles Murray ruled that homeschools were to be considered private schools and allowed to operate freely. This case resulted in the dismissal of approximately twenty criminal prosecutions of HSLDA families throughout Texas.

May 6, Colorado

The district court in Gunmson County ruled in favor of an HSLDA family in *Hinsdale County School Board v. Main*. The court granted the family a religious exemption from the approval requirement based on their First Amendment rights.

August 7, Ohio

As a result of a dramatic turn of events in the middle of trial, in which the super-intendent testified that he had conferred with the trial judge prior to filing the complaint for truancy, the judge ruled that Robin Diegel had not been given an opportunity for a hearing before the superintendent and granted HSLDA's motion for dismissal.

August 7, Rhode Island

In the HSLDA case *Kinstead v. East Greenwich School Committee*, home visits were declared unconstitutional and removed as a requirement for approval.

August 19, Iowa

The Iowa Supreme Court handed down a victory for HSLDA and remanded *Iowa v. Trucke* to the district court for dismissal, because charges against the family had been filed prematurely. The statute requires parents to send their children to school 120 days each year. The Truckes were charged with truancy thirty days into the school year, when no parent could possibly have been in compliance with the law.

September 3, North Dakota

In *North Dakota v. Melin* the judge ruled that the teacher certification require-ment was unduly burdening the Melins' religious freedom, was not necessarily fulfilling the state's interest, and was not the least restrictive means available to the state to preserve its interest. Although this decision was later reversed by the state supreme court, it was a surprising victory in a hostile state.

September 29, Pennsylvania

The eleven school district superintendents in *Jeffery, et al v. O'Donnell, et al* entered a motion requesting the appointment of guardians for the home-schooled children in the case. Federal Judge Kosik denied the motion and pro-tected the parents' rights.

1988

This year homeschool statutes or regulations were adopted in Colorado, New York, South Carolina, North Carolina, and Pennsylvania.

February 12, Kansas

A case was dismissed against the Wilms family, HSLDA members who were operating as a "satellite" of a local private school board.

April 27, New York

In an educational neglect case against the Blackwelder family, one of the families involved in HSLDA's federal civil rights action, the judge ruled in favor of the family and dismissed the case, saying that there were no grounds for an educational neglect verdict.

May 2, Michigan

The circuit court's ruling, in *Sheridan Road Baptist Church v. State*, provided the legal alternative for nonpublic schools (and homeschools) to use the third-party reporting procedure and thereby avoid the teacher certification requirement.*

May 10, Colorado

A new homeschool bill, SB 56, was signed into law by the governor. The new law repealed the former arbitrary approval process.

May 31, North Dakota

In *State v. Lund/Reimche*, the North Dakota Supreme Court ruled in favor of the families and reversed their truancy convictions, since the prosecutor could not prove the age of the children.

June 17, New York

District Court Judge Munson upheld the restrictive law for homeschoolers; however, new homeschool regulations were passed that set forth a clearly defined process for notification.

June 17, New York

In the federal case *Blackwelder v. Safnauer*, District Court Judge Munson ruled that the old law was constitutional. However, because the new regulations were passed on the same day, the negative ruling had no adverse effect on the families.

June/July, North Dakota

State v. Anderson and *State v. Dagley*: In both HSLDA cases the North Dakota Supreme Court ruled against the families, and the teacher certification requirement remained intact.

July, Hawaii

New homeschool regulations, which eliminated all teacher qualification and approval requirements, were adopted by the Hawaii Department of Education.

August 24, Pennsylvania

U.S. District Court Judge Edwin M. Kosik ruled in HSLDA case *Jeffery, et al v. O'Donnell, et al* that "the tutorial provision of Pennsylvania Compulsory Attendance Law . . . is unconstitutionally vague" and therefore, unenforceable. As a result of this victory, more than twenty cases in court against HSLDA families were won or dismissed.

October 26, Oregon

The first National Christian Home Education Leadership Conference was held as a part of *The Teaching Home's* National Home School Convention.

December 1, Colorado

The court of appeals affirmed the lower court's ruling in *People in Interest of D.B.* that children enrolled in an independent or parochial school can be allowed by the school to be taught at home. HSLDA wrote an amicus brief in this case supporting attorney Bill Moritz.*

1989

This year homeschool statutes or regulations were adopted in North Dakota, Hawaii, Maine, and Ohio.

February 20, North Dakota

As part of a rally at the state capitol, 150 homeschoolers from eleven states celebrated a "Bismarck Tea Party," flooding the offices of legislators with hundreds of tea bags with the attached message: "The consent of the governed for homeschooling, too!"

February 27, North Dakota

Judge Dennis A. Schneider dismissed the child neglect charge of HSLDA members Barry and Kim Fischer and, in a five-page decision, ruled that simply proving that a child is not receiving an education as required by law is not sufficient to sustain such charges.

April 7, North Dakota

Governor George A. Sinner signed into law HB 1421, North Dakota's new homeschooling law, which repealed the state's former teacher certification requirement for all teachers.

August 9, Michigan

The court of appeals rendered its decision against the DeJonge family. HSLDA appealed the case to the Michigan Supreme Court.

1990

This year homeschool statutes or regulations were adopted in New Hampshire and Connecticut.

April 17, Washington, DC

The U.S. Supreme Court's *Smith II* decision undermined one of the foundational freedoms of homeschooling—religious liberty.

April 28, New Hampshire

The governor's signature gave New Hampshire its first homeschool law, which is favorable to home education.

June 22, Alabama

HSLDA succeeded in getting a case dismissed against a homeschooling family in *Fort Payne City v. Johnson*, when HSLDA proved that the family was about one thousand feet outside the school district's jurisdiction.

July 2, Rhode Island

In three separate decisions for HSLDA, the Commissioner of Education ruled that the school district's demand that students participate in the school's testing program violated the religious freedom of three homeschooling families.

September 4, Massachusetts

The District Court of Amesbury Division ruled in favor of a homeschool family in the *Searles* case. The Court agreed with HSLDA that the family could homeschool even though they had not been officially approved.

September 6, Pennsylvania

HSLDA's civil rights suit *Stobaugh v. Wallace* was heard. Pittsburgh Superintendent Richard Wallace had issued orders requiring homeschooling families to participate in the district's own testing program and, when they refused, retaliated by issuing a portfolio demand. The judge dismissed the suit for prematurity but blasted Superintendent Wallace for choosing to "arbitrarily flout state law." The heart of the ruling was a clear homeschooling victory.

November 16, Washington

The National Home Education Research Institute (NHERI) released its first report *A Nationwide Study of Home Education*.

December 5, South Carolina

The South Carolina Board of Education won the first round in *Lawrence*, HSLDA's challenge to the law requiring parents without a bachelor's degree to pass a teacher's examination before being allowed to teach their own children.

1991

This year homeschool statutes were adopted in Iowa.

February, Kansas

Kansas homeschoolers and HSLDA defeated HB 2392, which would have required homeschool children to be taught by certified teachers.

April 19, Virginia

The Supreme Court of Virginia, in *Johnson v. Prince William County*, ruled unanimously in favor of a homeschool family on the legal issues, thereby setting precedent across the state to streamline religious exemption requests. However, the Court ruled four to three against the Johnson's religious beliefs. HSLDA immediately filed for a new religious exemption for the family, which was subsequently granted.

May 3, Iowa

The Iowa legislature passed House File 455 into law, allowing parents to homeschool without having a certified teacher involved in the teaching or supervision of the children's education. The bill was signed by Governor Terry Branstad shortly thereafter.

June 17, Michigan

A motion to dismiss was granted in *People v. Pebler*, supporting HSLDA's position that homeschoolers do not have to file the "Nonpublic School Membership Report" and that the compulsory attendance law is vague and basically unenforceable. This same year, a total of twelve other Michigan families were criminally prosecuted for not having teaching certificates. Every case was won or dismissed.

August 3, Alberta

Home School Legal Defense Association of Canada, Ltd., was established.

August 30, District of Columbia

HSLDA convinced the District of Columbia school district to revoke its restrictive policy of unannounced home visits and teacher certification requirements.

November 27, Texas

The court of appeals of Texas issued a landmark decision in *Texas Education Agency, et al v. Leeper, et al*, protecting the rights of parents to homeschool their children throughout the state. The TEA appealed this ruling.

December 9, South Carolina

South Carolina's requirement that parents without a college degree take a "basic skills" qualification test was overturned. The State Supreme Court unanimously ruled in favor of homeschoolers and HSLDA in *Lawrence v. State Board of Education*.

1992

January, Michigan

HSLDA filed a civil rights case against a prosecutor (*Arnett v. Middleton*) to protect seven homeschool families targeted for prosecution. HSLDA dropped the suit when the prosecutor quickly prepared an opinion stating that homeschooling was presently legal and that the law in Michigan was vague.

March 10, Michigan

Police officers arrived on the Loudon family's doorstep with a warrant for the arrest of their six-year-old daughter. She had been below compulsory attendance age the previous year, when a case charging the family with criminal truancy was dismissed. The court canceled the warrant after HSLDA intervened.

April 2, South Carolina

The General Assembly passed legislation naming the South Carolina Association of Independent Home Schools as a legal alternate source of approval for homeschooling parents.

April 6, Pennsylvania

The Pittsburgh School District agreed to settle HSLDA's federal lawsuit, dropping all criminal charges against Mrs. Deely, expunging her criminal record, clarifying their notification requirement, and paying damages and attorney fees.

May 15, Alabama

A homeschooling father's criminal truancy conviction was reversed by the Alabama Court of Civil Appeals in *Maas v. State* based on the violation of his statutory due process rights.

August 28, Alabama

HSLDA member Helene Richards, a mother of four children, had been the subject of an anonymous child abuse hotline tip and had refused to let a social worker into her home without a search warrant. The Court of Civil Appeals held that an invasion of a parent's home was a violation of the legal right to privacy.

September 25, Ohio

The NCAA announced that it was reinstating homeschool graduate Jason Taylor's football scholarship to the University of Akron. The organization had earlier pulled his scholarship because of a rule involving the calculation of grade point averages.

October 15, Oregon

The National Home Education Research Institute released *Marching to the Beat of Their Own Drum: A Profile of Home Education Research.*

November 3, Illinois

HSLDA worked with Illinois homeschoolers to defeat narrowly a statewide referendum that would have made public education a "fundamental right."

December 14, North Dakota

HSLDA won a major victory in *Birst v. Sanstead* before the North Dakota Supreme Court, which ruled that under state law homeschoolers may choose whether they wish to operate under the homeschool law or the private school law.

1993

January 25, South Dakota

HSLDA filed *Davis v. Newell School District*, challenging the state's unconstitutional home visit requirement.

January 26, Texas

The Texas Supreme Court heard oral arguments in the case of the *Texas Education Agency, et al v. Leeper, et al.* On the same day, a homeschool rally of five thousand people was held at the state capitol in Austin.

January, Virginia

The Congressional Action Program (CAP) was established by the National Center for Home Education to target federal measures that will have a direct impact on homeschooling.

March 5, South Dakota

After making it through the Senate Education Committee with the help of an amendment, HB 1260 passed, repealing the South Dakota home visit law. As a result, HSLDA's previously filed *Davis v. Newell School District* was dismissed.

March 15, Virginia

HSLDA established its Special Education Department.

March 19, New Mexico

Senate Bill 202 was signed into law by the governor, striking the requirement for the parent-teacher to possess "at least a baccalaureate degree" and in its place requiring the parent to have a "high school diploma or its equivalent."

April 11, Arizona

Governor Fife Symington signed Arizona's new homeschool law. Parents no longer have to pass a proficiency exam (ATPE) in order to teach their children at home. One must only be the "parent" in order to teach a child at home.

April 26, Virginia

Cumberland County Circuit Court reversed a school board's denial of a home-school family's religious exemption request in *Dusan v. Cumberland County School Board*, stating that the school board does not have the right to determine if homeschooling is in the child's best interest.

April, Virginia

Virginia homeschoolers and HSLDA worked successfully to override the governor's line item veto and defeat a mandatory kindergarten provision by a huge margin. A bill was also passed to lower the cutoff score from the fortieth to the twenty-third percentile.

May 11, Washington, DC

The Religious Freedom Restoration Act (RFRA) passed the House.

May 18, Oklahoma

A homeschooling father regained custody of his children after a lower court ruled homeschooling was harmful. The court of appeals stated that the

"Oklahoma Department of Education has no jurisdiction over homeschooling."
HSLDA had filed an amicus brief.*

May 25, Michigan

HSLDA won two major victories. In *Michigan v. DeJonge* the Michigan Supreme
Court, in a four to three vote, transformed Michigan from the worst homeschool state in the nation to one of the best. Michigan became the final state
in the country to strike the teacher certification requirement for religious
homeschoolers. Additionally, the Court ruled in *People v. Bennett* that homeschoolers are entitled to an administrative hearing before any criminal charges
can be brought against them. The criminal convictions of both families were
reversed.

June 10, Massachusetts

The federal district court in Boston ruled against the Pustell family, upholding the constitutionality of the Lynn School District's home visit requirement.
HSLDA appealed the case to the federal appeals court in Boston.

June 29, Washington, DC

Michael Farris and J. Michael Smith cohosted *Home School Heartbeat—Live*, a
live nationwide satellite broadcast featuring distinguished guests, discussion of
current legal and legislative battles, and call-in questions from viewers.

July, Washington, DC

HSLDA led other pro-family groups and thousands of informed families in an
opposition blitz against the Comprehensive Child Immunization Act. This bill
would have usurped parental rights by creating a federal vaccine mandate for
all children, as well as a national child registry and computer tracking system.
These dangerous provisions were successfully omitted from the bill while in
the House.

July 7, Washington, DC

A letter from Dr. Sellman announced that the United States Navy has developed "a compensatory screening model" that will allow individuals with alternative high school diplomas (including homeschool graduates) to become eligible

for enlistment. Dr. Sellman's letter indicated that the army is considering a similar program.

November 16, Washington, DC

President Bill Clinton signed into law the Religious Freedom Restoration Act of 1993 (RFRA). Michael Farris was one of the original drafters of the bill. Passage of the RFRA reinstated religious freedom as a fundamental right, securing parents' liberty to homeschool their children in peace and freedom.

December, California

During the 1993 legislative session, homeschoolers were instrumental in convincing Governor Pete Wilson to veto three bills potentially harmful to homeschooling. The first was the California Children's Bill of Rights, an act that would guarantee all children the right to "quality education" by the state, subjecting homeschoolers to intense state scrutiny. The second would have attempted to provide early childhood home visitation programs for families. The third piece of legislation would have implemented the first phase of a state-wide student tracking system.

1994

January, South Dakota

HSLDA worked with South Dakota homeschoolers to defeat legislation requiring all homeschool teachers to be state certified by the year 2000. The sponsor withdrew HB 1262 after being informed of its potential constitutional problems by HSLDA.

January 11, Virginia

Following arguments from HSLDA, the Prince William County Circuit Court ruled in favor of the Berlin family. The court decided that homeschool parents who are certified teachers may operate under the certified tutor statute rather than the more restrictive homeschool statute. An official memo from the state superintendent to school districts applied the decision across the state.

February, Illinois

Senate Bill 159, "Parents as Teachers" legislation, was defeated because of the work of HSLDA, pro-family legislators, and Illinois families. This bill would have given authority to the state board of education to implement mandated humanistic parenting programs and home visits for all families.

February, Virginia

Alerted by HSLDA, Virginia homeschoolers were able to derail legislation that would have repealed the homeschool religious exemption statute. Contributing to their successful efforts, HSLDA commissioned a study of students' test scores demonstrating the academic excellence produced by families homeschooling under the religious exemption statute.

February 15–24, Washington, DC

In a now-famous weeklong battle over House Resolution 6, homeschoolers demonstrated to Congress the power of grassroots political action. A provision in HR 6 would have threatened the existence of private and homeschools by requiring all teachers to be certified in each subject they teach. After more than one million calls from concerned parents poured into Capitol Hill and literally shut down the phone lines, the House voted 424–1 to delete the teacher certification provision and voted 374–53 to add Rep. Dick Armey's (R-TX) "Home School/Private School Freedom Amendment" to HR 6. The Armey amendment specifically excluded home and private schools from any federal control of education codified by HR 6.

March 1, Texas

Tarrant County Judge Scott Moore dismissed a Child Protective Services motion to prosecute a family who refused to cooperate with a child abuse investigation based on an anonymous tip. Michael Farris defended the family before the county juvenile court, resulting in the dismissal of all allegations and a new precedent that will help HSLDA protect other homeschoolers.

March 12, West Virginia

Governor Gaston Caperton signed House Bill 4546, which provided home-schooling families with two evaluation alternatives to standardized testing requirements and allowed students who fall below the fortieth percentile mark three years to catch up instead of two.

March 28, Tennessee

With encouragement from the Tennessee Home Education Association and HSLDA, the state legislature passed Senate Bill 1159, which eliminated the bachelor's degree requirement for homeschool teachers affiliated with a Tennessee church-related school.

April 6, Illinois

The Illinois Appellate Court ruled in favor of a homeschooling mother who had lost custody of her child based on her decision to homeschool in the case *In re Marriage of Riess*. HSLDA provided financial assistance and legal advice in the appeal.

April 14, Colorado

Governor Roy Romer signed Senate Bill 4, a new homeschool law drafted by HSLDA attorneys, which eliminated written notification and relaxed testing requirements.

April, Maine

HSLDA attorneys protected the Green family from a potential lawsuit brought by the Maine Commissioner of Education over the legitimacy of home-based, nonapproved private schools.

June 15, Texas

After an almost ten-year legal battle, the Texas Supreme Court ruled in favor of the homeschooling parents in the *Texas Education Agency, et al. v. Leeper, et al.* case. This landmark ruling reaffirmed the legality of homeschools to operate as private schools without regulation.

July 5, Oregon

The National Home Education Research Institute released *A Nationwide Study of Home Education in Canada*.

August, Nevada

HSLDA, together with the Northern Home School Advisory Council, objected to an attempt by the state department of education to require homeschool students to take the writing proficiency examination developed for public school students. After the state attorney general denounced the testing requirement, the state education department rescinded it.

September, New York

HSLDA attorneys defended the Brown family's religious freedom in negotiations with the commissioner of the Department of Social Services. All charges against the family were dropped, and the parents were removed from the child abuse registry.

October, Washington, DC

In response to an alert from HSLDA, homeschoolers from around the nation bombarded their senators' offices with phone calls and letters stopping the UN Convention on the Elimination of All Forms of Discrimination Against Women.

1995

January 3, New York

In December 1994, the Department of Social Services petitioned a Bronx family court to allow entry into the home and a full investigation of an HSLDA member family accused of neglect and abuse by an anonymous tip. The case was put on fast track, and HSLDA attorneys quickly presented a motion to quash the court order. The judge agreed to stay the order for three weeks to allow time for DSS to respond to the motion. When the court reconvened, the Department of Social Services withdrew its petition. New York law was upheld: Entry into a private home may not be ordered without evidence of probable cause, and an anonymous tip is not probable cause.

February, Virginia

After years of persistent opposition by HSLDA, the Fairfax County Public Schools relented on their requirement to have homeschooling families submit a "description of curriculum."

February, Virginia

In the case *In re Brianna*, the court ruled in favor of parents' rights to make medical decisions for their children and honored the religious exemptions from immunizations allowed by Virginia law. HSLDA defended this family, who were charged with child neglect because they chose not to immunize their children.

February 3, Georgia

Debbie Gaskin was arrested and jailed for contributing to truancy after she decided to homeschool her daughter, in full compliance with the law, following her daughter's absence from public school due to a sprained ankle. Mrs. Gaskin was released on $500 bond, and HSLDA immediately and successfully worked to have the truancy charges dismissed.

March, Utah

The legal status of homeschoolers was greatly improved by a new child neglect law that clarifies the standard for prosecuting homeschool families for educational neglect.

March, Arkansas

The Arkansas Senate Education Committee voted four to two to kill Senate Bill 583. This bill would have required homeschool students to take and pass the high school exit examination based on public school curriculum.

April 13, Arizona

The legislature passed Senate Bill 1348, making Arizona the first state in the country to remove completely a homeschool testing requirement. SB 1348 also allowed homeschoolers to participate in interscholastic competition at public schools.

May 16, Nebraska

In a precedent-setting opinion, a Nebraska hearing officer ruled that although Congress requires each state to offer free special needs services, the states are not empowered to make enrollment in these services mandatory. All children, even those with special needs, enrolled in a bona fide homeschool program in compliance with Nebraska law are exempt from public school attendance.

May, California

Three cases, one in San Diego and two in the Chowchilla School District, were won in juvenile courts by HSLDA. The families were accused of truancy by local public school officials but were cleared when HSLDA presented proof of their validity and compliance with the private school statute in the California education code.

July 24, California

In the *Calabretta* case, a California federal district court judge denied the police and social worker's motion to dismiss, indicating that he was aware of no binding precedent which excludes child welfare investigators from Fourth Amendment Law.

November 9, Vermont

Ken and Sheree Hadley of Granitville were granted the right to homeschool under the religious exemption statute after extensive negotiations between the Vermont Department of Education and HSLDA.

November, Washington, DC

Nineteen-year-old Makala Racobs was denied entrance into the Navy because she is a homeschool graduate. After HSLDA filed *Makala D. Racobs v. William Perry, Secretary of Defense*, the Navy agreed to an out-of-court settlement, offering Makala an opportunity to be reexamined for admission and setting up an experimental attrition rate study for homeschoolers.

December 15, Newfoundland

The Supreme Court of Canada found that Charles and Sandra Butler have the right to homeschool under section 7 of the Canadian Charter and reunited them with their three children. Child welfare officials had placed the Butlers' children into foster care after the Butlers refused a court order to enroll their children in public school. HSLDA of Canada helped the family appeal this court order to the Supreme Court of Newfoundland.

1996

This year homeschool statutes or regulations were adopted in Michigan.

January 9, Michigan

As a result of the *Michigan v. DeJonge* case won by HSLDA in 1993, Governor John Engler signed into law Senate Bill 679, Amendment A. This new law freed all homeschooling families from teacher certification and reporting requirements, transforming the state into one of the most favorable for homeschooling.

January 9, Michigan

Governor Engler signed Act No. 289, which designated as "fundamental" the right of parents to direct the education of their children.

March 4, South Dakota

Governor William J. Janklow signed into law two excellent pieces of legislation, drafted for homeschoolers by HSLDA. The first, House Bill 1286, freed homeschoolers to use any type of national achievement test they choose. The second, HB 1279, provided safeguards against false and malicious reports of abuse or neglect.

March 19, Hawaii

Legislation that would ultimately result in criminalizing corporal punishment was introduced and sent before the Committee on Human Services. Michael Farris and other HSLDA attorneys prepared a memorandum of law analyzing the legislative proposal and its unconstitutionality. With the help of the memorandum, Hawaii families demonstrated strong opposition to the legislation, resulting in its defeat at the final committee vote.

May, Washington, DC

After several nationwide alerts and intensive lobbying, a major threat against the right to privacy is averted. Pressure from homeschoolers and HSLDA convince Congress to amend S 269, The Immigration Act, removing its mandatory tracking provisions and preventing the establishment of a national ID card for every employee in America.

October, West Virginia

Legal action by HSLDA forced the Mercer County school superintendent to grant West Virginia's first "religious exemption," enabling the Minton family to continue homeschooling.

October, Indiana

HB 1259 died in committee after homeschoolers, alerted by HSLDA, flooded their legislators with calls and letters opposing the bill. HB 1259 would have required homeschoolers to take the statewide IPASS test, which is based on OBE skills and politically correct ideas.

October 2, Georgia

Five days before the Gaskin trial date, the defendants agreed to settle the case by paying Debbie Gaskin $13,750 for her malicious prosecution and false arrest.

October 25, Maryland

In *State of Maryland v. Cheryl Ann Battles*, Mrs. Battles was acquitted in criminal court of the charge of violating the state's compulsory attendance act. This homeschool mother had been prosecuted for refusing to sign the Maryland assurance of consent homeschool form because of her sincerely held religious convictions. The judge ruled that failure to comply with Maryland's regulations was not a crime because Mrs. Battles provided enough evidence to satisfy the court that she was providing her daughter with the "regular and thorough instruction" required by state statute.

November, South Carolina

The Department of Social Services wrongly pursued intrusive investigations of two homeschool families for child abuse and truancy allegations. As a result of intervention by HSLDA attorneys, the allegations against one family were declared unfounded and the investigation of the other family was dropped.

November, Alaska

Organized resistance from homeschooling parents and legal arguments from HSLDA led the Anchorage assembly to remove all curfew provisions from a proposed truancy prevention ordinance.

1997

January 7, California

In HSLDA's *Calabretta* civil rights case, a federal judge ruled that social workers and police officers who enter a family home to investigate child abuse without a warrant or proper evidence of an emergency violate the Fourth Amendment rights of the family.

February 14, Georgia

State representative Carolyn F. Hugley introduced House Bill 586, which would change Georgia's homeschool law from one of the best to one of the most oppressive in the country. Alerted by HSLDA, Georgia homeschoolers delivered an estimated 8,000 calls to the legislature, effectively tabling the legislation and sending it to a study committee.

February 28, California

In *Robert and Maria Kennedy v. Doonan, et al.*, a federal judge agreed with HSLDA and ruled that police officers violated the Fourth Amendment when they forced entry into the Kennedy home without a warrant to investigate a child abuse allegation on August 19, 1995.

March 5, Washington, DC

In a press conference, HSLDA and the National Home Education Research Institute released the largest and most comprehensive homeschool research study to date, *Home Education Across the United States*.

March 7, Arkansas

Governor Mike Huckabee signed House Bill 1157, now Act 400, which revolutionized the homeschool law, transforming Arkansas from one of the worst to one of the best states for homeschoolers.

March, Maryland

A coalition of concerned parents, the Maryland Association of Christian Home Educators, the Christian Home Educators Network, and the American Civil Liberties Union joined forces to defeat House Bill 486, a statewide daytime curfew bill.

April 3, North Dakota

The efforts of the North Dakota Home School Association were rewarded when Governor Edward T. Schafer signed House Bill 1368, which significantly improved the 1989 homeschool statutes. Later that week two more pro-home education laws were enacted. One made it easier for homeschooled high schoolers to obtain diplomas, and the other allowed parents to teach their autistic children.

April 9, Wisconsin

Alerted by HSLDA and Wisconsin Christian Home Educator's Association, homeschoolers rallied at the state capitol to oppose Senate Bill 106, which would have outlawed homeschooling for children who were found "truant" or "in need of services." In response the Senate shelved the bill indefinitely.

April, Minnesota

Alerted by HSLDA, Minnesota homeschoolers let their legislators know they adamantly opposed House File 1932, which would have extended public school testing requirements to private and homeschools. Because HSLDA testified and because of the opposition from homeschoolers, HF 1932 died in committee.

April, New Hampshire

Because of the courageous efforts of State Senator David Wheeler and New Hampshire homeschoolers, House Bill 211 was sent back to committee for further study. The bill would have defined "isolating" as a form of child abuse in a way that social workers could apply to homeschooling families.

April 22, Oklahoma

The state supreme court upheld Lynn Martin's right to direct the education of her children despite her ex-husband's challenge to her custody in *Lynn Stephen (now Martin) v. Mark Stephen*. Reversing the trial court's decision that her children attend traditional school, the supreme court reaffirmed the custodial parent's right to direct the education of her children without court intervention unless there is evidence of harm to the children. HSLDA filed an amicus brief supporting Mrs. Martin.*